Water for Life

Water Management and Environmental Policy

Successful water management is crucial for the proper operation of
natural environmental systems and for the support of human society.
These two aspects are interdependent, but decisions about one are
often made without regard to effects upon the other. A persistent
challenge is to consider them together. This book is the first to
explore fully the relationship between water management,
environmental conditions, and public policy. It combines a careful
review of the character and evolution of water management, and
evaluates management from the standpoint of the quality of the
natural environment. Topics covered include domestic and industrial
water supply and waste disposal, groundwater use, river channel and
floodplain management, and integrated river basins. The processes of
social decision making are examined against a backdrop of
plant–soil–water–ecosystem relationships and ecosystem change.
Examples are drawn from around the world, from local watershed
management to international river basin planning, with emphasis on
integrative approaches.

JAMES L. WESCOAT JR. is a Professor of Landscape Architecture at
the University of Illinois at Urbana-Champaign.

GILBERT F. WHITE is Distinguished Professor Emeritus of
Geography at the University of Colorado, Boulder.

Water for Life

Water Management and Environmental Policy

JAMES L. WESCOAT, JR.
University of Illinois at Urbana-Champaign

GILBERT F. WHITE
University of Colorado

PUBLISHED BY THE PRESS SYNDICATE OF THE UNIVERSITY OF CAMBRIDGE
The Pitt Building, Trumpington Street, Cambridge, United Kingdom

CAMBRIDGE UNIVERSITY PRESS
The Edinburgh Building, Cambridge CB2 2RU, UK
40 West 20th Street, New York, NY 10011–4211, USA
477 Williamstown Road, Port Melbourne, VIC 3207, Australia
Ruiz de Alarcón 13, 28014 Madrid, Spain
Dock House, The Waterfront, Cape Town 8001, South Africa

http://www.cambridge.org

First published 2003

Printed in the United Kingdom at the University Press, Cambridge

Typeface Swift 9/13 pt.   *System* LaTeX 2_ε [TB]

A catalog record for this book is available from the British Library

Library of Congress Cataloging in Publication data
Wescoat, James L., 1952–
    Water for life: water management and environmental policy / James
    L. Wescoat, Jr., Gilbert F. White.
        p.   cm.
    Includes bibliographical references (p.).
    ISBN 0 521 36211 3 (hardback) – ISBN 0 521 36980 0 (paperback)
    1. Water-supply – Management.   2. Integrated water development.
    3. Water-supply – Government policy.   I. White, Gilbert F.   II. Title.
TD345. W46   2003
333.91 – dc21   2003046034

ISBN 0 521 36211 3 hardback
ISBN 0 521 36980 0 paperback

Contents

Figures

Tables

Preface

To arrive at truly integrated water management no aspect has been more difficult than the joint evaluation of social and environmental consequences. For example, not until 2000 was there a systematic examination of methods to evaluate the social benefits of flood protection projects along with the social costs of altering the floodplain environment through such management.

This book reflects our attempt to canvass the need and suitable methods for carefully combining the two. It seeks to appraise the range of problems and the available methods of addressing them in the broader context of integrated management. It does not attempt to describe all relevant efforts from around the world but it does seek to evaluate some representative examples of problems and of constructive methods of addressing them.

The idea for this book initially emerged in the mid 1980s after a period of intense conflict between proponents of continued water development and activists for environmental protection. Although considerable progress had occurred in water resource systems modeling and environmental science and policy, they seemed to develop to a significant degree along separate lines. One of the more extreme cases was the parallel development of water laws related to supply and of environmental laws that dealt with water quality: in some countries and states these integrally related topics are administered by different agencies in different ministries and with different bodies of law.

Although inefficient and unnecessary in many ways, conflict between these two fields has in some cases been productive, yielding innovative solutions to complex water and environmental problems. Protracted conflict over dam operations on the Colorado River in the USA, for example, led to an adaptive management program linking scientists, stakeholders, and river managers in a science-based program of experimentation, monitoring, and management. Conflict between India and Pakistan over the Indus River led to the Indus Waters Treaty, which has endured through more than a half-century of unrelated regional conflicts.

At the same time, collaborative and cooperative processes have also yielded increasing harmonization of water and environmental management. Community-based watershed movements arose in many regions of the world in the late twentieth century, in some cases driven by legal requirements but in other cases driven by educational and place-based movements, designed to experience, understand, and enjoy local resources. Although clearly successful in terms of human coop-eration, how long can these local coalitions be sustained? Which ones will make an enduring ecological or cultural difference?

To address these questions, this volume adopts a broad perspec-tive, developed in its first four chapters. It begins by probing in gen-eral ways the problem of conflict, gaps, and harmony between water management and environmental policy. The second chapter considers how these phenomena serve jointly as challenges and opportunities, which it compares with the intense international interest at the turn of the present century in envisioning future trends, problems, and solu-tions. However, whether one considers watershed movements or global change, the third chapter reminds us that some aspects of emerging proposals have been attempted previously. How did gaps between wa-ter and environmental management arise in the first place? How did earlier societies address and transform them? When did they do so sus-tainably, and when not? By retracing the unfolding consciousness of ecosystem effects of water use back to its roots, we arrive at a topic that sets the stage for the rest of the volume – natural waters and the inherent variability of water supplies and water quality in ecological as well as hydrologic terms.

Five chapters address key intersections between water and en-vironmental management, starting with the soil–water–plant relations that support all ecological and agricultural systems. Beginning with soil moisture dynamics and associated processes of irrigation and drainage, the book then digs deeper into ground water resources, described in at least one legal case as "so secret, changeable and uncontrollable" as to lie beyond regulation (*Roath* v. *Driscoll*, 20 Conn. 533, 541 [1850]) – a frontier for science, management, and policy. As a high water table rises to the surface, from springs to great lakes, Chapter 7 reflects upon wetlands and lakes. This is followed by a chapter on river channels, which encompasses competing and sometimes complementary perspec-tives on river channel engineering, riparian ecosystems, and floodplain management. In the late twentieth century few topics were as controversial as large dams with the jointly social and environmental impacts of their reservoirs upstream and altered flows and river ecology downstream. The final chapter in this series turns to domestic and industrial water use, which are sometimes regarded as driving forces of aquatic environmental depletion and degradation. But scholars like Anne Spirn (*The Granite Garden: Urban Nature and Human Design*, 1984), along with scientific serials like *Environment and Urbanization, Journal of Industrial Ecology, Environment*, and *Water and Environment*, remind us that cities, industries, and societies are inseparable from the ecosystems they inhabit.

The final two chapters of the volume reflect upon how individuals and groups make decisions about water and environmental management. Chapter 11 compares and contrasts the extraordinary wealth of human experience in different regions, cultures, and environments around the world, which is a collective resource for all, but until recently accessible only to a few. However, an appendix to the volume highlights the dramatically increasing access to international water and environmental information through the Internet. As this information is increasing faster than our capacity to identify, synthesize, and use it, the appendix provides a guide to using Internet resources, as well as a list of water websites pertinent to each chapter of the book and region of the world. The final chapter returns to the theme of integrated water and environmental management, envisioned for centuries, and occasionally achieved. That chapter highlights three current and emerging approaches for their challenges and opportunities: community-based watershed management, adaptive management, and global environmental policy.

This volume is the fruit of several years of collaborative discussion and writing, between the authors and colleagues in related fields. It has been a pleasure to write. We are grateful for support from the University of Colorado Distinguished Professor program; to James Robb, Cartographer in the Department of Geography; and to Sugandha Brooks of the Institute of Behavioral Sciences for her patient and careful preparation of the manuscript. Hugh Brazier provided excellent editorial advice, which helped clarify our writing and ideas. We thank our editors at Cambridge University Press – Alan Crowden, Maria Murphy, Claire Nugent and Carol Miller – for their sustained encouragement over the years. Our main hope is that our book contributes to the further harmonization of these two vital fields of water and environmental management for the joint benefit of humans and their fellow creatures and the waters of the planet.

Abbreviations

BCE	Before Common Era (= BC)
CE	Common Era (= AD)
CEQ	United States Council on Environmental Quality
EPA	See USEPA
ESCAP	See UNESCAP
FAO	United Nations Food and Agriculture Organization
GEF	Global Environmental Facility
GEWEX	Global Energy and Water Cycle Experiment
GIS	Geographic Information Systems
GWP	Global Water Partnership
ICID	International Commission on Irrigation and Drainage
ICOLD	International Commission on Large Dams
ICWE	International Conference on Water and the Environment
IDNDR	International Decade of Natural Disaster Reduction
IGBP	International Geosphere–Biosphere Programme
IHA	International Hydropower Association
IIASA	International Institute for Applied Systems Analysis
ILEC	International Lake Environment Committee
ILRI	International Land Reclamation Institute
IPCC	Intergovernmental Panel on Climate Change
IUCN	International Union for Conservation of Nature and Natural Resources (also known as IUCN – the World Conservation Union)
IWA	International Water Association
IWMI	International Water Management Institute
LUCC	Land Use and Cover Change
NAS	National Academy of Sciences
NOAA	National Oceanic and Atmospheric Administration

NRC	National Research Council
NRCS	National Resources Conservation Service
PWRPC	President's Water Resources Policy Commission
SCOPE	Scientific Committee on Problems of the Environment
TNC	The Nature Conservancy
UNCED	United Nations Conference on Environment and Development
UNCHS	United Nations Centre for Human Settlements
UNEP	United Nations Environment Program
UNESCAP	United Nations Economic and Social Commission for Asia and the Pacific
UNFCCC	United Nations Framework Convention on Climate Change
USBR	United States Bureau of Reclamation
USDA	United States Department of Agriculture
USEPA	United States Environmental Protection Agency
USFWS	United States Fish and Wildlife Service
USGS	United States Geological Survey
USHUD	United States Department of Housing and Urban Development
USSL	United States Salinity Laboratory
WASH	Water and Sanitation for Health
WATMANET	Asian Watershed Management Network
WCD	World Commission on Dams
WCED	World Commission on Environment and Development
WHO	World Health Organization
WMO	World Meteorological Association
WRC	United States Water Resources Council
WWC	World Water Council

Conversions of selected units of hydrologic measurement

Length
    1 centimeter (cm) = 0.3997 inch = 0.01 meter
    1 kilometer (km) = 100 meters (m) = 0.62 mile (mi)
    1 foot (ft) = 30.48 cm = 0.3333 yard
    1 mile = 5280 ft = 1.609 km

Area
    1 hectare (ha) = 2.471 acres
    1 square kilometer (km^2)= 100 ha = 247 acres
    1 acre = 0.40469 ha

Volume
    1 liter (l) = 1000 cm^3 = 0.2642 gallon
    1 gallon = 3.785 liters
    1 acre feet = 1233.48 m^3

For details and other units see Gleick, 2000a, pp. 300–309.

1

Water and life

THE ROLE OF WATER IN THE LIFE OF ECOSYSTEMS
AND OF PEOPLE

The significance of the role of water in the life of planet earth can only be understood fully from analysis of its part in the sustenance of natural environmental systems and in the support of human society. The two aspects are interdependent in the long run, but decisions about one are often made in the short run without regard to effects upon the other, as when a city withdraws stream flow without considering the consequences for fish life, or when wetlands drainage reduces quantity and quality of water for urban use. A persistent challenge is to consider them together. From speculations as to the possible effects of global climate change upon water supply at one extreme of generalization to estimates of the essential daily needs of one isolated family at the other extreme, it is desirable to assess both aspects in relation to each other, as photographs from South and Central Asia in this chapter attest (Figure 1.1).

The problem of viewing the full importance of water on the global scene is introduced by briefly examining the global water budget, how elementary notions of the role of water in global life have evolved, how they at times have been in harmony or in conflict, and how they present themselves in miniature as well as on the world scale. A broad-brush sketch of the world situation helps us to recognize the importance of water at the local level, but there are gaps in knowledge at all levels. For example, some of the available statistics as to total quantities of water used by persons or plants in a particular area may be more nearly adequate than are the data on the effects of slight differences in water quality upon the health of either plant or human communities in that locality. The tremendous diversity in social and environmental

1

Figure 1.1   Fishing vessel on the Ganges River in India seeks sustenance from an increasingly polluted habitat.

characteristics around the world is illustrated by a description of 145 watersheds in terms of 15 global indicators of watershed conditions and their vulnerability to material and social change (Revenga *et al.*, 1998).

The evolution of thinking has been sporadic and has proceeded diffidently since the monumental 1864 study *Man and Nature; or Physical Geography as Modified by Human Action* (Marsh, 1864) directed attention to the many and varied ways in which the world population over time had changed its environment. That examination was brought up to date a century later by the symposium on *Man's Role in Changing the Face of the Earth* (Thomas, 1959), organized under the broad themes of retrospect, process, and prospect. Thirty years later, a group based at Clark University organized a symposium on *The Earth as Transformed by Human Action: Global and Regional Changes in the Biosphere over the Past 300 Years* (Turner *et al.*, 1990) in which the further environmental changes on a world scale were reviewed. New emphasis was placed upon "the tragedy of the commons" in which resources of water as well as land, vegetation, and animals had been exploited. Depending upon the human civilization involved, the emphasis varied greatly among the major societies of the globe, as reviewed at a Scientific Committee on Problems of the Environment conference on *Emerging Environmental Issues for the Twenty-first Century* (SCOPE, 1999).

In these and related analytical efforts the modifications in water and related ecosystems were examined primarily from the standpoint of how human activity had changed them. Some research also was directed at the consequences of water management for social purposes, as, for example, with the development of the concept of the "Hydraulic Civilizations" by Wittfogel, who asserted that complex societies arose along the large arid-zone rivers of the world (Wittfogel, in Thomas, 1959, pp. 152–164).

During the same period increasing attention was paid by hydrologists, engineers, and planners to the characteristics of natural systems that needed to be taken into precise account in planning and executing works for water and land management. Among the aspects of such systems requiring careful scientific analysis were factors affecting precipitation, evaporation, runoff, water loss by vegetation, flood flows, sediment production and transport, and physical, chemical, and biological quality of lakes and streams. (These are reviewed in Dunne and Leopold, 1978, and will be addressed in detail in later chapters.) That body of knowledge grew rapidly, and increasingly was used in the design and operation of relatively small water and water-related projects, which by the 1980s had begun to take increasing account of the interrelationship of both social and environmental factors in selected watersheds. (The growth of interest in smaller drainage areas is reviewed in Chapter 12.)

Environmental impacts

Between the 1930s and the 1960s evidence gradually accumulated that the construction and operation of water-control projects (dams, levees, channel control, and waste disposal facilities) could have an observable effect upon soil moisture, sediment movement, water quality, or other aspects of natural water resources as well as upon social systems (Figure 1.2). Experience with agricultural, urban water, industrial waste disposal, and many other projects from around the world began to accumulate and to challenge the promoters – private and public – of new projects (Farvar and Milton, 1972, pp. 155–365). Critical attention was turned to the effects of such problems as Nile River storage, irrigation in Southwest Asia, flood control in Southeast Asia, and salinity in the Colorado River.

Figure 1.2   Irrigation during the monsoon season in Punjab, Pakistan, supplies important food, fiber, and industrial crops – at the cost of forests, grazing land, waterlogging, and salinity.

This led in the United States to discussion of the need for federal legislation requiring that any proposed construction project be accompanied by an environmental impact statement (EIS) specifying the anticipated consequences for natural systems of soil, landform, vegetation, animals, and aquatic organisms. The prescribed EIS was to be accompanied by an indication of what measures, if any, might be undertaken to correct undesirable impacts. In many cases the estimation of possible environmental impacts was followed by major revision of federally-supported construction plans which might affect the environment. It was accompanied by specific federal initiatives to protect wetlands, water bodies, and other natural features as well as endangered species. National policy in 1969 required the completion of impact statements by sponsoring agencies (US Congress, 1969). The execution and further planning of prospective water management projects were widely affected.

AN OVERVIEW OF WATER IN SOCIAL AND ENVIRONMENTAL SYSTEMS

This book is directed at the interrelationship of water's role in both social and environmental systems. To show the major problems that are examined, the chief aspects are outlined here before examining each in detail in subsequent chapters. A perspective on the principal phases

Figure 1.3   Natural wetlands outside Dhaka, Bangladesh, serve key ecological functions in the metropolitan environment.

through which public action has evolved over the centuries concludes this introduction.

In natural systems relatively undisturbed by human action and not necessarily serving any human needs, water has at least four principal functions and processes that are usually variable over time and place (Figure 1.3). It:

- nourishes vegetation in soils and river beds;
- nourishes the full range of animal organisms, including fish in streams and lakes;
- removes organic material or transforms it through weathering; and
- moves soil and other inorganic materials.

In performing these functions water accumulates in soil moisture, plants, wetlands, lakes, rivers, and the oceans; moves on and through the soil, in streams, and underground aquifers; is transpired from liquid to vapor; and freezes and melts with fluctuations in temperature.

While the total volume of water on the globe as summarized in Chapter 4 does not change significantly over time, its form and location as precipitation, water, ice, or cloud does change. In those ways it also changes in the degrees to which it is essential to the life of all ecosystems – land or marine.

Although for a long time there has been recognition and relatively accurate measurement of the amount of water that falls as precipitation or dew on land areas, and of the amounts consumed by plants and animals for their survival and growth, it has been a very slow and irregular process by which the precise role of water in maintenance of specific ecosystems has been estimated.

WATER AND HUMAN WELFARE

The use of water for people

The most elementary human need for water is in support of life through drinking and eating. Next in importance is its use to maintain healthy households through washing of hands, bodies, dishes, cooking implements, clothing and linens, and floors. While Gleick (2000a, p. 11), drawing on data from the World Health Organization (WHO) and other sources, has suggested a minimum daily consumption standard of 25 l per person per day for drinking and hygiene, and 25 l for bathing and food preparation, this is subject to tremendous variance according to differences in climate, people, and mode of life (Figure 1.4).

Water serves an essential role in supporting the growth of plants cultivated by people for food and clothing. For example, depending upon precipitation and temperature, the volume of water required to grow enough maize to feed one adult for one day may be the

Figure 1.4   A waterhole for animals in Punjab, Pakistan, indicates the need of all organisms for minimum water requirements.

full crop water demand in irrigated regions, supplemental irrigation in other regions, and no irrigation at all in areas of rain-fed cultivation; and similarly, each of these areas will have varying drainage requirements.

Beyond elementary survival through drinking, eating, and other household uses the quantities of water required daily by one human, excluding water used to grow crops, varies tremendously according to its uses for:

- non-edible products
- water transport
- generating hydroelectric or fossil-fuel energy
- construction
- recreation in water and wetlands

Each of those uses has a wide range in the quantity of water withdrawn, and varies considerably in the extent to which the chemical and biological quantity is altered. Each has its own economic cost for a given area.

WATER AS A HAZARD TO HUMANS

Human society is subject to massive extremes in well-being according to the availability and quality of water. Droughts and floods are common manifestations of such extremes, and in some areas limit the long-term habitability of land by people. Ice storms, avalanches, and blizzards occur in cold environments. So, too, may salinity and other physical and biological quality of water adversely affect human health.

SOCIAL GOALS IN MANAGING WATER

Public aims in managing water have consistently combined two goals: (1) to deal with the social needs as then perceived, however incompletely, and (2) to assure that the efforts made by one or more segments of society were not rendered fruitless by subsequent actions of other interests. The classic case is that of water rights being guaranteed once an investment of effort or funds is made for irrigation of dry land (Figure 1.5). Similarly, rights are established for domestic and industrial users who take approved steps to withdraw water from surface or ground sources. Users of an improved waterway commonly are assured of continued use, subject in some instances to payment of fees. Recently, in some areas users of water who receive public support have been

Figure 1.5   The margins of arid-zone irrigation in the lower Amu Darya
Valley, Uzbekistan, adversely affected by upstream diversions, recession
of the Aral Sea, and local waterlogging and salinity.

required to show the results of inquiry into possible impacts of their
proposed actions.

MILESTONES IN THINKING ABOUT WATER MANAGEMENT

Human interventions in the water cycle for any of the foregoing purposes have unfolded around the world in a variety of ways but in
roughly the same order. At least eight major stages have been followed:

(1)   Initially, water is enjoyed in and withdrawn from natural
       sources – rivers, lakes, springs – to meet human needs without
       changing the source, and rivers and lakes are used for navigation,
       fishing, and recreation without changing the depth or flow.

(2)   Next, improvements are made to increase the accessibility and
       disposal of the water without changing the withdrawal capacity,
       as in changing the access to a river, lake, or spring and protecting
       it from land-originating pollution without channeling the natu-
       ral flow or providing storm drainage and sewers.

(3)   The natural water bodies and flows may be altered by simple con-
       structions that alter the place and direction of flow, as where
       spring flow is channeled into a pool or where a river bed is nar-
       rowed or deepened to improve its navigation, or a lake inlet is
       deepened to facilitate a boat landing, or a levee is constructed to

prevent overflow of a certain height from inundating the natural floodplain, or a run-of-the-river mill dam is built that has no storage and only retains water to alter the fall.

(4) When a storage work or diversion canal or treatment facility is constructed, the basic intervention changes fundamentally because the downstream flow is regulated in time and volume. Typically, this involves retaining water when flow is high to even out the flows downstream in a drier time or to assure, as in the case of hydroelectric power generation, a flow when the market demands it. In their first common form storage dams were for a single purpose such as navigation, power generation, irrigation, or flood control. Similarly, the addition of treatment works for domestic or industrial waste-disposal systems altered the quality of downstream flow for a specific purpose, such as drinking.

(5) A major advance took place when storage structures commonly were designed and operated for multiple purposes. This increased the complexity of criteria used in evaluating both the design and operation of storage structures. Beginning in the 1930s, the multiple-purpose dam became a common form of new large-scale water management.

(6) Beginning in the 1930s there was growing concern for designing systems of multiple-purpose and single-purpose storage structures for entire river basins. The age of so-called integrated river development had set in, with basins such as the Tennessee, the Columbia, the Seine, and the Snowy Mountains claiming attention. The chief purposes typically were electric power generation, irrigation, navigation, municipal water supply, and flood control.

(7) Although the heavy emphasis in multiple-purpose river basin development was on hydraulic structures, the numerous economic aims came to invite attention to alternative non-structural measures to achieve the same aims. For example, reduction of urban water demand through pricing, regulation, or improved technology was an alternative to storing more water for urban use; choice of different crops was an alternative to providing water for irrigation; relocation of urban activity out of the floodplain was an alternative to dams or levees to protect those activities from floods; and so on.

(8) From the 1960s, more specific attention was directed at the possible effects of water management upon elements in the natural environment. Initially, the consequences of dams were primary objectives, but other effects began to receive inquiry, including the

consequences of draining wetlands; the changes in irrigated soil resulting from applications of water, fertilizers, and pesticides; and the alterations in aquatic flora and fauna following construction of navigation channels and flood-control levees. In those efforts there has been a basically spiritual as well as functional concern that humans seek to live in harmony with the systems of the natural environment.

Simplifying these changes in emphasis in water management over human time, it is convenient to recognize a few times between 2000 BCE and 2000 CE when significant changes in management approaches took shape:

Time of initiation	Prevailing modes of water management
earliest to present	direct use and local withdrawals
earliest to present	improvements in water sources
2000 BCE	alterations in natural water bodies by channel deepening and straightening, levees, or run-of-river dams
500 BCE	single-purpose storage
1900 CE	multiple-purpose storage
1930 CE	unified river basin programs
1960 CE	non-structural alternatives rediscovered
1970 CE	environmental effect assessment, e.g., protection of endangered species
1980 CE	assessment of full effects of water use, e.g., dams

Since the 1980s, a revolution in information technologies has facilitated the expansion of computer data storage, modeling, internet communication, and decision support systems. The appendix to this volume provides a guide to Internet resources which lists websites relevant to each chapter and a set of methods for searching them efficiently and systematically.

CONFLICTS AND HARMONY

Looking over the record of efforts at water management, it is challenging to ask where and how particular efforts achieved their intended aims, and why; and where and how they were failures, or challenged, and why. This has often involved reassessment of standards for valuing the costs and benefits. In particular, it may be asked in what circumstances the social aims were satisfied without significant deterioration in the natural environment. Such observations are an essential part of estimating whether or not it will be practicable to satisfy the future needs of society for water without causing severe and irreparable harm to the human as well as natural environment. This is part of the basic inquiry as to whether or not use of water in the world of the future can be truly sustainable. The various connotations of sustainability as they apply to water will be examined in more detail in Chapter 2.

It is easy to point to concrete cases where water management has seriously degraded or destroyed a sector of the natural environment. The number is immense. It is extremely difficult to describe carefully areas where extensive water management for human use has been achieved without many negative effects on environmental systems. Every effort to identify positive and negative consequences requires a detailed ex-post evaluation, or post audit, of the human actions involved. While much effort is spent estimating the possible future effects of actions, detailed ex-post evaluations are rare (Wescoat and Halvorson, 2000).

Ideally, an ex-post evaluation would be comprehensive, integrated, long-term, cumulative, and adaptive (Figure 1.6). A "comprehensive" evaluation covers the full range of environmental, social, and institutional effects of a project. "Integrated" evaluation of these effects within an ecological context (both natural and human) involves an examination of their interactions and linkages. When evaluations are performed, they often occur relatively soon after project completion and fail to assess the "long-term" consequences of that action. One of the reasons why such evaluations are rare is that other actions are undertaken that contribute to the "cumulative" impacts of water management in both their river basin and ecosystem contexts. Nevertheless, to manage those water resources and environments, it is necessary to draw upon the results of comprehensive, integrated, long-term, cumulative study in an "adaptive" process, responding both to changing environmental conditions and to human needs.

While detailed ex-post evaluations are rare, there are some notable exceptions. For example, plans to develop the Columbia Basin in the northwestern USA established baseline conditions in the 1940s (USBR, 1941–47). Subsequent assessments in 1963, 1975, and 2000 shed light on the changing profile of positive and negative consequences, and the processes of adjustment that shaped them (Macinko, 1963, 1975; Ortolano et al., 2000). The Gal Oya irrigation and river basin project in Sri Lanka also had detailed baseline studies and evaluations over roughly the same period (Uphoff, 1992), which shed light both on the changing levels of concern about specific types of impacts over time and, more fundamentally, on evolving frameworks for evaluation.

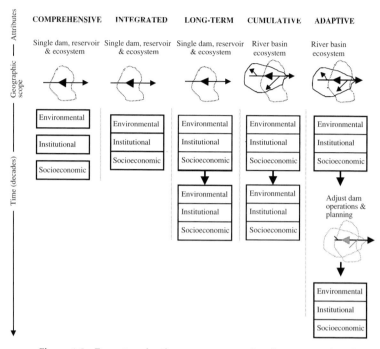

Figure 1.6   Ex-post evaluation concepts, ranging from comprehensive consideration of environmental, institutional, and socioeconomic impacts to adaptive management of river basin operations and planning. After Wescoat and Halvorson (2000).

Some studies offer valuable longitudinal perspectives on specific water issues. For example, in the field of flood hazards, ex-post evaluations have been prepared for flood control projects (Galloway, 1980); patterns of urban floodplain occupance (Gruntfest and Montz, 1986); flood disasters (Gruntfest, 1997); and floodplain management programs (White, 1988a). But these are exceptions, advanced by a handful of individuals and agencies.

As will be discussed in the next chapter, there are many other opportunities for continuous monitoring and evaluation of the complex relations between water and life. For example, many projects receive periodic attention prompted by regulatory requirements (e.g., relicensing of hydropower plants) or social movements (e.g., reservoir displacement). To understand the complex and changing relations between water and life, a more extensive and systematic pursuit of these opportunities is needed.

2

Challenge and opportunity

INTRODUCTION

The introductory chapter briefly described the state of water management and the natural and social systems principally affected during recent centuries. At the present time the challenge to concerned people is to ask what opportunities there are to recognize wise principles that might be applied in the years ahead to the correction of previous unwise activity and to the guidance of new activity. This chapter reviews the state of global water management at the end of the twentieth century as seen by selected analysts, and summarizes samples of thinking at that time as to policies that should guide further action.

As an aid to appraising both past and future water management it briefly examines the changing criteria for evaluating the effects of such management. General criteria which might guide future choice of policies and technologies are reviewed with attention to specific efforts made by non-governmental, national, and international agencies to specify their definitions of desirable policy. In a general sense, many of those criteria fall into the category of efforts at what is loosely termed "sustainable development." Because of the range of definitions often employed for those terms, an effort is made to express the various connotations of sustainable development more precisely as they apply to water management. They are then given meaning for the concrete aims of setting the demands for potable water, of meeting food needs, of supplying energy requirements, and of maintaining biodiversity in natural systems.

In broadest terms, the challenge is to find practical ways of so managing the available supplies of water on earth as to sustain likely future human populations at a desirable standard of life without widely degrading the basic environmental systems and their capacity to sustain

Figure 2.1   Temples in the rice fields of Bali, Indonesia, play important roles in irrigation scheduling and crop pest management as well as in religious life. Photograph courtesy of Andrew B. Wescoat.

humans in the future indefinitely (Figure 2.1). This will require drastic changes in the prevailing standards for evaluating new projects as well as radical measures to revise the design and operation of some existing water management.

An underlying condition for both efforts is relatively precise understanding of the consequences for both natural and social systems of the major management devices and methods that have been practiced. This also involves taking critical account of the many opportunities to affect the future quantity and quality of water and associated ecosystems and to change the character of related social systems. By 2002, there were numerous efforts to assess those opportunities in the century ahead (Gleick, 2002).

STANDARDS OF SUSTAINABILITY

The basic concept of "sustainable development" began to take shape in many areas during the 1980s. It was given concrete form in the report of the World Commission on Environment and Development (WCED, 1987), and found more explicit expression in the Rio Conference on Environment and Development in 1992 (UNCED, 1992). As later interpreted by the board of the US National Research Council (NRC, 1999d) it involved public policies directed to achieving a world society with the following primary goals: "to meet the needs of a much larger but

Figure 2.2   The early African-American settlement of Dearfield, Colorado, USA, was abandoned after climatic and economic crises of the 1930s.

stabilizing human population, to sustain the life support systems of the planet, and to substantially reduce hunger and poverty" (Figures 2.2 and 2.3). Specific international targets for meeting human needs included:

- providing food and nutrition;
- nurturing children;
- finding shelter;
- providing an education;
- finding employment.

Specific international targets for preserving life support systems included:

- ensuring the quality and supply of freshwater;
- controlling emissions into the atmosphere;
- protecting the oceans;
- maintaining species and ecosystems.

Specific international targets for reducing hunger and poverty included:

- encouraging social growth in income and employment;
- increasing the share of the increased income accruing to poor and hungry people;
- providing crucial public services for nurturing, education, and housing (NRC, 1999d, pp. 30–48).

Figure 2.3   Squatter settlements in Lahore, Pakistan, frequently occupy low-lying poorly drained areas. Their shallow handpumps and standpipes are subject to contamination from flooding and water disposal.

ASSESSMENTS OF THE WORLD WATER SITUATION

With these general criteria in mind, it is instructive to review briefly the assessments of the world water situation made by a variety of analysts at the end of the millennium (Figures 2.4 and 2.5). Increasing attention was directed to conspicuous failures in water management (Herring, 2003). There were many reports by various observing individuals and groups as the twentieth century drew to a close and attention turned to years when there were major international gatherings such as those at The Hague and Stockholm. The following reports are selected as representing a variety of approaches:

- World Meteorological Organization (WMO, 1997)
- United Nations Environmental Programme (UNEP, 1999)
- World Water Commission, *World Water Vision* (WWC, 2000)
- Gleick, *The World's Water*, 2000a
- Brown *et al.*, *State of the World*, 2001
- Bonn International Conference on Freshwater (Germany, 2001)
- United Nations World Summit on Sustainable Development, Johannesburg (Prince of Orange, 2002)
- Third World Water Forum, Kyoto, 2003

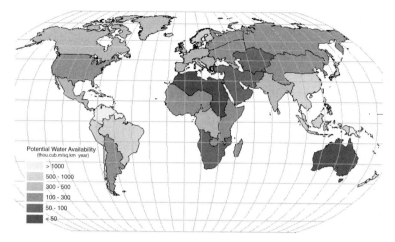

Figure 2.4   Potential annual water availability for natural-economic regions of the world (thousand m^3/ km^2), taking into account hydrologic relationships between rainfall, evapotranspiration, and runoff. After Shiklomanov (1999).

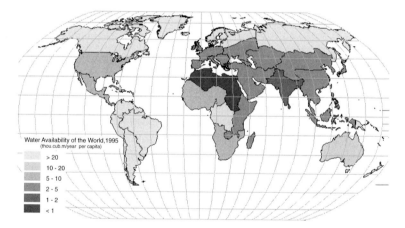

Figure 2.5   Potential water availability in 1995 (thousand m^3/ year per capita), ranging from "catastrophically low" (<1) to "very high" (>20). Mapped by natural-economic regions of the world. After Shiklomanov (1999).

The following observations are selected from that literature as they deal with three questions:

(1)   What are the major features of water management worldwide, particularly as it relates to the natural environment?

(2)   What are regarded as major problems of water management requiring attention in the future?

(3)   What are the more promising opportunities to deal with some of
those problems through policy, technology, or organization?

Observations on worldwide water management, particularly as
it relates to the natural environment, are selected from those sources.
The references are necessarily brief and do not pretend to cover the full
appraisal, but give a little of the flavor of selected thinking at the time
when many efforts were made to envisage the world water outlook.
It may be partly misleading to quote summary statements of views of
the situation without all relevant data, and the samples of responses
to the three questions that follow are given only to introduce the need
for more detailed analysis.

(1) Major features of world-wide water management

- The volume of total withdrawals of water continues to rise but at
a continually lower rate than was predicted in earlier years.
- The amount of crops requiring water continues to grow but with
declining volumes of water applied for given crop yields.
- Municipal water use per capita is rising sharply in developing
countries but declining in developed countries. Overall, 80 percent of the total population is estimated to have safe and affordable supply.
- While industrial water use per capita declines in developed countries it increases in developing countries.
- Recycling and increased productivity continue to lower the ratio
of water withdrawn to water consumed for all purposes.
- Pollution is becoming more widespread in underground aquifers,
many of which are declining.
- The population of amphibians is declining in many terrestrial
ecosystems.
- Fish populations decline in numbers in many coastal waters.
- Economic losses from natural hazards, much of which are floods,
hurricanes and landslides, continue to grow.

(2) Major problems for the future

- Pollution and overdraft of groundwater resources need to be
curbed and reversed.

- The quality of domestic water supply in developing countries does not keep pace with the volume of withdrawals.
- A large proportion of the world's wetlands have been destroyed with accompanying reduction in native vegetation and fauna that need to be restored.
- Water continues to be managed in many sectors by separate and often independent agencies.
- Chemical pollution of both surface water and groundwater is increasing in many areas.

(3) Promising opportunities to cope with current and emerging problems through improved water management

- Development of environmentally compatible techniques for treating both domestic and industrial waste and for avoiding the production of such waste (Figure 2.6).
- Applying economic and other social methods of reducing unnecessary withdrawals of water.
- Promoting agencies or policies to manage water and land with unified policies in small watersheds and large river basins, including international basins.

Figure 2.6   Advanced wastewater pond system in the Napa Valley of California, USA, combines low technology with high science in using biological treatment methods (designed by Oswald Green, LLC).

Figure 2.7   Urbanization poses challenges to productive irrigated areas involving adjustment of both water-management and land-use practices in Grand Valley, Colorado, USA.

- Carrying out research on the full impacts of various water management techniques upon the natural ecosystems, and on economic methods of curbing detrimental techniques.
- Definition and political application of a universal human right to water.
- Research leading to cheaper and more effective methods of desalting saline water in specific situations.
- Developing techniques for increasing food production with minor increases in consumptive use of water (Figure 2.7).

During the last quarter of the twentieth century and in subsequent years, a substantial number of projections were made, predicting global water withdrawal in the years 2000 and 2025, and in a few cases for 2050 and 2075. Those were reviewed by Gleick in *The World's Water, 2000–2001* (Gleick, 2000a, pp. 59–63). Account was taken of the differences in projection according to whether or not they included estimates of water lost from reservoir evaporation. Not accounting for reservoir evaporation, ten different forecasts of total withdrawal in 2025 ranged from 3625 to 5500 km^3 per year.

Looking at the supporting documents, Gleick observed two noteworthy trends:

First, the earlier projections routinely, and significantly, overestimated future water demands because of their dependence on relatively straightforward extrapolation of existing trends. Second, the methods and totals used for forecasting and scenario analysis have been getting more and more sophisticated, permitting a wider range of exploratory scenarios and a better understanding of the driving factors behind changes in demands for water. (Gleick, 2000a, p. 58)

In its comprehensive review of the state of the global environment the United Nations Environment Programme (UNEP) concluded:

Global freshwater consumption rose six fold between 1900 and 1995 – at more than twice the rate of population growth. About one-third of the world's population already lives in countries with moderate to high water stress – that is, where water consumption is more than 10 percent of the renewable freshwater supply. (UNEP, 1999, p. 41)

The UN Commission on Sustainable Development (1997) calculated that by the year 2025 as much as two-thirds of the world population may be subject to moderate-to-high water stress, in which more than 20 percent of the total naturally available annual water supply is withdrawn.

The World Water Council (WWC) convened a special Commission that prepared at the beginning of the twenty-first century its Vision of water and life in 2025 (Cosgrove and Rijsberman, 2000; WWC, 2000). The Commission concluded that the world was providing water for human use in quantities six times greater than 100 years earlier and that the current crisis was not about having too little water to satisfy needs but as "a crisis of managing water so badly that billions of people – and the environment – suffer badly." It also concluded that "while much has been achieved, today's water crisis is widespread. Continuing current policies for managing water will only widen and deepen that crisis."

Recognizing the belief that provision of safe and affordable drinking water had been achieved for an estimated 80 percent of the world population, and sanitation facilities for perhaps 50 percent, and that wastewater treatment had improved in many countries while food production kept pace with slowing population growth, the Vision noted six disturbing aspects of the water situation. In brief, these were:

(1)   As much as one-fifth of the world population lacks access to safe and affordable drinking water.

(2)   More than 15 percent of the world population eats less than 2000 calories per capita per day.

(3)   Much economic progress has caused severe impacts on natural ecosystems, such as destroyed wetlands and great reductions in river flow.

(4)   Water conservation techniques do not spread while water services are subsidized.

(5)   Groundwater supplies are being depleted by overpumping.

(6)   Water in many countries continues to be managed sector by sector by a highly fragmented set of institutions without effective allocations or effective participation of all concerned stakeholders.

In 2001, following the second World Water Forum, a conference on freshwater in Bonn, Germany, articulated five "keys" to sustainable water management:

(1)   The first key is to meet the water-security needs of the poor.

(2)   Decentralization is key. The local level is where national policy meets community needs.

(3)   The key to better water outreach is new partnerships.

(4)   The key to long-term harmony with nature and neighbors is cooperative arrangements at the waterbasin level, including across waters that touch many shores.

(5)   The essential key is stronger, better-performing governance arrangements.

The most important "water decision" taken at the global level is possibly the International Development Target set by the UN Millennium Assembly in October 2000. The target is "to halve, by 2015, the proportion of people living in extreme poverty and to halve the proportion of people who suffer from hunger and are unable to reach or to afford safe drinking water resources" (Prince of Orange, 2002).

In 2002, the results of these and other global water meetings and studies were presented at the second United Nations Conference on Environment and Development at Johannesburg, which reviewed progress toward the *Agenda 21* goals for freshwater drafted ten years earlier in Rio de Janeiro (UNCED, 1992). A summary document prepared for the ministerial conference by the Prince of Orange (2002), who opened and was a patron of the second World Water Forum, recommended seven targets and actions (Table 2.1).

In addition to the main UN conference a parallel meeting of water specialists was organized, called the Waterdome, which focused

Table 2.1 *Recommended targets and action in* No Water, No Future

Recommended targets	Recommended action
1. Halve the proportion of people who are unable to reach or to afford safe drinking water resources by 2015.	Mandate the World Water Assessment Programme of the United Nations to establish a baseline and monitor progress towards these targets and report to the Ministerial Conferences associated with the World Water Forum series or the UN's Commission on Sustainable Development.
2. Halve the proportion of people who are unable to reach or to afford sanitation by 2015.	
3. Increase water productivity in agriculture (rain-fed and irrigated) to enable food security for all people without increasing water diverted for irrigated agriculture over that used in 2000.	
4. Have at least 20% of all water infrastructure investments funded by alternative forms of financing by 2015.	Build capacity in local governments to assess alternative forms of financing for infrastructure, including capacity to identify, develop and negotiate sound projects that are financially feasible and environmentally sustainable as alternative solutions to large-scale investments.
5. Assess virtual water imports and exports through agricultural products for each country, or in other words, analyze the impact of changes in the subsidies in agriculture and the international system of trade in food and fiber, on national and local water demands, by 2015.	In the international trade negotiations on agricultural subsidies and trade in agricultural products, the World Trade Organization should consider the impact on water use in countries importing and exporting food.
6. Develop, by 2010, an agreed strategy for the use of molecular biology to increase drought tolerance and water productivity of crops to achieve water, food, and environmental security.	Have the Consultative Group on International Agricultural Research assess the potential for increased drought tolerance and increased water productivity in agriculture, including the potential of the use of functional genomics and other tools of modern molecular biology.

(*cont.*)

Table 2.1 (*cont.*)

Recommended targets	Recommended action
7. Have plans for resource allocation and investments, similar to those adopted for the Nile basin, agreed by the riparian countries for all of Africa's international basins by 2015.	Establish an African Water Facility to seed the investments in water-resources development and management to increase capacity to assess and manage water, and prepare an investment strategy for water resources development in Africa, within the framework of the New Partnership for Africa's Development.

Source: Prince of Orange, 2002.

in greater breadth and depth on the roles of freshwater in environment and development. The Waterdome agenda builds upon that of the Second World Water Forum, with the following themes:

(1)   water, regional integration, and finance
(2)   water and nature
(3)   water, energy, and climate
(4)   water and food security
(5)   water, health, and poverty
(6)   water and globalization

These international initiatives also stimulated a rich array of over 200 water management sessions for the Third World Water Forum in Kyoto, Japan, in March 2003. In addition to the environmental, engineering, social, and policy science themes, it was encouraging to see contributions from the arts (e.g., "Music in water") and humanities (e.g., "The wisdom of water"). The *World Water Development Report* released at that conference added four key challenges: water and industry, water and energy, water and cities, and ensuring the water knowledge base. Notwithstanding these professional advances, the report concluded that "worldwide, of the creatures associated with inland waters, 24 percent of mammals and 12 percent of birds are threatened, as are a third of the 10 percent of fish species studied in detail so far. Inland water biodiversity is widely in decline, mainly from habitat disturbance, which can be taken as evidence of declining ecosystem condition" (UNESCO, 2003, p. 14).

In undertaking each of these lines of research and administration essential elements are the criteria used for evaluation by the wide range of investigators and administrators who may pursue them. To that effort the criteria of sustainability as elaborated in *Our Common Journey* are essential.

The worldwide and complex assessment of water problems at the turn of the millennium set in motion a more complex and integrated approach than at any previous time in human history. A little of the extent and depth of that diverse analysis is suggested in the above references. Those and many related topics will be explored in the following chapters. They examine in more depth the principal facets of water management around the world as it is related to environmental policy.

A basic challenge to students of water management in the twenty-first century is to identify which combinations of research and administrative policy offer promising opportunities to exercise genuinely positive methods of achieving a sustainable world.

3

Unfolding recognition of ecosystem change

Many of the challenges and opportunities articulated in international water assessments of the 1990s indicated a growing recognition of ecosystem changes generated by human water use. Much knowledge has been gained in recent years about the human effects on aquatic, riparian, estuarine, and groundwater ecosystems. Some effects, such as eradication of native non-commercial fish, purposely accelerated environmental impacts, while others have occurred with little or no recognition until illuminated by scientific or public inquiry (Gosnell, 2001). Assessment of habitat conditions, along with distinctions among levels of species endangerment, has become increasingly refined (IUCN, 2000). But many human effects on aquatic, amphibian, invertebrate, and fish species and their habitats still lie beyond comprehension.

Each year new surprises occur: an amphibious population declines, a waterbird species experiences birth defects, an exotic mollusk invades new waters, a fish disease spreads, an insect disease vector adapts to control methods. With sufficient time, the surprise is recognized, management alternatives are formulated, and actions are taken. For example, the adverse water quality effects of irrigation return flows from pesticide contamination in the Aral Sea basin of Central Asia, like increased selenium concentrations from irrigation return flows to the Kesterson Reservoir of California, have opened up new lines of environmental impact assessment and adjustments in irrigated areas of the world (Ghassemi *et al.*, 1995; Kobori and Glantz, 1998; Micklin and Williams, 1996; NRC, 1989b). Remote sensing and aerial photography provide stark images of those impacts (Figure 3.1). Recognition of these environmental effects led to increasing public pressure on agricultural water users, organizations, and projects and to renewed questions about

Figure 3.1   Fishing boats stranded and abandoned along the former
Aral Sea coastline near Nukus, Uzbekistan, where commercial fishing
has collapsed.

the sustainability of irrigation agriculture (see ICID, 1957; MacDonnell,
1999; NRC, 1989b; and an international *Dialogue on Water, Food and
Environment*, facilitated by the International Water Management Institute, IWMI, 2001).

In some cases, unfolding recognition has followed advances in science and technology. For example, improved measurement techniques
have enabled increasingly precise monitoring, analysis, and explanation
of changing water stocks, flows, and quality conditions. Today, regulatory debates about acceptable arsenic levels in drinking water rely upon
measurements of concentrations in parts per million or $\mu g/l$, which
were not measurable until the late twentieth century. Advances in related fields of atmospheric, vegetation, and soil sciences have led to
increased understanding of nutrient cycling, climate variability, and
watershed changes that affect hydrologic processes and water quality
from microscopic to global scales. From early concern about acidification in boreal forest regions, atmospheric and watershed scientists have
traced the pathways and cycling of a wide range of chemicals emitted
by urban and agricultural activities and natural processes (Cowling,
1982; Cowling and Nilsson, 1995). At the global scale, an entire research field now focuses on the human dimensions of global environmental change, with particular emphasis on global and regional

hydroclimatic impacts and adjustments (Gleick, 2000b; Liverman *et al.*, in press; Lohmann, 2002). The 1990s also witnessed renewed scientific efforts to understand the water resources effects of land use policies and practices (e.g., Falkenmark *et al.*, 1999). Fluvial geomorphologists work with aquatic ecologists and ichthyologists on the flow regimes, flushing flows, and riparian landforms conducive, or destructive, to aquatic species and ecosystems (NRC, 1992; Pitlick and Van Steeter, 1998; Thorne *et al.*, 1997; Trimble, 1997).

APPROACHES TO HUMAN UNDERSTANDING OF ECOSYSTEM CHANGE

These examples invite broader questions about how human knowledge about environmental change unfolds. How do societies in different regions and time periods seek environmental knowledge? What roles do changes in perceptions, attitudes, social movements, and scientific processes play? What explains the rate and extent of change in specific areas? Of the many possible ways of addressing these questions, this chapter explores five broad processes of human understanding: (1) rapid innovation; (2) progressive development; (3) changing social values; (4) social rediscovery of integrated approaches; and (5) personal recognition of ecosystem effects.

(1) Rapid innovation

Some advances in water and environmental management have involved relatively rapid discoveries and applications. These may entail novel ways of observing water and related environmental phenomena. For example, development of the microscope, Louis Pasteur's theories of microbiology, and a host of related nineteenth-century scientific and social developments dramatically transformed the management of water quality for human health (Goubert, 1986). Rapid advances in remote sensing, high-speed computing, and international science organizations in the late twentieth century deepened social concern about global environmental change and its water resources implications (Gleick, 2000b; IPCC, 2001a, 2001b, 2001c).

Although none of these changes occurs instantaneously with a single observation or invention, they can occur quickly, for example on timescales of months to years, especially in the aftermath of disasters. An outbreak of *Cryptosporidium*-related diseases in Milwaukee, Wisconsin, in 1993 led water utilities in many cities and countries to test for that organism, issue warnings to vulnerable social groups, and work on technological solutions.

Similarly, publication of Rachel Carson's *Silent Spring* (1962) on pesticide contamination of freshwater ecosystems helped catalyze support for water quality testing, water pollution control, and pesticide regulation (Curtis and Profeta, 1993; Munn and Gilliom, 2001). It is sobering to realize that even in cases when rapid progress is made, initial plans may underestimate the amount and difficulty of what is involved. For example, the US Clean Water Act of 1972 called for all waters of the United States to be "fishable and swimmable" by 1983 and to achieve "zero discharge" of pollutants by 1985. These goals have not been met, and may never be met (Adler *et al.*, 1993).

As will be elaborated later, rapid regulatory changes do not always lead to rapid environmental improvement. Indeed, proliferation of environmental and water resources laws, regulations, and policies can actually constrain progress, as when different jurisdictions pass water laws that conflict with or encumber action. Efforts to undo bureaucratic knots face predictable, sometimes formidable, constraints. In the United States, a 1955 report on *Water Resources and Power* failed to lead to reorganization of entrenched federal water bureaucracies, as did subsequent reports in the 1980s and late 1990s (US Commission on Organization of the Executive Branch of the Government, 1955; Western Water Policy Review Advisory Commission, 1998; WRC, 1978).

An impressive example of rapid progress in the developing world involves flood hazards mitigation in Bangladesh, where cyclones killed an estimated 300 000 in 1970–71 and 139 000 in 1991 (Figure 3.2). A large-scale Flood Action Program, initiated in the 1980s, was strongly criticized for its emphasis on structural river engineering work (Haggart *et al.*, 1994; Islam, 1995; Rogers *et al.*, 1989, 1994). However, it and other programs also included non-structural measures, such as forecasting and warning systems, and innovative cyclone shelter designs, which helped reduce casualties in comparably severe cyclones in 1993 and 1998 (IDNDR–UNESCAP, 1999). Another example of rapid innovation in Bangladesh involved scientific advance and regional implementation of oral rehydration therapies for diarrheal disease. The scientific component of oral rehydration research determined the effective proportions of sugars and salts that enable fluid absorption in the gut (Ruxin, 1994). The practical diffusion of this knowledge in rural Bangladesh reached 13 million families within a decade through the efforts of the International Centre for Diarrhoeal Disease Research, Bangladesh, its MATLAB research station, and non-governmental organizations (Fauveau, 1994).

Figure 3.2   Low-lying settlements in Bangladesh exist in a delicate balance with floods and coastal storm surge.

It has been noted that major changes in environmental inquiry rarely originate solely in government agency programs. Examples ranging from flood hazards to global climate change have originated in research centers, universities, and local organizations. Government-sponsored inquiry later becomes important in sustaining those emerging lines of research, diffusing innovations through extension and outreach, and supporting the progressive development of human understanding of ecosystem change, as discussed below.

(2) Progressive development

While harmonization of water and environmental policy often begins with "new" knowledge, it also builds upon or reacts against previous approaches, which requires time for the progressive development and adoption of innovations. Thus, in addition to asking how major innovations occur, it is important to ask how recognition of the environmental effects of water use unfolds progressively over longer periods of time, from decades to centuries (Figures 3.3 and 3.4). Each innovation gives rise to processes of scientific and technological experimentation which refine understanding. For example, advances in soil physics have led to finer appreciation of the erosivity of different soils in different climates and under different land use management practices. Long-term

Figure 3.3   Ruined aqueducts in Rome, Italy, testify to the extraordinary technical ingenuity, and ultimate social or environmental unsustainability, of some major water projects.

Figure 3.4   The Trevi fountain in downtown Rome marks the terminus of a former Roman aqueduct that continues to run for both water supply and public enjoyment.

experimentation has likewise shed light on the efficacy of different combinations of erosion control technologies and policies (Helms, 1992; Hillel, 1992).

For long-term processes of scientific development and policy formulation, government programs and funding often play an important role. Improvements in the water and sanitation in urban environments, for example, required several centuries of progressive development (Melosi, 1999). In the early nineteenth century, few urban areas in the world had effective sanitation systems. Human and industrial wastes contaminated rivers and groundwater, drinking supplies, market gardens, parks, and urban ecosystems (Platt et al., 1994; Spirn, 1984). Cities were a sink for wastes of all sorts (Tarr, 2000). In many parts of the world, this is still the case. As cities initiate programs for improving household, street, and metropolitan sanitation, they transform environmental problems. These advances are progressive because many steps are involved. Initially, wastes are shifted from one location to another (and thus from one social group and ecosystem to others). Progress then entails cleaning up in these other areas, ultimately extending to a regional scale. They are also progressive because they entail social and political struggles that surmount administrative as well as political resistance to expanding access to water and improving standards of water and environmental quality (Swyngedouw, 1995). These changes are only progressive, in the fullest sense of the term, when they enable marginalized groups to gain their fair share of the resource and a secure place in a healthy ecosystem. As will be elaborated later, progress may also involve adapting traditional methods of turning wastes into wealth, e.g., by composting and reusing organic wastes; rediscovering local solutions, e.g., on-site cisterns and stormwater detention; and restoring local ecosystems, e.g., urban streams and floodplains. Emerging international programs of environmental sanitation (Esrey et al., 1998) include engineered pond and lagoon systems for sewage treatment (Oswald, 1995). As the ruins of sophisticated urban sewerage systems at sites such as Moenjo Daro in the Indus basin remind us, progressive development depends upon sustained human adjustment to changing political, economic, and environmental conditions (Jansen et al., 1991).

A second example of progressive recognition involves soil erosion, stream sedimentation, and soil conservation practices. Soil conservation has ancient roots in many parts of the world, but modern approaches advanced in the twentieth century through government-sponsored research, cost sharing, and local experiment stations

(Helms, 1992). Some modern assumptions about relationships between population growth and soil erosion have been challenged. A study in Tanzania associated higher population levels with increased soil protection (Tiffen *et al.*, 1994), but these results appear limited to special contexts (Boyd and Slaymaker, 2000). A study of farmers' decisions to conserve soil and water resources in developing countries indicates that progress depends upon expanding social capabilities to secure financial and administrative resources to address those problems, as well as recognition of them (Blaikie, 1985).

Education is an important vehicle for progressive development. Unfolding social recognition of ecosystem change, e.g., riparian impacts of streamflow diversions, may require decades of public education. Public support for wetlands protection has developed steadily but slowly from the 1930s to the present (Prince, 1997). The role of schools, universities, and public education in environmental understanding is increasingly appreciated. Schoolchildren and their teachers are learning how to measure streamflow, sample water quality, and observe aquatic species – and report their data to management agencies – in ways formerly used only by professionals. These activities are supported by curricula developed by professional water organizations (e.g., Project WET, Water Education Foundation, Children's Water Festival, and the Stockholm Junior Water Prize). Although relationships between water resources education and water use behaviors are not well understood, the ground has been prepared for examining them (Baumann and Haimes, 1988).

(3) Changing social values

Innovation and progressive change involve changing social values, as well as scientific knowledge and political action. Changes in social values, whether defined in attitudinal, ethical, or economic terms, can drive changes in water use behavior and water management policies that affect environmental quality (Kates and Burton, 1986).

Wetlands conservation provides a good example of these changes in many regions of the world. From antiquity, wetlands have been associated with disease vectors, insect pest habitats, and *miasma* (noxious vapors believed to upset the humors and thereby health) (Hippocrates, 1978). These views have promoted drainage and sewerage infrastructure from antiquity to the present (Figure 3.5). Except for cultures specifically adapted to wetland conditions and resources as in the Shatt al-Arab estuary of the Tigris and Euphrates rivers, theories about the

Figure 3.5   A sewer (*cloaca*) that drained the Circus Maximus in Rome improved a low-lying area but drained storm and sanitary sewage directly into the Tiber River.

unhealthy nature of stagnant waters and wet soils persisted through the nineteenth century. While theories of microbiological contagion displaced the *miasma* hypothesis (Blake, 1956), concern about aquatic insect disease vectors continues (Cairncross and Feachem, 1993).

As a result, many nineteenth-century water policies purposely advocated "swamplands reclamation" through dredging, drainage, filling, and plantation as in the lower Mississippi River valley (Harrison, 1961). It is estimated that wetlands comprised some 6 percent of the world's land surface, a large portion of which were drained in the twentieth century (Williams, 1991). Richards and Flint (1994) estimate that 36 percent of the wetlands in South and Southeast Asia were converted to other land uses between 1880 and 1980. A comparative study of land-use transformations in China, India, and the USA indicated extensive wetland losses in all three regions (NRC, 2001). The International Union for Conservation of Nature and Natural Resources (IUCN, 2002) estimates that wetland losses worldwide may be as high as 50 percent. Some midwestern states of the USA have drained over 90 percent of their wetlands (Prince, 1997).

At the same time, there has been unfolding social recognition of wetland values and benefits. Ecologists have drawn attention to the biological productivity of wetland ecosystems (Mitsch and Gosselink, 2000). Wetland scientists have also striven to estimate the economic value of wetlands for ecological productive fisheries, recreation, and aesthetic enjoyment. Photographers, environmentalists, and artists have deepened aesthetic appreciation through a wide range of media. Finally, leading wastewater engineers and environmental designers are rediscovering and refining the functional value of wetlands for waste assimilation, wastewater treatment, and environmental education (Campbell and Ogden, 1999; Sheaffer and Stevens, 1983).

All of these forms of appreciation supported changing social attitudes toward wetlands, which are increasingly perceived as beautiful, beneficial, and necessary (Prince, 1997; White, 1976). Attitudinal changes have contributed to legislation to protect wetlands, ranging from regulation of dredging and filling (e.g., section 404 of the Clean Water Act in the USA) to a National Wetlands Inventory by the US Fish and Wildlife Service. At the international level, the Ramsar Convention on the protection of wetlands, passed in 1971, two decades later listed 1109 sites comprising 87.25 million hectares of protected wetlands in 2002. It establishes international criteria for wetland conservation and promotes an international wetland conservation ethos, as will be elaborated in Chapter 7.

Even so, recognition of wetland impacts continues to shift as society weighs wetland values against other land, water, and environmental values. Policy debates over delineation of wetland boundaries, which affect the extent of area regulated, reflect on-going and unresolved negotiation of social valuation of wetlands and alternative resource uses (NRC, 1995).

Another example of changing social values concerns fisheries – native, sport, and commercial – and protection of the habitats that support them. Fishing occupation groups in some regions of the world have lower social status than other branches of agricultural and industrial activity. Twentieth-century water development favored large-scale irrigation projects over artisanal fishing communities, even when the latter contributed greater economic and dietary benefits to a region. However, when water development and overfishing depleted fish habitats and populations, changing social values have helped support native, commercial, and sport fisheries.

At the same time, tensions persist among fishing communities. For example, while sport fishing may require the types of cold-water temperatures found below dams, native fish prefer the warm turbid waters of unregulated rivers. Aquaculture has boomed in Asia and other regions of the world, but construction of fishponds displaces other aquatic habitat, and flushing of aquaculture effluents pollutes in-stream and nearshore fisheries.

Each example reminds us that changing social values have shaped all of the water and environmental problems that exist today. The beliefs that water not consumed is wasted, that water acquired as a property right should be transferable as a commodity separate from the land, and that non-human organisms have no inherent rights to water they require, are social values that have aggravated environmental problems. In each of these cases, unfolding recognition entails changing social values, which do not follow a straight path, but instead are continually renegotiated in the face of competing social demands. Sometimes recognition entails historical reflection, back upon earlier approaches to water management and environmental planning that have renewed potential, as discussed below.

(4) Social rediscovery of integrated approaches to water and environmental management

Public investment in a new line of water resources management may displace earlier approaches that are deficient, in one respect or another, in addressing water problems. The new approach may decrease costs, increase reliability, or increase certain types and levels of control. While providing these improvements, however, the new approach may also deflect attention from historically effective approaches to water and environmental management. After the passage of time, and the experience of new environmental consequences, society may rediscover these earlier approaches and adapt them to address more effectively its environmental problems and water needs.

For example, in the twentieth century there were identified four "watersheds," in which water scientists and managers chose some scientific approaches over other approaches that were more integrative (White, 1997, pp. 90–91):

- focusing on soil class rather than landscape type as a basis for study, teaching, and administration;
- focusing on downstream channel flooding and sedimentation rather than upstream watershed processes;
- concern with quantities of water rather than sediment flows from non-point sources affecting quality of water; and
- emphasizing the needs of individual land managers rather than larger organizations as primary managers of natural resources.

In each case, the latter approaches were rediscovered when the consequences of the less integrative approaches became clear.

Individually and collectively, these choices by scientific organizations contributed to the fragmentation of water and related environmental sciences and hence to delayed recognition of some types of ecosystem effects, notwithstanding other scientific advances. The historical definition of management agencies by different types of resource use and industrial organization (i.e., forestry, grazing, irrigation, etc.) – and fierce resistance to more integrative river basin, watershed, water quality, floodplain, community-based, and landscape alternatives – further delayed understanding of and comprehensive approaches to the environmental effects of water resource use.

Social rediscovery of neglected alternatives may involve decades to centuries, and be especially difficult if overlain with decades of scientific practice, education, and neglect. In the modern era, it also risks charges of romanticism about purportedly harmonious earlier, primitive, or distant societies that in fact had, at best, mixed environmental records (Tuan, 1968b). While some of these charges are well founded, they may belittle genuine yearning for more integrated, sustainable, and meaningful relationships between water and environmental management (Figure 3.6).

Some rediscoveries of integrated water management approaches are bearing substantial fruit. Watershed coalitions of the 1990s have antecedents in the 1950s, 1930s, 1910s, and 1890s (Wescoat, 2000).

Figure 3.6   Petroglyph of animals at the base of the Grand Canyon and Colorado River corridor in Arizona, USA, indicates the importance ascribed to the river canyon as the source of life.

Landscape classification of the 1890s re-emerged as landscape ecology and planning in the 1980s (Forman, 1995). Israeli and Jordanian scientists were able to reconstruct and adapt Nabatean water harvesting techniques in the Negev (Evenari *et al.*, 1982; Rogers and Lydon, 1997).

Other traditional water harvesting and irrigation methods have potential that has yet to be fully realized – though they may seem, as Agarwal and Narain (1997) warn in India, a "dying wisdom." The Centre for Science and Environment in India has promoted the identification, study, preservation and improvement of traditional water harvesting methods, adapted to different cultural and hydrologic regions. In five years, they established a nationwide water harvesting network, implemented projects in New Delhi, and expanded the range of choice for supplying local water needs (Agarwal *et al.*, 2001).

Some of the key challenges in rediscovering the potential environmental benefits of historic water systems are: first, recognizing their existence; second, analyzing how they did and did not work; third, adapting them to address current needs; and finally, monitoring their performance to promote further adjustments and diffusion. For this to occur, the historical geography of water management must be part of the curriculum in water resources programs, and must become part of the consciousness of individual water managers.

(5) Personal recognition

Many of the innovations described above involve large numbers of water users, activists, and social organizations working over, in human terms, relatively long periods of time. However, it is important to remember that each of these processes is experienced, and in significant ways affected, by individual recognition of the environmental effects of human action – and most immediately by one's own impacts. Individual recognition may lead to profound changes in individual and, by example, collective behavior. Aldo Leopold's *A Sand County Almanac* (Leopold, 1991) recorded his changing views of wildlife and natural habitats, and influenced generations of subsequent readers. Mahatma Gandhi (1957) described his personal habits and simple lifestyle as "experiments with truth," which influenced millions.

The history of late-twentieth-century environmentalism, experienced at a personal level, would yield myriad accounts of attitudinal and behavioral change. They may be rapid or gradual, active or reflective. Individual transformations may involve years or decades, but the ways in which they occur collectively shape broader processes of social change.

In the water conservation field, James Knopf (1991) developed a love of drought-adapted plants in Colorado, and has spent much of his career sharing that with others and encouraging them to adopt "xeriscape" approaches to planting that require minimal irrigation. Akhtar Hameed Khan (1996) in Karachi, Pakistan, became convinced that squatters could improve their household sanitation, and work with neighbors to upgrade large squatter settlements.

Whether individual or collective, historic or modern, value-driven or functional, rapid or gradual, each of these processes contributes to unfolding human recognition of the environmental effects of water use and of ways to harmonize those uses and effects. These five types of unfolding human recognition occur at all times, in all regions, in varying combinations, and with varying effects – as illustrated in the following section.

AN HISTORICAL-GEOGRAPHIC PERSPECTIVE ON HUMAN RECOGNITION

Many aspects of water and environmental understanding developed in the last quarter of the twentieth century, and they will be highlighted in subsequent chapters. Here we explore longer-term, and longer-distance, processes of human understanding that are sometimes overlooked in studies of water management and environmental policy. Recognition of water pollution problems often begins with environmental movements of the 1960s, and resultant water quality legislation such as the Clean Water Act of 1972, the Safe Drinking Water Act of 1974, the National Environmental Policy Act of 1969, and the Fish and Wildlife Coordination Act of 1958. The European Parliament (2000) and European Environment Agency (2001) have developed a broad far-reaching framework that strives to integrate sustainable water and environmental management. A similar perspective prevails in international water resources research. Although important, these benchmarks provide only a recent historical perspective. In this section we work backwards, from the mid twentieth century to earliest evidence of consciousness of environmental effects of water use (Delli Priscoli, 2000).

Concern about environmental, social and aesthetic impacts of dams in the 1960s, for example, had antecedents in the 1940s (USBR, 1946). The mid twentieth century witnessed water development experiments in many regions, some aspects of which extensively transformed natural ecosystems while others sought to conserve them:

- Tennessee Valley Authority (USA)
- Gal Oya Valley Authority (Ceylon)
- Damodar Valley Authority (India)
- Cauca Valley Authority (Colombia)

These regional experiments included dams for hydroelectric power along with erosion control and watershed management. They had earlier antecedents. For example, effects of land use on soil erosion were drawn in part from experience in China and Palestine (Kluger, 1992; Lowdermilk, 1944, 1953; cf. Brush et al., 1987). Multipurpose hydroelectric systems had been developed in Europe in the early twentieth century (United Nations, 1949; White, 1957).

Earlier, in the 1890s, Progressive Era resource managers developed integrated perspectives on forest management, urban water supply, and irrigation agriculture (Wescoat, 2000). Irrigation engineers traveled around the world to understand soil salinity and alkalinity (i.e., excess alkali metals, especially sodium, which cause a breakdown of soil structure, reduced water percolation, and increased plant toxicity), as well as irrigation development (Deakin, 1893; Hilgard, 1900; Whitcombe, 1994). State legislatures passed statutes protecting fishing and recreational water uses from pollution, as well as withdrawals for booming mining and agricultural industries. However, these initiatives did not sufficiently counterbalance single-purpose resource development or preserve wilderness areas such as the Hetch Hetchy River in Yosemite National Park (Muir, 1910) or drowned fjords in Scandinavia.

A half-century before the Progressive Era, George Perkins Marsh (1864) compiled and disseminated the results of European research on "waters" as well as other landscapes. He focused, in particular, on how forest clearance exacerbated "torrents" (floods) in alpine watersheds. Urban and industrial water pollution concerns figured prominently in nineteenth-century urban sanitary reform movements (Duffy, 1990), colonial water and sanitation programs (Arnold, 1993), and international water treaties on the Rhine, Rhone, and Danube rivers (Wescoat, 1995a).

Indeed, extending back much further in time, Clarence Glacken (1968) has documented the long history of western ideas about nature and society in *Traces on the Rhodian Shore*, which reveals that human recognition of effects on land and water environments existed in every period from antiquity through the eighteenth century. Plato's *Critias* (1965), for example, lamented the effects of grazing and farming on hillslope erosion so severe that the rocky subsoil was exposed like a "skeleton" (Hughes, 1994). Guillerme (1983) offers a similarly sweeping view of evolving urban water systems and environmental pollution in northern France from 300 to 1800 CE. The explanations for environmental change, and social justifications for managing human actions, have varied dramatically over these historical and geographic scales (as well as among individuals). But recognition of some connection between water use and environmental quality seems deeply rooted in most peoples and places.

If recognition of at least some ecosystem changes has existed in all historic eras, processes of progressive development and social rediscovery take on added importance, as does conservation over long timescales from decades to centuries.

But recognition may extend deeper still. Cultural ecologists have documented complex adaptive strategies for harmonizing irrigation systems, pastoral ecosystems, and social systems in some areas (Figure 3.7). Irrigators in the Andean highlands adjust cropping patterns, field selection, and complementary livelihood strategies in response to demographic, hydroclimatic, and socioeconomic change (Knapp, 1991; Mitchell and Guillet, 1994). Irrigators from the Middle East to Spain have adjusted surface and groundwater management to environmental and social variability over periods of centuries (Beaumont *et al.*, 1989; Butzer, 1990; Lightfoot, 1997). Others have

Figure 3.7   Pastoralists in the Ashkhabad area of Turkmenistan live in
close proximity and relationship with irrigators, and jointly adjust to
subtle changes in water and environment.

analyzed collapse of historic irrigated systems, again in response to joint
social and environmental change. Bennett (1969) compared the differential vulnerability of ethnic groups to environmental variability in the
northern Plains regions of North America, and showed that communities with strong social ties and sharing arrangements, e.g., Hutterite
religious communities, fared better over the long term. By comparison,
displacement of indigenous irrigators onto marginal hillslopes, flood-
prone lands, and saline areas aggravates environmental impacts, such
as vegetation clearance, accelerated hillslope erosion, and landslides,
which tends to lead toward field abandonment (Blaikie and Brookfield,
1987). In these cases, recognition is not the problem. People understand
both the environmental consequences of their actions and that their
choices are constrained by poverty, bias, and political weakness.

These perspectives from cultural ecological and historical research on water use and environmental problems lead further back in
time and prompt us to ask whether similarly adaptive strategies were
attained by prehistoric water managers. Archaeological research on irrigation and drainage systems indicates complex prehistoric processes of
water and environmental management (Denevan, 2001). Butzer (1976)
surveys long-term local irrigation successes and failures in the Nile
River valley, though the failures seem more attributable to political,
economic, and health hazards than to environmental degradation.

Climatic variability does seem to have played a role in regional abandonment of prehistoric canal irrigation systems in the southwestern United Sates (Doolittle, 2000), as did flooding and salinity in irrigated areas of Mesopotamia (Adams, 1981). In those areas, as in the sedimentation and reclamation of tank irrigation in Sri Lanka (Dikshit, 1986), it is not clear to what extent abandonment should be regarded as failure or successful adjustment. When social and environmental conditions improve, these lands and water systems may be reclaimed successfully. Irrigation in the Phoenix area of central Arizona (whose very name connotes a rebirth from the ashes of collapse) has collapsed and been rebuilt several times over the past two millennia (Haury, 1976). It is more difficult to make inferences about the extent to which recognition of environmental effects of water use influenced actions, relative to other knowledge and forces, and it seems reasonable to assume that motives, justifications, and values have differed widely across peoples, places, and times. But prehistoric water and environmental management behaviors (and thus perhaps some level of recognition) appear comparable with some historic and modern patterns.

Pushing back still further, it may be asked, if prehistoric societies recognized connections between their water uses and ecosystem changes, as part of their basic livelihood strategies, when and how did their consciousness of these connections arise?

It seems reasonable to assume that some human water-seeking and waste-disposal behaviors were, and are, instinctive and physiological, with little conscious recognition of the act itself or its consequences. Plant gathering in floodplain environments selects for some species, cultivars, or genetic strains over others (i.e., it favors those species) without necessarily recognizing changes at the landscape scale. However, floodplain farming involves human introduction of some species or strains over others in a favorable environment, altering that ecosystem in the process. But which seed dispersal processes were motivated by a conscious understanding of their effects? Defecation of partially digested grain in floodplain areas may involve little consciousness, while planting seed and clearing competing vegetation involves more.

If archaeological evidence indicates that protohistoric irrigators of the Nile, Mesopotamian, and Indus valleys were aware of their environmental effects six millennia ago, and similar inferences may be drawn from prehistoric agricultural sites, albeit with less certainty, how deeply do the roots of environmental consciousness extend? It seems reasonable to hypothesize that some effects may have been recognized during hominid evolution, e.g., association of different hunting and harvesting strategies with different water bodies, and perhaps the pollution of small ponds by excreta.

These possibilities raise similar questions about the environmental consciousness of other species. Does the beaver "know" when it creates a dam that it alters its habitat? In some sense, it must. Does it know that other species may be captured in, or excluded from, its habitat? Perhaps. Does it know that some humans downstream may contract giardiasis from its defecation in that habitat? Certainly not. Can it learn where humans are less likely to disturb its habitat? Probably. Can it adjust to human disturbances of its habitat by migrating upstream or to a less developed riparian environment, which it then transforms? Often it can.

The plant senses when soil moisture is readily available. Some plant roots emit toxins that prevent other species from competing for moisture. Others make stomatic adjustments to water scarcity. Some exotic phreatophytes invade disturbed river shorelines. Some endangered waterbirds nest in the branches of these exotic invasive plants. Some cultures believe these plants and water bodies, and the spirits that dwell in them, sense these interactions and support them.

Pushing back still further, what do the algae know about their pond environment? They certainly "know" how to reproduce when nutrients are available. They may suffer as reproduction continues, nutrient supply diminishes, and they die. But surely they do not know that their death depletes the oxygen necessary to sustain other fauna in the pond.

But neither do many humans recognize the environmental consequences of their water uses. Few urban dwellers recognize that the water in their tap came at the cost of complex riparian and aquatic habitats. Few realize that every article of food, clothing, and shelter also required the withdrawal and consumption of great amounts of water from such habitats. And regrettably few recognize how the waste streams from those products and their own bodies affect the habitats that remain. Indeed, all human beings fail to recognize some of their consequences – like the beaver, the tree, and the algae. The differences between the actual, as opposed to potential, environmental consciousness of humans and other species may not be as sharp as is often assumed.

To understand human recognition more fully, it may be asked which of its practices intend to produce an environmental effect, and which have an habitual, or magical, association with desired results but without recognizing their causes. Presumably, as some causal relationships between water use and environmental effects, e.g., floodplain planting and harvesting, become conscious and purposeful, other related environmental processes and effects remain outside consciousness for an indefinite period of time.

This point seems as applicable to the twenty-first century as to prehistory. Indeed, it invites the converse question: when modern societies lose consciousness of earlier water–environment relationships, how do they regain it? What similarities and differences exist between the earliest human recognition of ecosystem effects, the newest scientific discoveries, and the most belated rediscoveries of them?

These questions remind us that recognition, by itself, is of limited consequence. It is essential for consciously acting to harmonize or reduce conflict between water and environmental management. But purposeful action also depends upon a transformation of that recognition by perceptions, attitudes, and values that guide behavior (White, 1976). It is for that reason that processes of changing social values and personal commitment, discussed above, are important in linking perceptions and behavior.

These linkages do not diminish the importance of recognition, for it is impossible to value or act on knowledge one does not have. Moreover, certain types of recognition seem particularly difficult for human beings and other species as well. It has been noted that human beings do not readily recognize the water and environmental needs of other species outside their various commodity chains. Few societies recognize the needs of their lower status members, as evidenced by extensive squatter settlements today. When these needs are recognized, historians inform us that they often arise from self-interested concern about the spread of disease or fire, perhaps more than from ideals about a human or natural right to water (Rosen and Keating, 1991; cf. Gleick, 2000a).

Finally, recognition is crucial in the process of identifying, and taking seriously, alternatives for water use and environmental protection. On many occasions water managers unduly restrict the "range of choice" among practical alternatives (White, 1997, 1998). Even when policies require identification and consideration of alternatives, their implementation is often flawed (Gosnell, 2001; Michel, 2000).

Explanations for these failings range from simple lack of awareness to more complex political, economic, and social structures that constrain public choice. Less attention has focused on the failure to *imagine* the full range of possibilities for change. Synthesis of three broad approaches can help societies envision sustainable landscapes of water management (Wescoat, 2002):

(1)   *Humanistic–geographic approaches*, e.g., historical-geographic imagination (Prince, 1997), perceptual imagination (Litton *et al.*, 1974), material imagination (Bachelard, 1983), symbolic imagination (Dundes, 1988; Kumar, 1983; Tuan, 1968a).

(2)   *Critical social-geographic approaches*, e.g., political-economic imagination (Wittfogel, 1981), post-colonial imagination (Cosgrove and Petts, 1990), feminist imagination (Feldhaus, 1995; Halvorson, 2000).

(3)   *Global environmental approaches*, e.g., global environmental change scenarios (Riebsame *et al.*, 1995), emerging global water management programs (UNESCO, 2003), anti-globalization movements (Barlow, 1999), and local initiatives linked with global and meso-scale processes (Swyngedouw, 1995).

The point of this exploration has been to situate the challenges of increasing recognition of water–environment relationships in the broadest possible environmental and social perspective. By relating the varied human recognition of environmental effects with that of other creatures, we have set the stage for a more balanced consideration of natural waters in the chapter that follows. Natural waters are not just H_2O, cycling through the biosphere, but waters that give life to, constitute cherished habitats for, and are precariously transformed by all of the creatures of the biosphere, with varying degrees of recognition, consciousness, and sound judgment.

4

Natural waters

A logical point of departure for analysis of water management and natural environment would be a description of the natural state of waters worldwide before human alterations of their quantity and quality began to take effect. For a variety of reasons, this is possible only to a very small extent. Any presentation of the natural condition of waters of the globe necessarily must also take account of the magnitude and diversity of ways in which alterations have been taking place independent of human influences, and in which for more than five thousand years humans have changed inputs and outputs. It is difficult to estimate all of those changes accurately. Only a few rough estimates can be made of the truly natural state of the hydrologic cycle worldwide and in the United States, taking account of major components of precipitation, streamflow, groundwater and transpiration, and their chemical and biological quality.

HYDROLOGIC CYCLE

In simplest terms, the natural waters of the globe may be viewed at any one time as atmospheric moisture plus precipitation plus soil and underground storage plus glaciers and ice fields plus oceans plus moisture stored in or transpired from plants and animals. The concept of a hydrologic cycle has evolved from very simple to very complex (Figure 4.1). There is rich literature in hydrology and hydraulic engineering that defines and examines ways of measuring the various elements in the hydrologic cycle (Chow, 1964; Grigg, 1996; McCuen, 1989). The major elements of definition and measurement are not described in detail here, beyond identifying the principal components and their

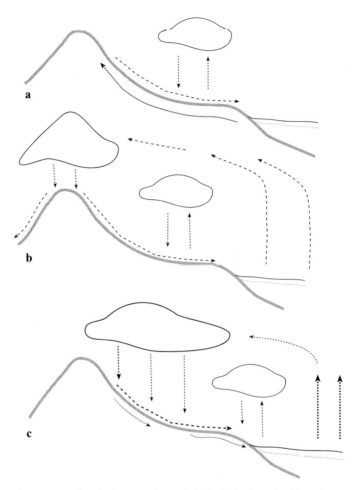

Figure 4.1   Historical conceptions of the hydrologic cycle: (a) ancient to Renaissance conceptions that posited uphill subterranean return flows; (b) the global hydrologic cycle according to John Ray (seventeenth century); (c) a highly simplified modern rendering of the hydrologic cycle which includes groundwater flows and discharge. After Tuan (1968a, p. 51).

interrelations and providing a table showing the major units of measurement, both metric and English (page xx). A modified calculation by Schlesinger (1991) outlines the components of the world hydrologic cycle. This estimates the volume of water in the pools of groundwater, ice, and oceans, and the annual fluxes through precipitation, evaporation, evapotranspiration, and river flow.

Table 4.1 *Estimated distribution of water in continental USA*

Form of liquid water	Approximate volume (%)	Estimated replacement period (years)
Groundwater – shallow	43.20	>200.00
Groundwater – deep	43.20	>10 000.00
Freshwater lakes	13.00	100.00
Soil mixture 1 m root zone	0.43	0.20
Salt lakes	0.04	>10.00
Stream channels – mean	0.03	<0.03
Water vapor in atmosphere	0.13	>0.03
Glaciers	0.05	>40.00

Source: Van der Leeden *et al.*, 1990, p. 56.

Each region within a continent has a distinct distribution. For example, the pattern for the continental United States in Table 4.1 is similar to the global distribution in its rough proportions of groundwater to lakes and streams. However, the United States has far less glacial water than Canada to the north, but more glacial water and snowmelt than Latin America to the south.

The major components of the hydrologic cycle are now included in elementary school science education. However, not very long ago, leading scientists had diverse, and sometimes erroneous, impressions of how the global hydrologic cycle functions. Indeed, major efforts are under way in programs such as the Global Energy and Water Exchange (GEWEX) project to clarify global hydrologic processes, in which the oceans, which are not considered in most water resources texts, play a central role. At the landscape scale different environmental factors may be closely related to water flow and quantity for that landscape in a variety of ways. Similarly, at the smaller scale of hillslope hydrologic processes (Figure 4.2) the roles of rainfall interception, streamflow, infiltration, percolation, adsorption, pipeflow, and springflow for a hillslope must all be considered – as must physical, biological, and chemical properties of soil at the even smaller scale of the field plot (Kirkby, 1978).

Additionally, new computer modeling and animation tools now make it possible to analyze those elements and interactions in detail.

A further reason that precise estimation of the natural waters of any part of the globe is difficult is that in recent years there has been serious challenge to the view that the total volume of water on

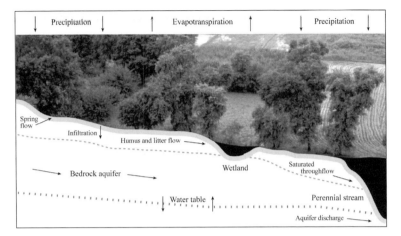

Figure 4.2   Components of the hillslope hydrologic cycle include manifold surface and subsurface runoff processes. After Kirkby (1978, p. 5).

earth has not changed since earth took shape. The prevailing view was that after the planet was formed roughly four billion years ago, the water molecules were subject to change between solid and gaseous states, but that their total number remained approximately the same. Beginning in the 1980s, however, ultraviolet images of the upper atmosphere began to suggest to some scientists that there was a continuing stream of water-bearing objects, such as comets, reaching the atmosphere, thereby increasing the total supply of water (Gleick, 1998b, pp. 193–199).

Major international scientific efforts are analyzing significant changes in climate, hydrology, and related elements of the environmental system. These include the International Geosphere–Biosphere Programme (e.g., Lohmann, 2002) and the Intergovernmental Panel on Climate Change (IPCC, 2001a, 2001b, 2001c). This theory has received further support and, if correct, implies that the water resource may be changing significantly.

The water resource at any scale is subject to a variety of management measures, and natural waters may be viewed as what the resource would be without any of those human interventions affecting both quantity and quality. Human actions have altered the basic distribution and quality of precipitation, streamflow, and groundwater in a number of ways, and continue increasingly to do so. Those actions include not only direct manipulation of quantities in the hydrologic cycle by diverting precipitation and streamflow, by storing water, and by altering evaporation, but actions that change the quality of air, water, and soil. A bit of that complexity is suggested by a diagram of the hydrologic cycle for a temperate climate hillside (Figure 4.2). This chapter suggests the intricacy and extent of such activities in a summary fashion by outlining the theoretical natural hydrologic cycle and noting briefly only a few of the principal human influences on it. Those influential actions are analyzed in more detail in subsequent chapters.

Thus, the basic elements in the natural distribution of water on the earth are precipitation, snow and ice, streamflow, water stored in plants and animals, groundwater, and the seas and oceans. Any diagram of the natural water cycle for a specific area should recognize the influences on it of elements of climate, terrain, and ecosystems that are relatively constant for periods of decades to a century but that have changed drastically over thousands of years, as illustrated by climatic ice ages, by continental drift, and by periods of intense volcanic activity. Since the beginning of human history, the effects of human actions on ecosystems and thereby on that system's influence on the natural water cycle have multiplied. The changing human factor thus directly affects not only the immediate distribution and quality of water but also affects the natural systems of atmosphere and landscape that in turn influence water quantity and quality.

PRECIPITATION

It has been variously estimated that approximately 110 300 million km^3 of water fall on the earth as precipitation in an average year (L'vovich and White, 1990, p. 236). The distributions of recorded mean annual precipitation for global ocean and land areas are shown in Figures 4.3 and 4.4. It is not established that there has been any major change in the average amount and spatial distribution in the past 400 years when there have been recurrent droughts (Kates *et al.*, 2001), but there now is question as to potential effects of climate change in the near future. Typically, there are significant departures from the normal in any one year. Thus, the deviation – positive or negative – as shown in Figure 4.5 indicates various degrees of departure in the year 2000.

The mean volume of water falling annually as precipitation is essentially unaffected by human action, except that since the 1980s

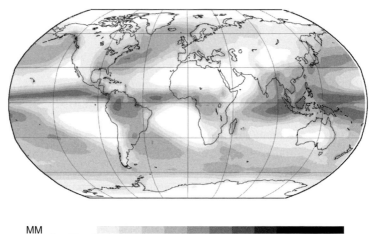

MM
1 10 25 50 75 100 150 200 300 400 600 800 1000

Figure 4.3   World distribution of mean precipitation, 1980–2000
normals in mm/month, mapped on a 2.5 degree grid. Dark areas
indicate heavy precipitation over the oceans of the equatorial
intertropical convergence zone. From Deutscher Wetterdienst (DWD),
Global Precipitation Climatology Centre Visualizer.
http://www.dwd.de/research/gpcc/visu_gpcc.html. Last visited March 21,
2003.

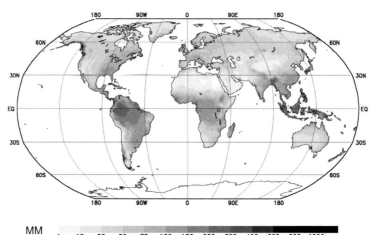

MM
1 10 25 50 75 100 150 200 300 400 600 800 1000

Figure 4.4   World distribution of mean precipitation over the
continents, 1961–90 normals in mm/month, mapped on a 1.0 degree
grid. Light areas indicate low precipitation over subtropical
high-pressure zones in the continental interiors. From Deutscher
Wetterdienst (DWD), Global Precipitation Climatology Centre Visualizer.
http://www.dwd.de/research/gpcc/visu_gpcc.html. Last visited March 21,
2003.

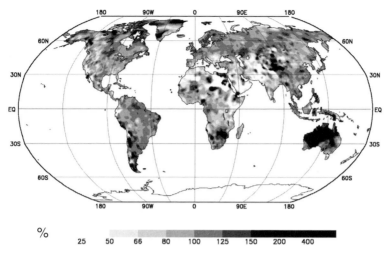

Figure 4.5   Departure from precipitation normals (percentage of
1961–90 values) in the year 2000 (January–December). The lightest areas
indicate abnormally low precipitation while the darkest areas indicate
abnormally high precipitation. Overall, this map reveals the high
interannual and spatial variability of precipitation. From Deutscher
Wetterdienst (DWD), Global Precipitation Climatology Centre Visualizer.
http://www.dwd.de/research/gpcc/visu_gpcc.html. Last visited March 21,
2003.

there has been increasing analysis of the significance of climate change
as a result of alterations in flows of carbon dioxide and other greenhouse gases to the atmosphere. Growing out of early reports by SCOPE
on the possible effects of greenhouse gases such as carbon dioxide on
temperature and precipitation, and supported by analysis showing increases in average air temperatures over large areas, and by evidence of
receding glaciers particularly in mountainous areas and polar ice fields,
and of rising ocean levels, the synthesis by the Intergovernmental Panel
on Climate Change (IPCC, 1995) led to the World Conference at Kyoto
in 1997, which initiated international negotiations to curb the emis-
sion of greenhouse gases (UNFCCC, 1997). A position that in the face of
continuing scientific controversy commanded increasing support was
that global warming was under way (IPCC, 2001b). This implied rising
average atmospheric temperatures and evapotranspiration in some
regions, melting of some ice fields, and rising sea levels. Additionally, with new computer animation tools, interannual and seasonal processes and patterns of global precipitation could now be visualized as
changing (Figure 4.5).

Figure 4.6   Orographic storm bringing atmospheric moisture and precipitation from the Pacific Ocean to the Rocky Mountains of the USA.

It is difficult to estimate the relative proportions of precipitation falling as rainfall compared with snowfall, as the measurement error for the former is roughly 5 percent while snowfall measurement error over large areas can exceed 50 percent (Figures 4.6 and 4.7). The amounts of precipitation in different forms are also variously related to season of the year and to land elevation.

In terms of the hydrologic cycle for regional land areas, climate change was seen as possibly increasing total precipitation and evaporation, and as altering the patterns of intense rainfall and drought (IPCC, 2001a; Liverman, 1999). Thus, the basic relationships of elevation, temperature, precipitation, evaporation, water use, and runoff were recognized as subject to significant change. In this fashion the role of human action in altering the volume and timing of available water was also seen as increasing. While it was not practicable to make confident quantitative predictions of precisely what changes would occur in specific areas, it was reasonable to begin with effects on the water cycle that already were measurable.

In these circumstances it no longer was possible to judge that any parts of the global water cycle are not subject to some form of human manipulation. Conversely, if the temperature–precipitation regime changes so does the water cycle independent of local management.

Figure 4.7   Water stored in high-altitude snow fields of the Rocky Mountains is used for recreational purposes and melts with the onset of warmer temperatures as streamflow for subsequent use on irrigated farms and cities.

EVAPOTRANSPIRATION

Evapotranspiration refers to the total amount of water that is used in an area by evaporation (from plant surfaces, upper soil profiles, and water bodies) and transpiration (from natural vegetation and crops).

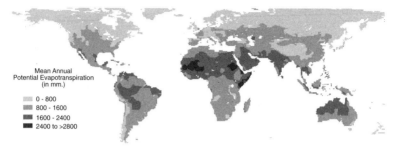

Figure 4.8   World distribution of mean annual potential evapotranspiration (millimeters). From UNEP Global Resource Information Database (GRID) and University of East Anglia, Climate Research Unit. http://www-cger.nies.go.jp/grid-e/gridtxt/petgeo.html. Last visited March 21, 2003.

Evaporation involves latent heat exchange and absorption of heat as water is converted from liquid to gas while transpiration involves gas exchange through the stomata of plant leaf cells. Standard-sized evaporation pans are used to measure evaporation from open water bodies in a given set of climatic conditions, while lysimeters are used to measure both transpiration and evaporation for specific soil, crop, and climatic conditions (Dunne and Leopold, 1978).

Potential evapotranspiration (PET) refers to the amount of water (depth in mm) that would be consumed if water supply were continuously available to meet the needs of a given crop as well as any evaporative losses that may occur. Actual evapotranspiration represents the amount of water that is actually available and consumed. The difference between precipitation and actual evapotranspiration describes the amount of water available in natural ecosystems and natural processes of surplus, deficit, and soil moisture storage and discharge. Thus, the difference between precipitation, actual evapotranspiration and potential evapotranspiration indicates the potential for increased crop production with supplemental irrigation water.

These two processes are commonly lumped together as a measure of climatic water demand, irrigation efficiency, or water lost to the atmosphere that will not be available for reuse by others in a basin. In equatorial regions PET is relatively constant during the year, and it is more seasonally pronounced with increases in latitude (Figure 4.8). Actual evapotranspiration, by contrast, varies with available precipitation, ranging from the total amount of precipitation in arid environments to a variable fraction of precipitation in humid regions.

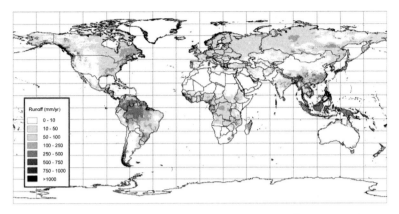

Figure 4.9   World distribution of mean annual runoff (mm per unit
area per year). Dark areas indicate relatively high runoff in the
equatorial tropics and maritime temperate zones. Data are mapped on a
30' grid (c. 50 km at the equator). From University of New Hampshire/
Global Runoff Data Centre, Koblenz, Germany: Global Composite Runoff
Data Set version 1.0. Runoff Data Explorer. http://www.grdc.sr.unh.edu/
html/Runoff/ index.html. Last visited March 21, 2003.

STREAMFLOW

Streamflows reflect, to a significant degree, the positive difference between precipitation and evapotranspiration. They are also affected by
vegetation, soil, slope, infiltration, and storage capacity. While measurement of stream elevation dates back to ancient Egypt with the
famous Nilometer (Biswas, 1970), and channel cross-sections and slopes
were calculated in Roman aqueducts, accurate measurement of stream
discharge in volume per unit of time developed in modern times.
Measurements have been refined with improved methods for detect-
ing and integrating variations in velocity across different parts of the
channel cross-section from its bed to its banks and surface. Estimates
of regional and global runoff volume are also a relatively recent development, compiled by the Global Runoff Data Centre in Germany
(Figure 4.9) (Fekete et al., 2002).

It has been variously estimated during recent decades that the
mean annual flow of streams to the ocean or to inland seas is approximately 25 000 km^3. These flows represent the volumes remaining in
streams after melting and runoff, minus losses through surface evaporation, transpiration by plants and animals, and charging of underground aquifers. As elaborated in Chapter 8, human modification of

Figure 4.10   Cold spring meltwaters have high water quality for
drinking and recreation (Colorado, USA).

streamflows is one of the oldest dimensions of water management, from
the headwaters to deserts and deltas (Figures 4.10 to 4.14).

GROUNDWATER

In estimating the global water cycle it is necessary to take into account
the volume of water that accumulates over various periods of time
in underground aquifers, and, likewise, the current discharges from

Figure 4.11   Overland flow from rainfall events is a major source of non-point-source pollution to streams and lakes (Boulder, Colorado, USA).

Figure 4.12   Narrows along the main stem of the Indus River at Attock in Pakistan have provided a strategic ford and bridge location from antiquity to the present.

those aquifers to surface streamflow or the oceans. With few exceptions, the discharge from aquifers as a result of human withdrawal exceeds the natural inflow, and to that extent the natural stream discharge is reduced while the managed outflow is increased.

Figure 4.13 In arid and semiarid regions, natural channels like Mamm Creek, Colorado, USA, run dry in late summer, conditions aggravated by irrigation withdrawals and invasion of exotic species such as *Tamarix* spp.

Figure 4.14 Deltaic channels in coastal Bangladesh return continental freshwater to the sea where it becomes once again the principal source of evaporation for the world's freshwater supply.

The role of aquifer use in affecting streamflow differs tremendously from one area to another, and their return flow rates and paths are highly complex; but in a state of no human management, the function of aquifers as storage places is relatively simple. They store water and release it to evapotranspiration or discharge it to streamflow or the oceans by gravity, and as their capacities are exceeded by inflow. Their volume may be altered by tectonic change as, for example, when subsidence reduces recharge and storage, or when geologic faulting alters flow paths.

SNOW AND ICE

While there is fairly accurate estimation of the volume of water falling as precipitation in the form of either rain or snow it is more difficult to estimate the amount and changes of water stored in glaciers and long-term snow fields (Figure 4.15 to Figure 4.16). There is little doubt as to the present extent of glacier ice, but there is less precision as to the full magnitude and extent of past glacial accumulations. The extent of past glaciation has been mapped from present physical evidence, and rough calculations have been made of the volume of water stored at various periods. It has been estimated that approximately 5.8 million square miles (15 million km^2) of land surface are covered by glacial ice, with roughly nine-tenths of the coverage in South Polar regions.

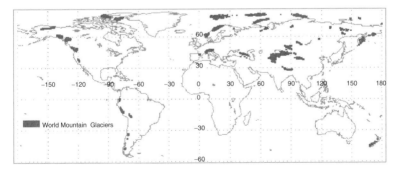

Figure 4.15   The World Glacier Inventory includes some 67 000 glaciers along zones of high altitude tectonic collision. Mountain glaciers are receding in most regions of the world. Data from National Snow and Ice Data Center, http://nsidc.org/data/glacier_inventory, with new mapping tool at http://map.ngdc.noaa.gov/website/nsidc/glacier/viewer.htm. Last visited March 21, 2003.

Figure 4.16   Grand Pacific Glacier, St. Elias Mountains, Glacier Bay Tarr Inlet, Alaska, USA. Source: US Navy photo SEA, July 26, 1948, archived at the National Snow and Ice Data Center. http://nsidc.org.

Until the 1980s and 1990s, changes in glacial water were considered as products of physical forces unrelated to human activity (though some traditional societies have long believed that human actions and rituals can alter glacial meltwaters). As indicated above, attention turned to the possibility that human-generated climate change was altering the volume of glacial accumulations and melting. Thus, the perception of those water accumulations as wholly natural began to alter. Human activity came to be seen as affecting not only the proportion of precipitation falling as snow, but also its frozen storage in polar icecaps, ice sheets, glaciers, and icebergs.

WATER QUALITY

All of the above elements refer to the quantity of water, and omit the specific physical and biological quality of the water. As will be outlined in other chapters, quality varies in time and place, as it relates to precipitation, streamflow, soil moisture, or groundwater. In their natural state both surface and ground waters vary tremendously in their quality from place to place, independent of human management. Extreme cases are in the salt content of inland waters such as the

Pyramid Lake in the United States or the Aral Sea in Central Asia. They also display highly variable concentrations of different minerals. For example, extensive deposits of groundwater in sections of northern Bangladesh have natural concentrations of arsenic as high as 2500 µg/l (Nordstrom, 2002). The exposed population may be as large as 30 million in Bangladesh, and 6 million in West Bengal, India. Arsenic concentrations ranging from 1800 to 9900 µg/l are reported in parts of Argentina, Thailand, Inner Mongolia, and Vietnam. Some of these loadings vary annually with the season while others, such as some of the groundwater concentrations, are not affected in significant degree by time of year. In general, it is grossly misleading to assume that surface water or groundwater in its natural state is of the same biological and physical quality from place to place.

Water quality and quantity interact with one another in important ways. Water with high concentrations of natural minerals or metals may be unsuited for various uses, no matter how abundant the supply. On the other hand, natural waters with small concentrations of minerals may be highly valued, and priced, for their taste and nutritional qualities. The concentration of sediment in a stream favors some species over others and in ways that may be independent of the amount of water in the stream. Heavily sediment-laden water smothers spawning habitats for some species, while creating ideal spawning habitats for others. Indeed, clear waters can strip the fine sediment fraction out of a riverbed, contributing both to increased seepage losses from the bed and to the loss of fine particles in spawning habitats. Periods of naturally low water flow, e.g., during droughts, are negatively correlated with concentrations of dissolved and suspended solids. Conversely, flood flows transport large sediments and boulders and resuspend organic and inorganic matter on floodplains, which subsequently alters water quality and habitat conditions in the stream channel. In each of these and many other ways water quantity and quality are closely associated with ecosystem processes.

ECOSYSTEM CHANGE

All of the characteristics of natural waters as outlined above have been subject in some degree to alteration independent of human action over very long periods of time by changes in ecosystems as a result of natural climate change. The density and composition of trees, for example, has shifted with the coming and going of glacial climate. Those effects are most pronounced where there is marked difference in altitude over short distances as in mountainous landscapes. Such evolving landscapes thus are among the first to experience visible changes in the natural waters as a result of climate fluctuation as well as from human action. Commonly, the volume, sediment load, and timing of stream flow may shift rapidly in response to changes in vegetative cover, agricultural practices, urban withdrawals, and other ecosystem alterations.

In these and other ways water and land management alter the natural hydrologic regime so that it is no longer possible to regard the distribution and seasonal and annual variation of the waters of the globe as strictly natural. Any comprehensive view of water management encounters a wide variety of changes in water quantity and quality, which are affected by concurrent and interrelated efforts to use and preserve other environmental resources.

5

Plant–soil–water–ecosystem relationships

INTRODUCTION

The previous chapter on natural waters concluded with a discussion of natural ecosystem changes on the earth's surface. This chapter extends that analysis to encompass both intentional and inadvertent modifications of evapotranspiration, plant–soil moisture relations, and related ecosystem processes for human ends. These human ends range from use of forest, grass, and shrubland watersheds to irrigation and drainage schemes in large river basins, to stormwater management and non-point-source pollution control in urbanizing environments.

Every human activity affecting land use and land cover not only affects the hydrologic processes of interception, infiltration, evapotranspiration, aquifer storage, and runoff discussed in the previous chapter, but by altering water quality it also modifies plant–soil–water relationships. In addition to their feedback effects on land use productivity, these hydrologic processes affect natural ecosystems through erosion, sedimentation, and changes in soil organisms and habitats. A cubic meter of soil contains millions of bacteria and fungi, as well as hundreds of springtails, nematodes, and earthworms, all of which are directly affected by everyday soil–water management. In addition to these local effects, this chapter discusses recent research on effects of atmosphere–land surface fluxes on the global hydrologic cycle.

Table 5.1 indicates the extraordinary diversity and plenitude of life in the soil. While algae are primary producers that photosynthesize on wet soil surfaces, most soil organisms are secondary and tertiary consumers, converting dead plants and animals to humus. Through these processes and their movement through the soil, they also affect the porosity and moisture holding capacity.

Table 5.1 *Types and numbers of soil organisms in the surface 15 cm of soil*

Organisms	Number (per m^3)	Biomass (g/m^3 live weight)
Microflora		
Bacteria (aerobic/anaerobic)	10^{13}–10^{14}	40–500
Actinomycetes	10^{12}–10^{13}	40–500
Fungi	10^{10}–10^{11}	100–1500
Algae	10^9–10^{10}	1–50
Fauna		
Protozoa	10^9–10^{10}	2–20
Nematodes	10^6–10^7	1–15
Mites	10^3–10^6	0.5–1.5
Collembola (springtails)	10^3–10^6	0.5–1.5
Earthworms	10–10^3	10–150
Other fauna[a]	10^2–10^4	1–10

[a] Macrofauna: include vertebrates, e.g., gophers, moles, snakes; arthropods, e.g., ants, beetles, maggots, termites, grubs, spiders, millipedes, woodlice; mollusks, e.g., slugs, snails.
Source: Brady and Weil, 1999, pp. 291, 297.

Soil moisture regimes in turn affect the species present, their abundance, and population dynamics (Table 5.2). Moisture conditions reflect climate and physiography as well, ranging from saturated aquic soils of permanent wetlands to the aridic soils of deserts and xeric soils of Mediterranean regions.

Within a given climatological region, the structural and physical properties of soils play major roles in soil moisture conditions, both for natural and agro-ecosystems. The supply of water, porosity, and structure of soils affect soil moisture conditions and problems (e.g., soil cracking, shrink–swell clays, piping, and salt movement. It is useful to distinguish five types of soil moisture, their associated types of energy, and implications for natural vegetation and cropping systems:

(1)   Submergence potential in saturated soils drives groundwater movement (discussed in Chapter 6), as well as the moisture for plants that tolerate saturated conditions. Saturation occurs when all soil pores are filled with water.

(2)   Gravitational potential causes water to percolate through a soil by gravity, unhindered by other forces, and to be readily available to plant roots of all types. When all gravitational water has leached out of a soil it is said to be at field capacity.

Table 5.2 *Soil moisture regimes*

Regime	Description
Aquic	saturated on a semi-permanent basis; common in wetland, low-water mark, and nearshore environments
Perudic	perennial excess moisture and leaching; common in wetland margins, high-water mark and nearshore environments
Udic	plant-available moisture on an interannual basis; common in humid well-drained environments
Ustic	plant-available moisture for most but not all months and years; common in sub-humid and semiarid environments of dryland farming
Aridic	plant-available moisture for less than three months of the year; or dry for more than half the growing season; common in semiarid and arid environments
Xeric	Mediterranean soils with soil moisture available primarily in cool winter months and long dry summer periods in the northern hemisphere (with the opposite seasonal pattern in the southern hemisphere)

Source: Brady and Weil, 1999, pp. 64–65.

(3) Osmotic potential refers to the attraction of water to dissolved solids (e.g., salts), which reduces its gravitational potential and thus its availability to some species.

(4) Soil water potential involves the relatively weak attraction of water molecules to other water molecules (cohesion), which reduces gravitational potential but helps retain water in soil for capillary action, surface tension, and uptake by plant roots.

(5) Soil matric potential refers to water held by relatively strong molecular bonds (adhesion or adsorption) to colloids and soil particles, especially clays, which is generally not available for plant use (referred to as the "wilting point").

Physical and chemical changes in soils affect water flow paths, storage and availability. For example, soil desiccation can cause cracking which leads to differential patterns of soil wetting and percolation when moisture becomes available (Figure 5.1). Extreme soil shrinking and swelling can cause substantial damage to buildings and infrastructure that are improperly located and designed. Excess sodium in alkali soils, whether from natural causes or leaching of other minerals, causes a breakdown of the crumb-like structure of a soil surface

Figure 5.1   Soil cracking in desiccated area of the Badlands, South Dakota, USA.

(slaking), which greatly reduces moisture infiltration and requires applications of gypsum and other treatments to restore soil structure. By contrast, salt crusts aggravated by deficit irrigation or waterlogging do not radically alter the soil structure and can be leached with sufficient moisture, provided first that there is sufficient drainage and second that drainage water does not simply transfer the problem to another location (Figures 5.2 and 5.3). Soil clearing in humid environments exposes soils to the full impact of raindrops, which can reduce infiltration and accelerate erosion. In humid tropical soils, clearing may leach organic matter, lead to iron concentrations, and soil hardening and sterility. Similarly, irrigation and cultivation methods can contribute to the development of "hardpan," or relatively impervious shallow layers in many types of soil that limit their further agricultural use unless broken up by deep tillage methods.

Concern about such human effects on soil moisture has ancient scientific and practical roots in the field of agronomy (e.g., Cato, Varro, and Columella in Roman Italy alone; see Butzer, 1990). In medieval times, an eleventh-century Arabic text by the *Ikhwan al-Safa* (Brethren of Purity) of Baghdad sympathetically describes the plight and significance of soil organisms.

These perennial concerns about food, fiber, and soil are addressed in modern times through satellite remote sensing, geographic

Figure 5.2   Salinity from canal seepage near the Karakum Canal, Turkmenistan.

Figure 5.3   Salinization from waterlogging and rising lake levels at the Salton Sea, California, USA.

information systems (GIS), agro-meteorological forecasting, and spatial decision support systems. The *WWW Virtual Library Irrigation* (2003) lists irrigation management software, as do an increasing number of water resources and environmental research centers. These tools help farmers and water managers estimate soil moisture conditions and trends, storm and drought effects, and linkages between food production, transportation, and consumption in different regions. By monitoring crop growth and weather conditions, they help forecast regional food production, support famine early warning systems, and guide regional food supply planning, e.g., the US Agency for International Development's Famine Early Warning System in Africa. Although these emerging methods require ground-truth surveys and local analysis of human and environmental impacts and adjustments, they can provide extensive real-time information for water and environmental managers.

A key scientific challenge associated with plant–soil–water relationships is the high spatial and temporal variability that occurs at every scale of soil water management, from a small field plot to a large agricultural region (Becker *et al.*, 1999). Farmers know that slight differences in terrain and soil texture on a single field can produce significant variations in soil moisture, drainage, and attendant crop yields. Wheat farmers in the Punjab region of India and Pakistan cultivate several fields in locations that have different soil moisture conditions in order to manage the risks of too much or too little soil moisture, and associated conditions of beneficial or destructive soil organisms (Astroth, 1990) (Figures 5.4 and 5.5).

From micro-irrigation technology to neutron probes and laser leveling, farmers seek to manage local soil moisture variations. In rural

Figure 5.4   Water distribution during the monsoon season in Sheikhupura district, Punjab, Pakistan, viewed from the Hiran Minar.

Figure 5.5   Water harvesting tank from the Mughal period (early seventeenth century) in Sheikhupura district, Punjab, Pakistan, viewed from the Hiran Minar.

and urbanizing watersheds, land cover conservation strives to manage runoff, recharge, erosion, sedimentation, and riparian habitats. Urban stormwater planners combine soil infiltration management with on-site detention ponds, roof gardens, storm sewers, and pump stations to manage local stormwater flooding and pollution problems (France, 2002).

Increasingly, these plant–soil–water management activities inter-sect with larger-scale environmental management. Afforestation of up-land watersheds is linked with regional wildlife habitat and biodiver-sity. Irrigation affects soil and water salinity balances in arid river basins. Agricultural drainage reduces wetland habitats and discharges selenium, fertilizer, and pesticide-contaminated water into riparian, es-tuarine and coastal marine habitats, as has occurred from Mississippi River valley drainage into the Gulf of Mexico (Meade, 1995) and drainage from the irrigated Central Valley of California (NRC, 1989b). Industrial discharges contaminate soil particles and moisture with heavy met-als such as cadmium, chromium, lead, and hydrocarbons in ways that require expensive remediation and forgone food production opportuni-ties (NRC, 1999a).

Thus, this chapter uses the expression "plant–soil–water–ecosys-tem relations" to highlight the connections between soil water manage-ment and environmental policy. Managing plant–soil–water–ecosystem relations at the scales of irrigation canal commands and river basins is difficult due to the spatial, temporal, and social complexities of those larger systems. A salinity problem solved through leaching of one field in the upper Colorado River basin aggravates river and soil salinity on fields downstream in Mexico (USBR, 2001). Increased con-sumptive use in irrigated areas and reservoirs decreases return flows to streams, wetlands, and aquifers – thereby concentrating river salinity levels. Stormwater problems addressed by drainage and channelization in one suburb may promote environmental and flood hazards down-stream, and reduce riparian habitat at the regional level.

At every scale, it is important to link well-established concerns about plant–soil–water relationships in agriculture to associated prob-lems of environmental management. Each innovation generates new problems. Reforestation may protect upland riparian and aquatic habi-tat while reducing water runoff and increasing long-term fire hazards that increase episodic erosion and sedimentation. In plains environ-ments, low tillage methods may conserve soil moisture while leading farmers to increase chemical treatment of plant pests, which pollutes the conserved water (NRC, 1990). Changes in irrigation management alter plant pest and disease vector ecologies (Lansing, 1991; van der Hoek et al., 2001). Cultivation of dryland regions alters soil salinity and alkalinity balances in those areas. Groundwater pumping in coastal en-vironments aggravates saltwater intrusion.

At the farm level, organic farming strives to harmonize soil, water, and environmental conservation problems (Duram, 1999). At the regional level, efforts are made to integrate watershed ecology, agro-ecology, irrigation ecology, restoration ecology, and wastewater ecology. It is increasingly feasible to identify scientifically the relevant processes involved in plant–soil–water–ecosystem management at field and farm scales. These processes include: (1) maintaining soil water infiltration capacity; (2) retaining plant-available soil moisture; (3) managing soil moisture drainage to regulate stormwater runoff and resultant streamflows (cf. Chapter 8 for related issues of floodplain management); (4) managing soil water chemistry and toxicity for plant, animal, insect, and human habitats; and (5) managing some of the keystone, native, and exotic species in these habitats.

These processes have been analyzed and translated into scientific practice in various fields of agronomy, watershed hydrology, irrigation engineering, agricultural drainage engineering, and stormwater engineering (NRC, 1989b). Progress is also under way in emerging fields of restoration ecology, non-point-source pollution control, and bioengineering, e.g., of riparian, wetland, and aquatic ecosystems (Federal Interagency Stream Restoration Working Group, 2001).

However, it remains extremely difficult to scale those interventions up to larger systems of regional water and environmental management. The measurement problems are formidable due to the dynamic spatial, temporal, and social variations mentioned earlier. Nevertheless, this chapter seeks to survey the state of knowledge about emerging patterns, problems, and innovations in plant–soil–water–ecosystem relations, and to consider some promising management approaches, especially at the larger regional scales.

The chapter examines three major themes in plant–soil–water–ecosystem relationships:

(1) changes in land use and land cover that affect soil moisture in rural and urbanizing watersheds, from the local to global scale;
(2) changes in environmental aspects of agricultural irrigation and drainage, with an emphasis on dryland ecosystems;
(3) changes in urban stormwater management

The chapter begins with an overview of how changes in land use and land cover alter soil moisture and associated hydrologic and ecological processes. The second section of the chapter links global trends in irrigation and drainage with regional changes in environmental systems, beginning with salinity and alkalinity and continuing to encompass environmental aspects of agricultural drainage. The final section focuses on hydrologic and environmental changes brought about by urbanization, and on emerging methods for integrating stormwater management with urban environmental planning and rural land use.

The first set of linkages concerns land use, land cover, soil moisture, and their environmental and water resources management implications. These linkages are significant from the scale of individual fields to the watershed, regional, and global scales, as discussed below.

Watershed and river basin soil moisture management

Local soil water management has ancient roots. European scientists began systematically to document effects of deforestation on erosion and flooding at the watershed scale in the seventeenth century (Biswas, 1970). George Perkins Marsh (1864) compiled this early scientific literature for a broad readership in the USA in the mid nineteenth century. Land cover experiments in the Wagon Wheel Gap Experimental Watershed Study used paired watersheds in Colorado, from 1910 to 1928, to measure water yield effects of different forest and grassland treatments, which helped support passage of the national watershed protection act (US Congress, 1911) (Figure 5.6).

Figure 5.6   First paired experimental watersheds used to evaluate the hydrologic effects of different land-use and land-cover treatments at Wagon Wheel Gap, Colorado, USA.

These early experiments gave rise to the scientific fields of hill-slope hydrology (Kirkby, 1978) and rural watershed management in temperate (Haan et al., 1982), tropical (Easter et al., 1986; Pereira, 1989), and mountainous environments (Sharma, 1995).

Rural watershed management involves a continuous process of harmonizing changing forestry, grazing, rainfed and irrigated cropping practices, and population pressures with variable slopes, aspects, soils, and vegetation cover. Just as advances in air photo interpretation complemented earlier field mapping techniques for land classification, computer cartography and GIS systems are increasingly used to monitor watershed conditions and problems, such as erosion, sedimentation, and land exhaustion (Harlin and Lanfear, 1993). A rough survey of historical land classification methods would include the following:

- Tennessee Valley Authority – Unit Area Land Classification System (1930s), which used alphanumeric numerator and denominator descriptors of soil conditions and capability.
- US Bureau of Reclamation – Land Suitability for Irrigation (1951), which distinguishes six classes of arable, non-arable, and limited suitability types of irrigable soil.
- US Department of Agriculture – Land Capability Classification (1961), which distinguishes eight capability classes and further subdivision into soil subclasses and units.
- Natural Resources Conservation Service – Seventh Approximation of Soil Taxonomy (1975), which classifies soils in a hierarchical system of seven levels, according to the genetic processes that produce them.
- Food and Agriculture Organization – Framework for Land Evaluation (1976), which distinguishes major kinds of land use, detailed land use types, land use requirements, land qualities and land characteristics.
- Food and Agriculture Organization – Agro-Ecological Zoning (1978), which is applied at large regional and national scales to map and assess land use and environmental types.

Reviews of watershed management in the Asian tropics by the East–West Center at Hawaii (Easter et al., 1986) and the World Bank (Doolette and Magrath, 1990) have shown how upstream land uses impact downstream water environmental quality and that ad hoc adjustments to these impacts are rarely cost effective and sometimes exceed upland project benefits. However, they also indicate that upstream–downstream linkages can be harmonized by downstream financing of upstream land use management, controlled livestock feeding, and participatory approaches to watershed management. The UN Food and Agriculture Organization (FAO) has stressed the need for much stronger planning, monitoring and evaluation (PME) of watershed projects. For example, the Asian Watershed Management Network (WATMANET) has developed methods for participatory processes, land tenure reforms, and empowerment of women to clarify and achieve economic and environmental benefits (Sharma, 1997).

In India, the Centre for Science and Environment (Agarwal and Narain, 1997) has promoted conservation and revival of traditional water harvesting methods, in part through land cover and soil water management. Water harvesting, mulching, and dew harvesting methods have received attention in arid regions of the Middle East (Evenari et al., 1971), North America (Lightfoot and Eddy, 1995), and Asia (UNEP, 1998).

The last decade of the twentieth century witnessed a revival and bold conceptual extension of watershed management to encompass ecosystem quality and citizen-based planning (Brunner, 2002). Some of these watershed initiatives have combined scientific investigations of watershed hydrology with policy discussions, archival research, public education, and the arts (Natural Resources Law Center, 2000). The Long-term efficacy of local watershed initiatives, and their potential implications for regional sustainability, have yet to be determined (MacDonnell, 1999).

Regional land cover and soil moisture management

Some of the watershed and river basin examples discussed above are planned and carried out by national organizations (e.g., in the United States the Soil Conservation Service, USGS, and EPA). National organizations have attempted, and with varying success, to implement uniform programs over large regions. For example, geographers engaged school children to develop a national land use map of Britain – an intensive field technique over a large area that has not to our knowledge been replicated, though an effort is currently under way to scan those maps to analyze land use change over the past half-century (Brown, N., 2001). By the mid twentieth century, air photo interpretation was increasingly used to classify rural land use conditions and potential in river basins ranging from the lower Indus River basin to the Tennessee River basin.

The US Geological Survey (USGS) undertook national land use and land cover mapping in the 1970s at 1 : 250 000 with a 4 ha resolution, but the agency was not able to update land cover in areas of rapid change, to map changes in land cover, or to draw specific implications for water and environmental management.

More recently, the US National Oceanic and Atmospheric Administration's Climate Prediction Center began monitoring soil moisture over large areas and linking those measurements with other climatological and hydrologic conditions to make soil moisture and drought predictions. Such advances are, and will continue to be, made possible through integrated networks of remote sensing data and automated field measurement, which continuously update data and feed them rapidly and directly into GIS systems and models for climate forecasting, reservoir operations, and drought planning (Zagona *et al.*, 2001).

Before proceeding to global scale models, it is important to acknowledge the contributions of historical geographers and environmental historians, who use archival sources and repeat photography to document land cover changes and environmental impacts. For example, Williams (1991) and Darby (1956) use archival data to document wetlands drainage in the United States and United Kingdom. Richards and Flint (1994) use imperial records and gazetteers of South and Southeast Asia to analyze regional changes in forest cover, cropland, pasture, wetland, and water surfaces over a 100-year period from 1880 to 1980.

The FAO provides data on irrigated areas, as well as other agricultural land uses, but it does not link these variables with one another in a way that enables analysts to understand how changes in land cover affect soil moisture and environmental quality.

Global land cover, soil moisture and climate change

Land cover and soil moisture are key sources of uncertainty in global climate models, and have thus become scientific priorities in global change research since the 1990s. Three international research programs address different aspects of the issues raised above at the global scale.

Land-Use and Land-Cover Change

An international project on Land-Use and Land-Cover Change (LUCC) was organized by the International Geosphere–Biosphere Programme's (IGBP) International Human Dimensions of Global Change Programme. The LUCC project addresses five main questions:

(1)   How has land cover been changed by human use over the last 300 years?

(2)   What are the major human causes of land use change in different geographical and historical contexts?

(3)   How will changes in land use affect land cover in the next 50 to 100 years?

(4)   How do human and biophysical dynamics affect the sustainability of specific types of land uses?

(5)   How might changes in climate and global biogeochemistry affect both land use and land cover, and vice versa?

These questions are currently being addressed in a series of case studies, including one of Belize in Central America, a region that in some areas has had high levels of population density and land use intensity in the past, followed by periods of depopulation, extensification, and repopulation in recent centuries (Turner *et al.*, 1995).

In contrast with earlier mapping and statistical efforts, the LUCC project seeks to focus on the dynamics of land use and land cover change. It plans to add those processes to global models, and incorporate feedbacks from those models. Although soil moisture effects and feedbacks are not the primary concerns of these broader scientific activities, they are a key parameter in many processes of land use change, land cover change, and global modeling efforts.

Biospheric Aspects of the Hydrological Cycle

Soil moisture is a primary variable in the IGBP's project on Biospheric Aspects of the Hydrological Cycle (BAHC). The BAHC concentrates on soil–vegetation–atmosphere transfer processes at the patch, regional and continental scales. It synthesizes field and remote sensing data to evaluate soil moisture flux, below-ground processes, and spatial and temporal variability – and to parameterize these variables for the land–atmosphere interaction components of global models. BAHC includes a cross-cutting study to "analyse impacts of environmental change and climate variability on water and land systems" in different biomes (Pielke and Bravo de Guenni, in press). International soil moisture datasets employed in these hydroclimatological and environmental studies include the ISLSCP (International Satellite Land Surface Climatology Project) Global Soil Wetness Project; the University of Maryland's Global Soil Moisture Data Bank; and Oak Ridge National Laboratory's datasets on Global Distribution of Plant-Extractable Water Capacity of Soil and Global Soil Texture and Derived Water-Holding Capacities.

Global Energy and Water Cycle Experiment

A third IGBP initiative gives an early indication of how these datasets will likely be used. In May 2000 a joint international workshop of BAHC and GEWEX focused directly on "Soil moisture monitoring, analysis and prediction." The workshop assessed the status of satellite remote sensing of soil moisture monitoring, current field experiments, and hydrometeorological modeling and prediction applications. The workshop acknowledged progress at the regional scale and debated the strategic goal of developing and implementing a "global system for monitoring, analysis, and prediction of soil moisture" by 2010. However, it was not clear how closely soil moisture flux will be integrated with land use and ecosystem change, though that is the long-term aim.

The past quarter-century has witnessed remarkable developments in landscape planning, from the local scale of citizen-based watershed initiatives to international soil moisture monitoring. The integration of these efforts over enormous ranges of spatial and temporal scale, heterogeneity, and variability seems at least a multi-decadal enterprise. In the meantime age-old practical problems of irrigation and drainage continue to demand short- and long-term initiatives, and it is those problems and initiatives that are discussed next.

ENVIRONMENTAL ASPECTS OF IRRIGATION AND DRAINAGE

Recall from Chapter 1 that irrigation agriculture constitutes the largest consumptive use of water worldwide, and in most regions of the world, especially Asia. While arid zone irrigation has leveled off, and even declined, in some industrialized regions of the world where higher-value urban, environmental and industrial water uses have expanded, irrigation continues to expand in other regions of the world, notably sub-humid regions, where it supplies supplemental water and increased water supply reliability, and in areas of high population growth and low industrial development. By some accounts, world population growth will necessitate intensified food production through irrigation and other means (Rosegrant *et al.*, 2002; WWC, 2000). One scenario modeled by the International Water Management Institute (Seckler *et al.*, 1998) envisages a 17 percent increase in irrigated land area by 2025, the environmental consequences of which are unclear.

These agricultural water withdrawals, applications, consumptive uses, and constraints – especially when combined with other agricultural practices and chemical applications – have profound

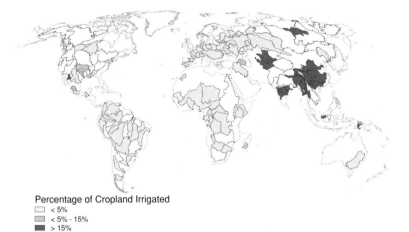

Percentage of Cropland Irrigated
☐ < 5%
▨ < 5% - 15%
■ > 15%

Figure 5.7   World distribution of irrigated cropland mapped by river basin. From Revenga *et al.* (1998, p. 1.26, map 8).

environmental effects, which this section examines. Because irrigation systems display great regional variations in technology, crops, social organization, and productivity, it seems useful to survey the major geographic patterns and types of irrigation, in tandem with common environmental effects and adjustments.

Interestingly, international irrigation organizations have not developed a framework to guide this line of analysis, though they have produced some useful components for such a framework. For example, the FAO publishes annual estimates of irrigated land by country (Figure 5.7). The data for 1998 indicate that India and China have twice the irrigated hectarage of the two next largest countries, Pakistan and the USA, which in turn have more than twice as much irrigated land as the next largest countries. However, these data encompass vastly different types of irrigation systems, environmental contexts, and potential impacts.

In an early attempt at a comprehensive survey, Leonard Cantor's (1970) *World Geography of Irrigation* distinguished the following irrigation types and regions:

- types of irrigation
  - traditional irrigation
  - modern perennial surface irrigation
  - modern groundwater irrigation
- storage and conservation

- human landscape of irrigation
- economic aspects of irrigation
- irrigated regions
  - Monsoon Asia
  - Southwest Asia
  - Europe and Russia
  - Africa
  - North America
  - Latin America
  - Australia

Although Cantor addressed environmental effects briefly in each of these sections, he did not examine them in detail.

In a framework that elaborated social aspects and consequences of irrigation, Wittfogel (1981) emphasized the correlation between aridity, topography, and social aspects of irrigation including property rights, state power, and economic modes of production (Figure 5.8). Although Wittfogel gave little attention to environmental effects or to environmentally sustainable irrigation, archaeologists working in many regions of the world that he discussed have examined long-term environmental consequences of irrigation, especially waterlogging and salinity, and their ramifications with, and for, social systems. Interestingly, comparison of the Nile and Tigris–Euphrates valleys indicates relatively sustained flood irrigation systems in the former, compared with dramatic processes of expansion and collapse, apparently for jointly environmental and social reasons, in the latter (Adams, 1981; Butzer, 1976). Irrigation in the central Arizona region of the United States has had at least three major periods of development and abandonment in the past two millennia. Long-distance transfer of rice irrigation techniques was carried out by west-African slaves in the southeastern USA (Carney, 1998).

The first congress of the International Commission on Irrigation and Drainage (ICID, 1957) asked "Can man develop a permanent irrigation agriculture?" Among arid regions, the lower Nile valley appeared to be a positive example, at least until recent decades of large up-stream impoundment and downstream groundwater extraction (Postel, 1999). Humid regions of rice irrigation and aquaculture simultaneously demonstrate large-scale environmental transformation and long-term sustained food production (Figure 5.9). The picture and prospect in the continuum from semiarid to sub-humid, and perennial to intermittent irrigation, are more complex.

Variables	Water, environment, and social relations		
Geographic location	Core	Margin	Submargin
Climate	Arid	Mesic	Humid
Water technology	Canal irrigation	Hydro-agriculture	Rain-fed agriculture
Hydraulic density [economic role of water]	Compact [national water economy]	Loose I [regional water economy]	Loose II [local hydraulic and non-hydraulic economies]
Property relations	Simple [state property]	Semi-complex [personal property]	Complex [private property]
State functions	Hydraulic works	Transport, communications	Defense and trade
Political organization	Despotism	⟶	Democracy
Human experience	Terror	⟶	Freedom
Hydrologic contexts	Broad alluvial floodplains	Major tributary watersheds	Alpine and perennial streams
Ecosystem types	Desert and semiarid grasslands	Temperate grasslands	Forest and alpine ecosystems
Ecosystem scales	Large landscapes	Meso-scale systems	Heterogeneous patches
Environmental policy types	State-based	Community-based	Property-based

Figure 5.8   The structure of Wittfogel's 1957 analysis of the relationships among "hydraulic societies," "oriental despotism," and bureaucratic social organization – expanded to include environmental variables. From Wittfogel (1981).

Figure 5.9   Cultivation of high-yielding basmati rice varieties in Punjab, Pakistan, resulted from intensification of water, agrochemical, and labor inputs associated with the Green Revolution and Indus Basin Development Programme.

The International Water Management Institute's "Indicators for comparing performance of irrigated agricultural systems" focuses on crop-production and water-use variables that imply but do not measure environmental indicators that affect the performance and sustainability of irrigation agriculture (Seckler *et al.*, 1998). The nine indicators are:

(1)   output per cropped area
(2)   output per unit of canal command area
(3)   output per unit irrigation supply
(4)   output per unit water consumed
(5)   relative water supply (ratio of water supply to crop demand)
(6)   relative irrigation supply
(7)   water delivery capacity
(8)   gross return on investment
(9)   financial self-sufficiency

This framework was developed, and is currently being used to evaluate and adjust irrigation systems, in South Asia (especially Sri Lanka, Pakistan and India). Its influence on irrigation policy and practice has yet to be determined. While it may improve overall crop water supply and demand planning, the framework lacks ecosystem indicators. Even a new and frequently updated *WWW Virtual Library Irrigation* (2003) lacks a major heading on "irrigation and environment."

The "Vision of water for food and rural development" presented at the Second World Water Conference in the Hague in March 2000 stressed the importance of a "healthy environment," "sustainability," and "environmental awareness." Although it effectively wove these concerns into each section of the report, it did not elaborate environmental aspects of irrigation in sufficient detail to guide policy. While it considered environmental constraints, it did not propound an ecosystem approach to agricultural water management (WWC, 2000).

The ICID has developed a matrix of environmental impacts associated with irrigation and drainage systems, which is elaborated in an FAO publication on *Environmental Impact Assessment of Irrigation and Drainage Projects* (Dougherty and Hall, 1995) and reproduced here as Table 5.3.

Although useful as an initial inventory, this framework, along with the others mentioned above, gives less attention to agricultural drainage than to irrigation. In addition to their separate effects, the relationship between irrigation and drainage systems is key for understanding impacts on plant–soil–water–ecosystem relations.

There are large engineering and scientific literatures on environmental impacts of specific drainage types and systems, but they are inadequately linked or balanced with irrigation research. The relative neglect of agricultural drainage parallels the relative neglect of urban wastewater management relative to urban water supply. For example, FAO has not published annual estimates of land drainage. There is to date no "World Geography of Drainage." ICID has not published a matrix on environmental impacts of drainage. And as of late 2000, a *WWW Virtual Library on Drainage* had yet to be developed.

The International Land Reclamation Institute in the Netherlands (ILRI, 2002) has, however, developed a database on environmental aspects of drainage in its DRAiNNET information network, though these aspects are not organized in an ecological or geographic framework. While some environmental effects of drainage are related to those of irrigation systems, others, like oxidation of humic and organic soils, accelerated subsidence of saturated and organic soils, and wetlands dewatering and destruction are specific to drainage.

Notwithstanding these conceptual weaknesses, detailed attention has been devoted to several broad types of environmental impacts, the most prominent of which involve soil and water salinity. The US Salinity

Table 5.3 *ICID checklist of environmental impacts*

Hydrology	1-1	Low flow regime
	1-2	Flood regime
	1-3	Operation of dams
	1-4	Fall of water table
	1-5	Rise of water table
Pollution	2-1	Solute dispersion
	2-2	Toxic substances
	2-3	Organic pollution
	2-4	Anaerobic effects
	2-5	Gas emissions
Soils	3-1	Soil salinity
	3-2	Soil properties
	3-3	Saline groundwater
	3-4	Saline drainage
	3-5	Saline intrusion
Sediments	4-1	Local erosion
	4-2	Hinterland effect
	4-3	River morpholoqy
	4-4	Channel regime
	4-5	Sedimentation
	4-6	Estuary erosion
Ecology	5-1	Project lands
	5-2	Water bodies
	5-3	Surrounding area
	5-4	Valleys and shores
	5-5	Wetlands and plains
	5-6	Rare species
	5-7	Animal migration
	5-8	Natural industry
Socioeconomic	6-1	Population change
	6-2	Income amenity
	6-3	Human migration
	6-4	Resettlement
	6-5	Women's role
	6-6	Minority groups
	6-7	Sites of value
	6-8	Regional effects
	6-9	User involvement
	6-10	Recreation
Health	7-1	Water and sanitation
	7-2	Habitation

(cont.)

Table 5.3 (*cont.*)

	7-3	Health services
	7-4	Nutrition
	7-5	Relocation effect
	7-6	Disease ecology
	7-7	Disease hosts
	7-8	Disease control
	7-9	Other hazards
Imbalances	8-1	Pests and weeds
	8-2	Animal diseases
	8-3	Aquatic weeds
	8-4	Structural damage
	8-5	Animal imbalances

Each item in the checklist is scored on a five-point scale ranging from *positive impact very likely to positive impact possible, no impact, negative impact possible or negative impact very likely*, with columns also for *no judgment possible at present* and *comments*.
Source: Dougherty and Hall, 1995.

Laboratory (USSL, 2002) has compiled a bibliography of thousands of scientific publications on salinity during the twentieth century.

Ghassemi *et al.* (1995) provide one of the most comprehensive international surveys of salinity causes, extent and management. They begin with a global overview, examine agronomic and soil water process, and then survey a broad range of engineering and management options. The bulk of their volume assembles detailed case studies from eleven countries, but does not make detailed comparisons across cases.

Human efforts to harmonize irrigation, drainage, and environmental quality in different geographic regions around the world have varied widely in their success and consequences. While it is not possible within the scope of this chapter to survey the efficacy of complex initiatives in different parts of the world, international commitment to a "Dialogue on water, food and environment," which began in 2001, indicates the growing salience of this goal (IWMI, 2001).

ENVIRONMENTAL APPROACHES TO URBAN
STORMWATER MANAGEMENT

Just as drainage from agricultural lands has important water resource and environmental implications, so too does drainage from urbanizing regions. This section focuses on emerging environmental approaches to urban stormwater management.

Concern about urban drainage has ancient roots. Roman water laws specified that the drip (*stillicidium*) from roofs must not cause harm to tenants of adjacent or downslope properties (Bruun, 1991; Evans, 1994; Scobie, 1986; Ware, 1905). At the same time, urban dwellers had an easement to convey drainage waters away from their property, even if it passed over a neighbor's property. But they could not discharge drainage waters onto public lands, and they had a responsibility to keep drains clear of debris. Poor people and slum tenements were located in low-lying poorly drained areas then as now.

The Greek geographer Strabo praised Rome more for its elaborate sewers than for its hilly setting or water supply (Strabo, 1917–32), though urbanization of the hills increased the need for urban drainage in low-lying regions such as the Forum. Unfortunately, sophisticated urban drainage works at Rome, Moenjodaro and other early cities collected, conveyed, and discharged water directly to rivers, which became increasingly polluted and prone to flooding downstream. They succeeded in draining surface waters, but at the same time destroyed wetlands, accelerated surface subsidence, and reduced aquifer recharge.

Unfortunately, this approach to urban drainage and its associated problems of water pollution, flooding and groundwater impacts prevails in many urbanizing regions of the world to this day. Similarly, the ancient view of urban stormwater as a "common enemy," which every landowner has a right to avoid and discharge as efficiently as possible remains a principle of common law in many parts of the world.

However, a corollary principle of common law, that one cannot alter drainage patterns to the detriment of a neighbor, has given rise to more harmonious environmental approaches to urban stormwater. While problems of urban soil moisture mismanagement spread in the most rapidly urbanizing and poorest cities of the world, innovative approaches are also entering the mainstream, which are the focus of the following sections on (1) on-site interception, infiltration and detention; (2) wetland, pond, and creek restoration; and (3) non-point-source water quality management. While these three processes are interrelated in metropolitan hydrology, innovations have developed semi-independently and need to be more fully integrated.

On-site water interception, infiltration, and detention ponds

While the "common enemy" drainage doctrine and modern sewer systems strove to collect and convey water off-site as quickly as possible,

environmental approaches seek opportunities to absorb and retain precipitation as close as possible to where it falls, without interfering with
other economic activities.

Maintaining the natural land cover of vegetation, soil litter, and
tilth are classic means of achieving this aim. Where land cover has
been disturbed, reforestation, mulching, soil aeration, and taking steps
to reduce the compaction and consequent reduction of infiltration are
likewise common steps. These principles were applied comprehensively
in a development known as the Woodlands near Houston, Texas, where
land uses were zoned for their infiltration capacity and recharge potential (Spirn, 2000).

At the regional scale, the Denver Urban Drainage and Flood Control District has a jurisdiction extending beyond the City and County
of Denver, Colorado, to include 33 municipal jurisdictions. The district
coordinates metropolitan plans for flood hazard reduction through infrastructure grants, master planning, drainage way design, floodplain
management, and maintenance programs.

Places that have adopted "no net increase in runoff" standards
have stimulated additional steps to reduce the area of impervious surface, and to increase the use of porous paving, "French drains" (vertical
trenches filled with coarse aggregate), detention ponds, and rooftop
water retention gardens. Runoff can be reduced 100 percent when formerly impervious areas such as rooftops and parking lots are restored
to pervious, vegetated, depressed land surfaces, provided local infiltration capacity and detention storage are not exceeded (Dreiseitl et al.,
2001; Fergusson, 1994; France, 2002).

Many of these features have jointly aesthetic and hydrologic
benefits, and handbooks of stormwater management now provide information both on calculating water volumes conserved and on improving the aesthetic value of, for example, ponds that formerly had
unsightly shapes and edges. Ecological approaches to detention pond
design – and the long legacy of urban wetland drainage and destruction – are stimulating increasing interest in urban wetland restoration (see Chapter 7 on lakes and wetlands). In some jurisdictions,
destruction of wetlands in one location must be mitigated by
constructing wetlands in other locations (NRC, 1995). There are many
unintentionally constructed wetlands – e.g., in areas of canal seepage,
over-irrigation, subsidence, and wastewater discharge – but the new
wetland restoration movements strive for scientific reconstruction and
management of plant–soil–water–ecosystem relations for jointly socioeconomic and environmental benefits.

There is great potential in extending these environmental approaches to urban soil moisture detention in many urbanizing parts and aspects of the world (Sheaffer, 2000). They intersect with techniques of urban flood-plain management (e.g., flood-proofing), discussed elsewhere in this volume. They entail increasingly sophisticated approaches to managing shrink–swell soils (e.g., through foundation engineering and drainage) and subsidence in clay soils. Subsidence accelerated by groundwater pumping and surface water drainage in compactable soils affects urbanizing areas ranging from coastal areas such as New Orleans and Houston to highland basins such as Mexico City.

At the same time, low-lying areas of low-income settlement, for example, in peri-urban areas from Nairobi to Mumbai, still present great challenges in conveying water off-site in environmentally sensitive ways.

From vegetated swales to urban creek restoration

Swales (shallow channels that carry occasional storm runoff) have been employed from agricultural fields to suburban towns to urban parks. They slow down the passage of water through vegetated sideslopes and beds that increase channel roughness and decrease channel erosion, while collecting and conveying water from broader areas to a channel and ultimately to a sink or outlet. Small swales may be constructed on agricultural terraces to remove accumulated runoff or redirect it to a drier field. Larger swales may carry the runoff from entire subdivisions. As with detention ponds, they can have aesthetic as well as functional value by sculpting the landscape in visually dynamic and coherent ways.

An early example involved Frederick Law Olmsted's work on the "Emerald Necklace" park system in the Boston region in Massachusetts, which was driven by sanitation and drainage concerns and accomplished through large-scale park development and grading (Spirn, 1984).

These jointly aesthetic and functional approaches have an added ecological dimension in emerging methods of urban creek restoration. While river channel and floodplain management are examined in Chapter 8, here the stage is set for that discussion by considering the new movements to reconstruct ephemeral and small perennial urban creeks. These methods include "daylighting" creeks that were channelized in stormwater pipes sometimes a century or more ago. It includes revegetation of sideslopes with diverse plantings that have higher roughness coefficients, higher evapotranspiration rates, and therefore altered runoff capacities and reduced flow of pollutants (Riley, 1999).

These integrated environmental and water resources approaches are increasingly justified on socioeconomic and cultural as well as engineering and ecological grounds. They restore sources of community landscape identity and enjoyment as well as dramatically improving disturbed urban environments. Urban creek restoration also contributes to the water quality aims of plant–soil–water–ecosystem management.

From sedimentation to non-point-source pollution management and bioremediation

As noted above, classical urban drainage approaches led to water quality and flooding problems that offset their local benefits. Water quality protection has become a major justification for integrating environmental and urban stormwater management. As in the case of grass swales, the initial water quality impacts considered were erosion and sedimentation. Erosion not only depleted agricultural resources, it also increased sedimentation and turbidity in streams, which disturbed aquatic habitat and river channel dynamics.

Publication of *Silent Spring* (Carson, 1962) raised public concerns about associated runoff of agricultural chemicals, especially fertilizers and pesticides, whose impacts ranged from eutrophication to aquatic mutagenicity and drinking water contamination. Although widely voiced by urban populations, these concerns diffused more slowly in urbanizing regions and on golf courses where lawn chemicals are applied at very high rates and have very short runoff paths to natural watercourses.

The Clean Water Act initially exempted these non-point sources of water pollution but there is increasing effort to redirect water quality policy toward them. Demonstration projects have been initiated to design, monitor and model non-point-source pollution control methods (Terrene Institute, 1995). For example, a demonstration project at the Land and Water Fund of the Rockies, in Boulder, Colorado monitors the performance of an urban non-point source runoff and pollution control project whose elements include on-site water collection, detention, infiltration, and transpiration (Heaney, 2002). Prince George's County in Maryland is moving toward a policy of "Low Impact Development" which focuses the "Smart Growth" initiatives emerging in areas of rapid urbanization on hydrologic issues and urban stormwater conservation.

However, some of the most challenging cases entail contamination of soils by spills, leakage, and chemical applications that have very slow and diffuse rates of movement that resist conventional clean-up and control methods. These situations have led to the emerging field of bioremediation (use of plants and microorganisms) to clean up contaminated soils and soil water. They have also led to increasingly sophisticated systems of land application of wastewater for fodder crop production, advanced sewage pond systems, and wetland restoration designs for waste management as well as other purposes (Campbell and Ogden, 1999). Phytoremediation uses plants to absorb, and thus at least temporarily collect and concentrate, chemicals from soil water and contaminated soils where they can be harvested and, if non-toxic, used for fuel or forage. Restoration of contaminated aquifers leads from this chapter on soil moisture to the next on groundwater and environmental management.

6

Groundwater

INTRODUCTION

Below the soil water in many continental areas not covered by snow and ice are porous lithosphere formations more or less saturated with groundwater. Those that occur in well-defined forms are commonly referred to as aquifers. These groundwater formations differ tremendously from place to place in at least nine different respects that are discussed below. Together, groundwaters account for a substantial proportion of all freshwater on the globe. They are used in various degrees from either springs or wells by a wide variety of technologies, and their wise use and protection calls for a large range of types of public measure.

It is estimated by Russian hydrologists that approximately 29 percent of the world's freshwater is stored at any one time in aquifers (Shiklomanov, 2000). About 33 percent of that volume is on the Asian continent, 23 percent in Africa, 18 percent in North America, 13 percent in South America, 6 percent in Europe, and 5 percent in Australia. Roughly one-half of the stored groundwater is estimated to be at depths of less than 200 m, and the remainder at depths up to 2000 m.

Around the globe, the actual net withdrawal of groundwater is affected by the conjunctive use of groundwater and surface water, and by the particular purpose for which it is used. In areas where the withdrawal exceeds either natural or artificial recharge, aquifers have been drawn down significantly. In some areas they have been largely or entirely exhausted. In those areas where exhaustion is threatened the human response is (1) to abandon the use of the aquifer, (2) to find and apply an artificial means of replenishing the formation, or (3) to reduce withdrawal to estimated approximate inflow. Often, the increasing cost of withdrawal leads to aquifer abandonment before it is exhausted. The effectiveness of the various possible measures is related to the confinement and porosity of the aquifer as well as to the natural or artificial rate of replenishment.

While there is outflow of groundwater in some places through springs and seeps, in many places the overwhelming outflow for human purposes is by means of wells of various depths and capacities. Customarily, the human use of an aquifer is described in terms of the flow from the springs or wells reaching the stored water.

The physical quality of aquifer water in its natural state ranges from completely salty (over 30 000 ppm total dissolved solids), as in some inland and many coastal areas, to relatively free from minerals. While many aquifers are protected from human pollution, and from drafts exceeding their natural inflow, others are heavily contaminated by waste disposal and are drawn down or exhausted by pumping. To combat such pollution and exhaustion, the range of social measures is large and diverse.

In some areas the organic growth on the land surface is influenced by the quantity and quality of natural flow from an aquifer. This is relatively uncommon except in the land around springs where very special combinations of plants and animals are supported in the immediate area of a springflow to the surface.

Because the scientific study of groundwater is generally less extensive than research on most other aspects of the hydrologic cycle, understanding of the effects of water management on its basic character as well as on related ecosystems is very rough in many places. Estimating the quantity and quality of water in an underground formation differs greatly in accuracy from place to place. Ideally, it would be desirable to know the precise physical and chemical character of a water-bearing formation, its full water-storing capacity, its actual water storage, the rates at which water is added and discharged, and the quality of stored water. This is rarely the case. In the United States, for example, the proportion of Federal research expenditures in the annual budget for hydrology that in the late 1990s was spent on groundwater was roughly 3 percent.

Underground water-bearing formations are classified according to a variety of features, including:

(1)   character of the water-bearing rock (age and rock type) including its porosity;
(2)   thickness of the formation;
(3)   depth below the soil surface;

(4)   relative impermeability of the formations above and below, and extent to which the aquifer can be replenished naturally;

(5)   volume of storage;

(6)   rate of natural replenishment;

(7)   quality of water (saline or fresh);

(8)   degree of pollution;

(9)   effect of flow upon organic life on surface.

The term aquifer commonly is applied to formations in which those features are relatively distinct. However, where some of those features are not well defined there may be extensive and significant storage of water below the soil surface, but without designating the storage as an aquifer. In some formations, for example, there may be areas of extensive seepage that does not appear in well-defined springs.

The major types of groundwater regions in the United States have been mapped by Heath (USGS, 1988). This broad classification does not reveal the tremendous diversity that may exist within relatively small spatial areas of soil surface. Depending upon the geologic age and rock type – from recent sediments through different geological formations to Precambrian crystalline rocks – there may be formations ranging from very important to insignificant water-bearing capacity at various depths.

An example of aquifer diversity can be found in the High Plains Aquifer, which is one of the great aquifers in the United States (Alley et al., 1999; Brooks Emel, 1995; Kromm and White, 1992). It covers an area from Nebraska to Texas including the Ogallala formation over a relatively impervious formation. It is overlain by an assortment of sands and gravels, with small groundwater content, and in a few places is eroded by streams with valley groundwater, cutting through surface sediments. It provides large supplies of water through wells but has a very low natural recharge capacity. Thus, the High Plains has been a cheap, readily accessible source of well water for irrigation since the 1930s, but it is not widely replenished by either natural or artificial means. Its net depletion has reached the point in some areas that the long-term use through wells is being reduced. The effects upon the natural ecosystems on the surface of the High Plains are not yet conspicuous, and natural water quality is not a matter of special concern. In terms of water management the urgent challenges are to cope with progressively larger withdrawals from the aquifer by reducing use or by planning for its exhaustion.

The situation in many other groundwater regions is much more complicated. Again, the High Plains region of the United States between Canada and the Gulf of Mexico alone includes at least four other major areas in addition to the Ogallala. Those are sand dune deposits, outwash plains, Dakota sandstones, and Oligocene clays (Chow, 1964). From early exploitation of about 480 million cubic feet (14 million m^3) per day in 1949, it increased to 2150 million cubic feet (61 million m^3) in 1980, and declined to 1870 million cubic feet (53 million m^3) per day in 1990.

To suggest the range and diversity of groundwater conditions and problems around the world, two tables show outlines of the major types of groundwater and the chief forms of human use of groundwater. Those are followed by a review of the principal ways in which the character of aquifer management has had consequences for the quality of environment, as well as notable problems of aquifer water quality, and problems of overdraft and exhaustion. A concluding section addresses the question of the relationship of aquifer management to the world water outlook.

MAJOR TYPES AND USES OF GROUNDWATER FORMATIONS

As outlined in Table 6.1, groundwater formations differ significantly in physical character. The major uses of groundwater are shown in Table 6.2.

The characteristics and extent of a water-bearing formation, and of any materials above and below it, have a powerful influence upon its quantitative role in the local hydrologic cycle, and its likely provision of sustainable supplies. Some of the relationships between aquifer characteristics and human use can be summarized in descriptions of a few examples from the USA.

A shallow, porous sand and gravel aquifer overlying an impervious formation can be used so long as annual withdrawal does not exceed

Table 6.1 *Common types of groundwater occurrence*

	Geologic formation	Confining strata	Replenishment
seep	soil	underlying	precipitation
spring	soil	underlying	seep or precipitation
aquifer	porous rock	relatively impervious above or below or both	depends on adjoining or upper strata

Table 6.2 *Major uses of groundwater in the USA, 1995*

	Groundwater used (millions of gallons per day)	
	Freshwater	Saline water
Public supply	15 100	—
Domestic	3350	—
Commercial	939	—
Irrigation	49 000	—
Livestock	2260	—
Industrial	4090	15
Mining	1070	1010
Thermoelectric	565	—
Total[a]	76 400	1110

[a]Figures may not add to totals because of independent rounding.
Source: Solley *et al.*, 1998.

infiltration from above, as in the Atlantic and Gulf coastal plain and the Florida peninsula.

A porous aquifer that is confined above and below by relatively impervious materials will be exhausted in time by human withdrawals, as in the Ogallala in the High Plains.

A deep porous aquifer that is subject to nourishment by disposal of surface water or through injection can be used so long as input is at least equal to the withdrawal, as in the Eastern River Plain in Idaho.

In both confined and unconfined aquifers, urban use of water can result in major declines in groundwater level. A confined aquifer of Cambrian Ordovician materials under the Chicago metropolitan area suffered a decline of 200–800 feet (61–244 m) between 1864, when the first deep well was drilled, and the 1980s, when providers of water began to shift from ground to surface sources (Alley *et al.*, 1999, p. 51).

An unconfined aquifer of glacial materials in Nassau County, Long Island, New York suffered from the installation during the 1960s of a sewer system that diverted water formerly discharged into the aquifer into the ocean. As a result of the diversion the groundwater surface dropped about 10 feet (3 m) in some places (Alley *et al.*, 1999).

NOTABLE PROBLEMS OF AQUIFER WATER QUALITY

In addition to questions of volume and stability of supply, some of the more troublesome problems of aquifer management relate to the quality of water withdrawn. This is a product either of the natural chemical constituents of the aquifer or of contamination from human sources. The natural chemical content of groundwater varies tremendously around the globe and so, too, does the pollution of shallow groundwater from human domestic waste or from industrial sources, many of which employ no or partial treatments.

In the late 1960s the most conspicuous case of a problem relating to natural aquifer water quality began to come to light with respect to arsenic in a number of Asian and Latin American countries (Chappell *et al.*, 2001; Nordstrom, 2002). In West Bengal and Bangladesh, as part of a government program to provide improved water supply for human consumption to villagers in the delta of the Ganges River, several million tube wells had been drilled to groundwater to replace contaminated surface water sources that were being used for human consumption. Belatedly in the 1990s, it was discovered that the aquifer, particularly in alluvial sediments, in some areas had arsenic concentrations up to 2500 µg/l. Over periods of months or years these concentrations of arsenic were found to be the cause of hypopigmentation, keratosis, skin cancer, organic cancer, and various other cancers, neurological, reproductive and cardiovascular problems. Perhaps 30 million people in Bangladesh villages and six million in West Bengal were exposed to water from contaminated wells, and it currently was difficult to provide ready substitutes. Effective mitigation was slow in coming in providing substitute uncontaminated sources or effective treatment (Hoque *et al.*, 1994). It was estimated that of the six million in West Bengal who were drinking arsenic-contaminated water, 300 000 already showed signs of some form of poisoning. Other areas of substantial population exposure were in Taiwan, Mongolia, Argentina, and Chile.

Around the world, exhaustion of soil moisture affected by drawing down of aquifers or by the reduction of aquifer discharge into streams has been found to have significant effects upon ecosystems, particularly during dry periods in weather.

Problems of pollution

Contamination of groundwater quality may occur either as a direct effect of waste discharge through wells or through filtration of surface materials into aquifers lacking upper confinement. Irrigation accounts for the largest volume of such pollution in many aquifers accessible to surface drainage. Because substantial volumes of salty water naturally occur adjacent to freshwater supplies, a reduction in aquifer level through pumping may induce inflow of the brine into a formerly fresh supply. This is a particularly widespread problem in coastal areas where increase in ocean level or withdrawal of fresh water from an aquifer adjoining salt water may lead to intrusion by salt water. Chlorides and dissolved solids move into what previously was a fresh-water aquifer.

As early as 1969 the Committee on Saltwater Intrusion of the American Society of Civil Engineers (ASCE) found that such intrusion was reported in some part of almost every state in the USA (Sherwood *et al.*, 1969).

The use of groundwater in most coastal areas is very much influenced by the degree to which the aquifer is subject to infiltration of salt water from the ocean. This hazard may have a powerful influence upon the place and volume of withdrawal, as along sectors of the southern Atlantic coast of the United States. It would become more acute as sea level rose with climate change.

Because of the tremendous differences from place to place in quality of groundwater linked with the many and various connections between surface and ground waters, the design of measures to manage groundwater is a complicated and highly variable exercise. The time in which the results of management may become apparent is very long in many places. In those circumstances a study by the US Geological Survey of the sustainability of groundwater resources in 1999 placed heavy emphasis upon long-term data collection linked with sophisticated modeling of the intricate interrelation of factors (Alley *et al.*, 1999). The USGS noted that if genuinely sustainable management of groundwater was to be assured careful observations needed to be executed over many years and that precise computer models of the numerous interrelated factors needed to be used.

A similar set of recommendations with respect to preventing contamination of aquifer quality came in 1993 from an interdisciplinary committee of the NRC (NRC, 1993a). Noting that all groundwater is vulnerable, that a variety of factors such as soil, geology, recharge rates, and the quality of contaminants are at work, and that a high degree of uncertainty applies to the various assessment methods, the committee argued for very careful and sensitive methodology adjusted to the particular environments. What might be optimal for a groundwater resource estimate on Cape Cod would require modification for Iowa or Florida. Vulnerability to pesticide contamination, for example, differs tremendously not only from one region of the country to another, but within regions as well.

GROUNDWATER MOVEMENT AND WITHDRAWAL

Movement of groundwater is very much affected by volumes and differences in pressure and elevation. Darcy in 1856 concluded that the flow through stratified beds of sand was proportional to energy loss, inversely proportional to the distance of the flow, and proportional to type of sand (*Encyclopedia Britannica*, 1974a). This is similar to the relations involved in average conditions of water flow through pipes. Darcy's Law has remained a standard law for estimating groundwater movement.

Springs

Springs may be classified in terms of (1) type of water-bearing material where they issue from that material, (2) their magnitude of discharge, (3) the degree to which their discharge is constant or variable, and (4) temperature as non-thermal or thermal (Maxey, 1964).

A small proportion of current groundwater use is from free-flowing springs, with the large proportion of use being from constructed wells. Springs commonly are divided between thermal and non-thermal flows reaching streams or surface pools, and differ greatly in mineral content and temperature. Thermal hot springs may range in temperature from as little as 30 °C in parts of the Sahara in Tunisia to over 50 °C in Thermopolis, Wyoming. The mineral content of the thermal water in those two springs, measured in dissolved solids, varies from 400 mg/l to 2600 mg/l. The chemical quality of thermal springs varies tremendously around the world, chiefly in areas of current volcanic activity (Waring, 1965).

Groundwater typically accumulates in rock pores that are saturated. The chief porous rocks are unconsolidated sand and gravel, limestone, sedimentary rocks, and basalt. In such formations springs commonly support streamflow. This means that the immediately adjoining soil and water maintain roughly uniform temperature and chemical conditions. Thus, the adjacent organisms will have a more constant environment. These tend to be relatively simple refuges for plants and animals, varying with the chemical quality of the rock and water.

Because of the differences in climate, water supply, and content, the plant and animal populations in the immediate vicinity of springs vary greatly, although all tend to support a large number of individuals of relatively few species. Three major types of springs are found according to water flow: those in which water flows rapidly from the source, those in which water flows into the bottom of a pool that feeds a brook, and those in which water seeps to the surface through the ground. Some springs support large numbers of algae and plants. Other springs support organisms that consume other matter such as leaves.

Spring isolation may support small-size organisms, and offer refuge to species that diminish after climate change and that are especially sensitive to changes in light. Thus, the natural diversity of spring organisms may be especially vulnerable to human management of springs (*Encyclopedia Britannica*, 1974b; Reid, 1961).

For these reasons the early and widespread practice of managing springs as sources of domestic water supply, for example, by clearing, lining, and diverting them, has over the years destroyed or greatly reduced the ecosystems associated with springs.

Many ancient cities in humid regions also have a long history of using springs. Early settlements on the hills of Rome, for example, relied upon springs (*fons*) that drained into the Forum (Smith, 1922). The ancient historian Livy (1960, p. 56) wrote that one of Rome's early rulers, Numa, known for his justice, piety, and contributions to Roman law, visited a nymph goddess named Egeria at a spring sacred to the muses for advice (Figure 6.1). The legal digest of Justinian includes laws on the right to use water from springs (Mommsen and Krueger, 1985, p. 43.22.1) and also requiring the cleaning and repair of springs (Mommsen and Kruegem, 1985, p. 22.1.6). Conversely, times of injustice were associated with drought and failure of springs. Livy (1960, p. 302) reports that in 430–428 BCE, "it was so bad that cattle lay dying of thirst near the dried up springs and along the banks of the parched brooks; others died of scab and the infection was passed on by contact to human beings."

Springs have been features around which many communities first developed, particularly in arid and semiarid climates (Figure 6.2). Damascus, Syria, and Caesarea in Israel are examples (Olami and Peleg, 1977). Likewise, many ancient cities constructed aqueducts to carry domestic water from distant springs (Crouch, 1993). Rome alone built eleven aqueducts for that purpose (*Encyclopedia Britannica*, 1974b).

Wells

The common human access to groundwater is through wells. These differ tremendously in depth, width, casing if used, and power used in raising water to the surface, and those factors together affect the total pumpage, its reliability and its cost. For depths up to 25 m the construction ranges from simple digging to augering and boring with driven-and-jetted devices (Figures 6.3 and 6.4). For deeper wells the method is

Figure 6.1   Springs of Egeria outside Rome, Italy, once deemed sacred by the pious king Numa who came here for advice from the nymph of the spring.

drilling. The casing varies roughly from 9 cm to 120 cm in width, and the yield varies according to diameter of casing and size of pump from 15 m^3 to 20 000 m^3 per day (Van der Leeden *et al.*, 1990, p. 458). The type of construction also varies widely in depth in relation to the geologic formation of the aquifer and the specific purpose of the well.

Some wells are solely for injection purposes but the prevailing number are for extraction. Purpose of use accounts for the time and volume of pumping. Injection wells serve to dispose of hazardous and

Figure 6.2 Eldorado Springs, Colorado, USA, sacred to the Arapahoe tribe of Indians, was converted for recreational swimming and commercially bottled mineral water in the nineteenth century.

Figure 6.3 Seventeenth-century brick well along the Yamuna River in Agra, India. Some of these old wells still operate or have been refitted with pumpsets to draw upon shallow alluvial aquifers.

Figure 6.4   Fortified stepwell (known as a *baoli* or *baori*) at Nagaur Fort in the desert region of Rajasthan, India, illustrates the architectural beauty and strategic importance of groundwater development in arid regions.

Table 6.3 *Number of extraction wells in operation in the USA, 1984*

Household	13 100 000
Irrigation	348 000
Community	98 000
Public – small group	283 000
Total	13 830 000

Source: USGS, 1989.

industrial wastes, to facilitate oil or gas production, to aid in mineral extraction, and for a wide variety of waste disposal. In the 1980s there were more than 220 000 injection wells in operation for the United States. With the inclusion of shallow non-hazardous Class V wells, that number could rise to almost one million (USEPA, 2002a).

In 1984 the total number of extraction wells in operation in the United States was approximately as shown in Table 6.3. The annual number of water wells drilled in the United States from 1964 to 1984 has ranged from 336 000 to 23 000, with the largest number each year in Florida (USGS, 1989).

As indicated in Table 6.3, the overwhelming proportion of wells is for domestic use. In an area such as the Ogallala, by contrast, irrigation

Figure 6.5   Center-pivot irrigation in the Great Plains region of the USA pump water from the deep and largely non-renewable Ogallala aquifer.

activities are dominant and the wells serving domestic use year-round are separate from the larger wells providing irrigation water during the growing season (Figure 6.5).

Problems of overdraft

In 1983 the National Water Summary of the US Geological Survey identified areas in 29 states where there had been a decline of more than 40 feet (12 m) in artesian water level in at least one aquifer as a result of pumping (USGS, 1984). More recently the overdraft situation has worsened, and in most regions of the world where groundwater is a major source of supply conditions continue to deteriorate.

An increasing number of urbanizing and intensively irrigated regions around the world are over-pumping groundwater at rates that exceed recharge capacity, leading to declining water levels, increasing pumping depths, well failure, and energy costs for pumping (Figure 6.6). Margat (1996) gives examples of net annual overdraft that help put the United States examples discussed here in an international context:

Algeria/Tunisia	0.16 km³/year overdraft
Saudi Arabia	1.13 km³/year overdraft
Gaza Strip	0.19 km³/year overdraft
Ogallala, USA	15.2 km³/year overdraft

Figure 6.6   Abandoned *qanat* water system in Turkmenistan, which
tapped into aquifers in piedmont areas and upper alluvial fans and
conveyed water by tunnels (with regularly spaced airshafts for
ventilation and maintenance). Abandonment of these systems may
result from upstream depletion or failure to maintain the system
during periods of economic or political stress.

Beyond these gross estimates, many local areas experience far greater
rates and consequences of groundwater overdraft. Municipal, industrial
and agricultural groundwater overuse in the north China Hubei plain,
for example, is so severe that into the late 1990s an estimated 300 towns

did not have adequate drinking water supplies, and 100 towns faced severe and worsening water shortages, leading to local water rationing and environmental problems associated with long-distance regional water transfers (Boxer, 1998; UNCHS, 1996; World Bank, 2001).

Comparative study of regional groundwater depletion in India has shed light on rates of overdraft. While these problems are especially severe in arid parts of Rajasthan and Gujarat, the broader Indo-Gangetic plains and Deccan plateau are increasingly affected. The percentage of state groundwater areas utilizing over 65 percent of their annual groundwater potential in 1992 was (Central Ground Water Board, 1992, reported in Saleth, 1996, p. 17–18):

Andhra Pradesh	17.15%
Bihar	9.35%
Gujarat	17.49%
Haryana	44.90%
Karnataka	10.28%
Madhya Pradesh	3.70%
Maharashtra	6.15%
Punjab	76.27%
Rajasthan	38.98%
Tamil Nadu	31.49%
Uttar Pradesh	10.50%
West Bengal	10.55%
All-India Average	13.54%

Research in India and Nepal has also identified key factors and behaviors that affect overdraft (e.g., subsidized or unpriced energy, dramatic increase in use of electric and diesel pumpsets), informal local groundwater markets organized in some cases by communities and in others by large landholders, and the relative efficacy of alternative local and state institutional strategies (e.g., power tariffs, rental markets, and groundwater laws) (Saleth, 1996; Shah, 1993). Groundwater use in India and elsewhere is so decentralized, and problems are so pervasive, that local individual and community solutions are perhaps more critical for sustainable groundwater management than state and national policies (Moench et al., 1999). Where shallow water tables occur, low-technology pedal pumps can be used, but as water tables drop, community and, increasingly, intergovernmental coordination is required (Shah, 2000).

In 1974 the Council on Environmental Quality (CEQ) estimated that there were many states in the USA in some part of which there had been critical groundwater overdraft of more than 500 million gallons (1893 million liters) per day (CEQ, 1981).

For these reasons parts of the Ogallala aquifer may be exhausted in places by withdrawals but some parts also may be maintained as a stable source where the volume of withdrawal does not exceed the low rate of natural replenishment plus artificial recharge. Few other aquifers have as relatively simple relations between sustained use and quality and recharge. Most aquifers are more complicated in terms of sustained quantity and quality.

A major hazard of groundwater withdrawal in some areas is land subsidence. Where water is pumped from some aquifers near the land surface, as in the Los Banos area of California, the surface may sink sufficiently to affect buildings and roads (as much as 5–10 m), and impose a severe social cost on pumping. It has been estimated that subsidence due to groundwater withdrawal had occurred in at least 17 areas in the USA prior to 1980 (Poland, 1981). In karst and cave environments groundwater drilling can produce dramatic sinkholes.

GROUNDWATER MANAGEMENT OPTIONS AND THE WORLD OUTLOOK

Practicable management measures by public agencies to deal with the effects of overdraft or pollution of groundwater cover a wide range of private or public initiatives. The principal ones are as follows:

- drilling permits: municipal or state permits setting the depth and diameter of new wells.
- withdrawal limits: regulation of the time and volume of pumpage from existing wells.
- regulation of injection well drilling depth, and pumpage of injection wells for recharging.
- regulation of volume and character of waste discharged into aquifers.
- regulation of land use affecting the functions of springs.

The continuing rate of exhaustion of aquifers indicates that many efforts to prevent deterioration of both quantity and quality of groundwater are ineffective or inadequate, but a few initiatives indicate conditions in which success is achieved.

The key questions are, first, whether these local cooperative groundwater management successes can be scaled up to the regional aquifer level and, second, whether the lessons of sustainable aquifer management in one region can be adapted and transferred to others. For example, local communities have successfully organized to recharge dug wells with declining water levels in Gujarat, India (Moench *et al.*, 1999, pp. 247–260). These institutional successes have also been linked with increasingly efficient irrigation technologies. But their potential impact within the broader context of regional canal irrigation, drainage, and tube-well projects and policies is unclear. Similarly, their relevance for other types of communities, aquifers, and water-use technologies has yet to be established, though comparative investigations by IWMI and other organizations focus on precisely that issue.

Advances in groundwater measurement, real-time monitoring, and aquifer modeling also promise to help scale up from intensive well observations in small areas to aquifer management (e.g., USGS, 2003). A study of 25 regional aquifers in the USA yielded an atlas of large-scale aquifer conditions as well as improved protocols for regional groundwater monitoring and assessing vulnerability to contamination.

However, many if not most users withdraw groundwater with little understanding of regional impacts; and many if not most jurisdictions still regulate groundwater withdrawals and pollution under separate laws and agencies. Groundwater resources will have increasing importance for the ways in which they are buffered from fluctuations in environmental and social processes, including interannual global climate variability and trends. But groundwater pumping and contamination are less subject to public monitoring and regulation, and they respond less quickly to management actions taken to mitigate depletion and pollution hazards. These aquifer characteristics argue for greater effort worldwide to anticipate long-term regional aquifer problems, to develop long-term regional strategies for groundwater management, and to coordinate those strategies with regional systems of water and related land resource management – all of which have proven elusive in most if not all areas of the world to date.

7

Lakes and wetlands

INTRODUCTION

The volume and quality of water accumulating in natural lakes and wetlands varies tremendously from place to place on the continents and over time (Figures 7.1 and 7.2). In most parts of the modern world wetlands have been subject to drastic changes caused by water and land management practices, and lakes generally have received much more attention than wetlands. The extent and types of change in both quantity and quality of water are influenced by a diverse combination of human techniques that are evolving rapidly (Figure 7.3).

The current situation is reviewed here in terms of the major types of lakes and wetlands, their more significant features, and the range of social measures that improve or degrade their quality. They exhibit a tremendous diversity in the effects of human management, ranging from virtual destruction of large areas, as in the case of sections of the Aral Sea, to the preservation of unique landscapes, as in the case of small lakes in the Adirondacks and Japan.

In some regions, such as in southern Florida, the distinction between gently sloping perennial wetlands and shallow lakes may be slight, and certain lakes are bordered by seasonal wetlands. In some other areas such as Lake Baikal, the boundaries between deep lake bottom and rugged shores are abrupt and well defined.

It is estimated that the earth's continents contain roughly 191 million km^2 of liquid surface water, and that 92.3 percent is in lakes. Sixty percent of that volume is fresh, with salt water accounting for the rest (Shiklomanov, 1993). The estimate of water in world marshlands or wetlands is that in volume they account for approximately five percent of the lakes, but because they extend seasonally

Figure 7.1   Small alpine lakes and wetlands form in glacial depressions during warm months of the year (Colorado, USA).

Figure 7.2   Although limited to brine shrimp, grubs, and flies, saline inland water bodies such as Mono Lake, California, USA, support diverse avian and terrestrial species, as well as recreational camping. A California court applied the public trust doctrine to protect ecological and cultural values at Mono Lake in 1983.

Figure 7.3   Receding shoreline of the Aral Sea near Nukus, Uzbekistan, indicates former beach ridges, exposed alkaline mudflats, and residual shoreline vegetation.

over large shallow areas, the total area of wetlands on continents in 2000 was highly variable and extremely difficult to estimate.

In the United States, as with other continental regions, the area in wetlands, including peatlands, changed drastically after early settlement. It was estimated in 1990 that more than half of the early wetlands in the USA, or approximately 100 million acres (40 million hectares), had been destroyed (Kusler and Kentula, 1990, p. ix). Accurate comparable data on wetlands destruction for most continents other than Europe are lacking. In the USA the annual rate of destruction by draining, filling, or clearing during the late 1980s was believed to be about 450 000 acres (182 000 ha) per year but diminishing significantly. In India, the destruction had been very large but public measures to reverse the trends began to take hold by the late 1980s (ILEC, 1996, pp. 53–60).

Historical perspectives on wetlands reveal a long record of drainage, accompanied by a dramatic change in human attitudes toward their ecological value. The Greek geographer Strabo mentions Roman drainage of wetlands (Strabo, 1917–32), while Darby reconstructs the drainage of the fens in the United Kingdom from medieval to modern times (Darby, 1956). Although many cultures have appreciated and successfully occupied wetland environments, from the lower Mississippi and upper Amazon floodplains to the Shatt al-Arab and Bengal deltas, negative attitudes among non-wetland dwellers toward these environments did not undergo major changes until the twentieth century in the USA (Prince, 1997) or internationally (Williams, 1991). Lakes have had more widespread human appeal but, nonetheless, severe environmental problems in many parts of the world.

SIGNIFICANT FEATURES OF LAKES

The distinguishing physical and biological characteristics of a lake typically embrace at least eight dimensions. Those are defined in the following general terms, and then are illustrated for eight sample areas. Obviously, there are many other types of lakes and wetlands that could be described. The samples are chosen to illustrate some but not all of the diversity that is found on and among the principal continents. For a more comprehensive sample of lakes see the International Lake Environment Committee's World Lakes Database (ILEC, 2002).

(1) Surface area and water volume

The surface area of individual lakes varies from less than 1 km^2 to more than 82 000 km^2 in the case of the Great Lakes of North America.

(2) Landform

The physiographic character of their location is highly varied, ranging from shallow pans in plains areas, such as the Great Plains of the USA, to deep lakes in areas of steep mountain faulting and folding, such as the Himalayas. The former include much sedimentary rock, and the latter usually include more faulted metamorphic and igneous rock.

(3) Climate: precipitation and temperature

While there are almost no lakes and wetlands in fully arid regions or in the polar ice caps, lakes and stream wetlands are present in all other climatic regions, and thus embrace a wide range of moisture, temperature, and evaporation.

(4) Water quality

The natural concentration of minerals in water varies tremendously from one climatic or landform region to another, ranging in mineral content from very fresh water to salt seas. More than half of the lakes of the Asian continent, for example, are somewhat salty. Water quality and lake water mixing processes also vary seasonally in different climatic and physiographic contexts. The principal measures of water quality are:

pH	the acid or basic condition of a solution, measured as the negative logarithm of the hydrogen ion concentration; natural waters range from 4 (acidic) to 9 (basic)
SS	suspended sediments affect turbidity and transparency; measured in mg/l
DO	dissolved oxygen affects aerobic plant and animal life in water; measured in mg/l
COD	chemical oxygen demand measures biodegradable and non-biodegradable organic matter; measured in mg/l
chlorophyll	green matter in plants that converts CO_2 and water to carbohydrates in the presence of sunlight; measured in μg/l
N	nitrogen concentration, a key nutrient and indicator of waste flows into a water body; measured in mg/l

(5) Plant and animal life

As a result of the diversity of climate and water quality the organic life of the lakes varies from nearly sterile pools in desert regions to tremendously rich assortments of plant, fish, and insect life. Aside from brine shrimp, fly grubs, and bacteria species there are few organic growths in the Great Salt Lake of Utah. In contrast, in one equatorial lake in western Thailand there are 19 different species of plants and 20 different species of fish and amphibians. The diversity of wetland organic growth from one climate region to another is even greater. Plant life includes phytoplankton and macrophytes (including plants that live submerged below the surface, emerge above the water surface, or float like water lilies upon the water surface).

(6) Human use of land

Similarly, there is enormous range in the type of human use of adjoining land and wetlands even for the same lake. For example, one sector of the waterfront of Lake Michigan in the USA is occupied by dense city buildings and industry, and another sector about 70 km away is a wildlife refuge with almost no permanent human settlement.

(7) Human use of water

The water from some lakes is not used by humans and is unsuitable even for fishing, but in many other lakes there is intensive withdrawal use for irrigation as well as for diversified fishing, recreation, transportation, and domestic and industrial human consumption.

(8) Human changes in natural systems

Some lakes have been changed drastically, or even destroyed, by human use, while a few others have remained essentially in their original condition (Figures 7.4 and 7.5). More complicated alterations have occurred in wetlands, ranging from complete eradication to systematic changes in life systems or to elaborate programs for restoration.

SUMMARY OF SELECTED LAKES

Samples of diverse lakes, each described briefly according to the foregoing categories, are summarized here to provide a rough indication of the range of conditions worldwide (ILEC, 1994–96).

Figure 7.4   Management of the coastal lake currents of Lake Michigan (Michigan, USA) often employs jetties that trap sand for one area, while aggravating erosion by increasing scouring down-current from the obstruction.

Figure 7.5   Notwithstanding lakeshore structural protection efforts, coastal erosion has led to the gradual collapse of entire settlements along the bluff of southeastern Lake Michigan (Michigan, USA).

Lake Biwa, Shiga prefecture, Japan

The largest lake in Japan, about 700 000 years old, Lake Biwa is located in tectonic depressions of much greater age. It covers 674 km², with a total length of 63 km and at one place a width of only 1.35 km, making it in effect one large and one small lake (Figure 7.6). The depth in the larger part reaches 104 m and is less in the smaller part, with very little fluctuation in water level. Residence time of the water is up to 5.5 years from a catchment area of 3174 km². Mean air temperature in the area ranges from 3 °C to 22 °C in an average year, and mean annual precipitation is 1741 mm. There is no freezing, and the mean monthly water temperature ranges from 6 °C to 26 °C according to season and month.

Water varies in transparency with depth, and at the surface varies seasonally from 4 m to over 8 m in the large lake, and from 1.1 m to 2.4 m in the smaller lake. pH and physical concentrations in the upper levels of the larger lake are as follows:

pH	7
SS	1 mg/l
DO	7–10 mg/l
COD	1.5–2.6 mg/l
chlorophyll	1.7–7.2 µg/l
N	0.0–0.01 mg/l

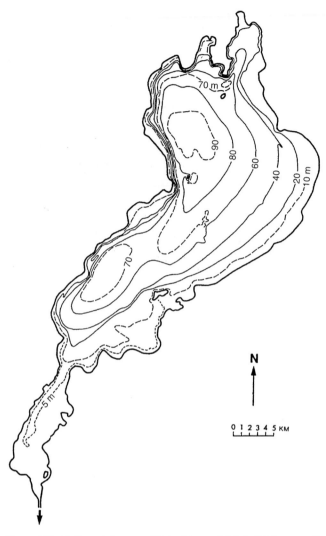

Figure 7.6   Bathymetric map of Lake Biwa, which is fed by more than 500 streams on the island of Honshu, Japan. Contours show depth in meters. After ILEC (1994–96); base map from Japan Map Centre (1982).

The number of distinct species found in the larger lake for each group are:

flora	macrophytes and phytoplankton	20
fauna	zooplankton	9
	benthos	15
	fish	15

The average annual fish catch was 3200 metric tons in 1977 to 1981. The phytoplankton population generally increased between 1950 and 1980. Fishery production increased slightly.

For the chief drainage areas of Shiga prefecture in 1970, 63 percent of the land was in woody vegetation, 2 percent in herbaceous vegetation, 25 percent in agriculture, 9 percent in urban and industrial, and 1 percent in open water. The total human population in the adjoining areas had been increasing from 1960 to 1980. Lake water was being used chiefly for a power plant, irrigation, and domestic supply. Toxic contamination of the lake was not serious, and was restrained by national, prefectural and local regulations, and by extensive wastewater treatment systems.

A major 20-year project, 1972 to 1992, had been initiated by national and local authorities to increase water supply downstream and to install advanced waste collection and treatment facilities, and this had substantial results (ILEC, 1995, pp. 7–35).

Lake Baikal, Buryat and Irkutsk, Russia

Located in a great continental rift in eastern Russia, Lake Baikal ranks as the deepest lake in the world, and stores approximately one-fifth of all the globe's freshwater (Figure 7.7). It receives the discharge of more than 300 rivers from surrounding mountainous terrain, and discharges it to the Angara River that flows to the north. There are 22 small islands in its long, narrow surface of more than 31 000 km^2. The maximum depth is 1741 m, the shoreline extends about 2000 km, and the entire catchment area is approximately 560 000 km^2. The climate is northern continental, with mean monthly temperatures ranging between $-19.7\,°C$ and $+17.7\,°C$, and mean monthly precipitation ranging from 8 mm to 109 mm for a total of 450 mm in an average year.

Water transparency at the surface during summer months is in the 10–12 m range and is in the 9–10 m range at the lowest depths. Dissolved oxygen in open water fluctuates between 10 and 14 mg/l.

Flora of the lake includes ten species of macrophytes, and 22 of phytoplankton. The fauna includes 16 species of zooplankton, 21 species of benthos, seven fish species, and one native mammal.

Until recent decades the regions adjoining the lake were largely underdeveloped, but exploitation of the mineral resources has led to increases in urban population and to demands for agricultural produce to feed the new areas. This has not thus far caused problems of nitrification or serious change in mineral loading of lake waters. But in the

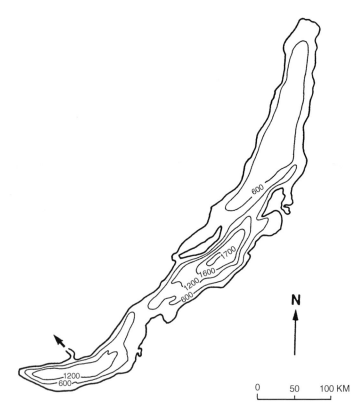

Figure 7.7   Bathymetric map of Lake Baikal, Russia, the deepest lake in the world. Contours show depth in meters. After ILEC (1994–96); base map from Hutchinson (1975).

latter part of the twentieth century there was only one major industrial wastewater treatment plant adjoining the lake. Thus, the chief changes in environmental system resulting from economic development have so far affected land rather than lake. A lake management program has been outlined (ILEC, 1995, pp. 241–251).

Lake Superior, Canada and United States

In surface area, Lake Superior ranks in size next to the Caspian Sea with an area of 82 367 km^2 (Figure 7.8). Located in a broad depression south of the retreating Ice Age glacier, in an area of sedimentary rocks, the maximum depth is 406 m and the volume is 12.2 × 10^{12} m^3. Water level fluctuations are small (0.3 m) and the shoreline is 4768 km. Residence time of water is 191 years, and the catchment area is 124 838 km^2. At the Marquette station, monthly temperature means fluctuate between

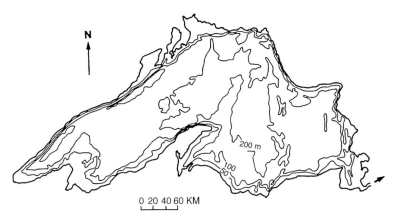

Figure 7.8   Bathymetric map of Lake Superior, Canada and USA, the western lake of the Great Lakes, which contain the largest volume of liquid freshwater in the world. Contours show depth in meters. After ILEC (1994–16); base map from Prof. F. M. D'Itri, Institute of Water Research, Michigan State University, USA.

−8.3 °C and 18 °C with a mean of 5.3 °C. Monthly precipitation for an average year varies from 43 mm to 89 mm for an annual average of 808 mm. Ice forms on the surface, but not on the shore, for varying times between November and April.

Average transparency of the water near shore ranges from 0.5 m to 15 m with the mean 8.5 m. Some of the principal measures of water quality near shore are as follows:

pH	7.7
SS	absent except in a few harbors
DO	0.8 mg/l
COD	—
chlorophyll	0.8 µg/l
N	230–280 mg/l

Numbers of distinct species found in the lake are:

flora	macrophytes	8
	phytoplankton	6
fauna	zooplankton	6
	benthos	4
	fish	8

Annual fish catch in 1977 was 4120 metric tons.

In the catchment area 94 percent of the land is in primary woody vegetation and 4 percent in herbaceous. Agricultural and residential use accounts for the remainder. Total human population in that area in 1970 was 533 000 with most of it in three cities (Duluth, Sault Sainte Marie, and Thunder Bay). The lake water was being used chiefly for industrial and power-plant purposes, with about half that volume being consumed for irrigation and mining, and a very small relative volume for domestic purposes. Toxic contamination is low overall, though mercury and other pollutants occur in seven coastal Areas of Concern. Eutrophication, acidification, and wastewater pollution loading were not major problems. Comprehensive lake ecosystem management was established in 1991 by a binational agreement (ILEC, 1994–96).

Lake Léman (Lake of Geneva)

Located in Switzerland and France, the Lake of Geneva, or Lac Léman, has a surface area of 584 km^2 and a volume of 88.9×10^6 m^3 (Figure 7.9). It drains a catchment area of 7975 km^2 and has a maximum depth of 309 m and a shoreline of 167 km. The climate is continental, with mean monthly temperatures ranging from 1.1 °C to 17.8 °C, and with mean monthly precipitation varying from 51 mm to 99 mm for an annual mean of 852 mm.

Water transparency reaches a maximum of 10–15 m in winter months and is 3–10 m during the remainder of the year. Dissolved

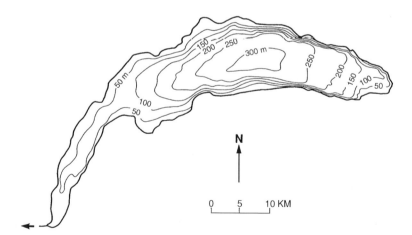

Figure 7.9   Bathymetric map of Lake Léman (Lake of Geneva), shared by France and Switzerland, and site of intensive urban recreation and resort activity. Contours show depth in meters. After ILEC (1994–96); base map from Lachavanne (1980).

oxygen for surface open water fluctuates between 10 mg/l and 13 mg/l annually.

Lake flora includes 12 species of macrophytes and eight of phytoplankton. The reported fauna includes seven species of zooplankton, six species of benthos, and four of fish, with an annual fish catch of 150–230 metric tons.

The catchment area includes major parts of three cities (Geneva, Lausanne, and Montreux) with a total population of over 950 000. About 30 000 persons were engaged in agriculture in the drainage area during the 1980s. Beyond urbanized areas, much of the land is in conifer forest, pasture lands, and grapes, maize, beets, and potatoes.

In addition to fisheries, navigation, and a wide variety of recreation, some of the lake water is used for domestic purposes for approximately 70 000 people. Deterioration of water quality shows in rising eutrophication, and in high loadings of nitrogen and phosphorus. Some of this is limited by national and cantonal water pollution regulation under a joint management plan.

Lake Nyasa (Lake Malawi), Mozambique, Malawi and Tanzania

Lying at the southern end of the north–south African Rift Valley, Lake Nyasa has a surface area of 6400 km^2 with a shoreline of 2450 km marked by relatively steep shores (Figure 7.10). The catchment area is barely larger than the lake surface with many steep shores. Lake depth ranges from a mean of 292 m to a maximum of about 700 m. The climate is continental with mean annual temperature 27 °C.

Average water transparency at one observation point ranges from 13 m to 23 m. The dissolved oxygen in the upper 200 m varies from 5 to 8 mg/l, and below that depth the water is anoxic.

The flora is very limited, with only one species of emerged macrophyte. There are four species of zooplankton and 19 species of fish. The annual fish catch has been estimated very roughly, reaching a total of 21 000 metric tons in 1971, and 9000 tons for Mozambique waters alone in 1983.

There is a very small human population in the catchment area, with some agricultural land use, and no accurate data on population numbers and industry. The use of water, beyond fisheries, for transportation, sightseeing, and tourism is very modest, and there is no evidence of significant deterioration in the lake environment from siltation, eutrophication, acidification, or toxic contamination. A Fisheries Research Institute is maintained at Metangula, and the existing

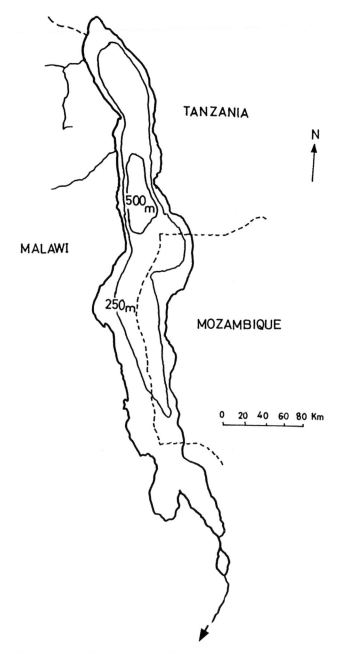

Figure 7.10   Bathymetric map of Lake Nyasa (Lake Malawi), shared by Mozambique, Malawi, and Tanzania, and southernmost lake in the Rift Valley system of Africa. Contours show depth in meters. After ILEC (1994–96); base map from Eccles (1974).

facilities for rural or municipal water supply and waste treatment are very limited (ILEC, 2002).

Pyramid Lake, Nevada, United States

Pyramid Lake is located in the western margin of the Great Basin Desert in Nevada with a surface area of about 453 km^2 and a volume of 27 $\times$ 10^6 m^3 (Figure 7.11). It drains 4730 km^2 and is known as the deepest

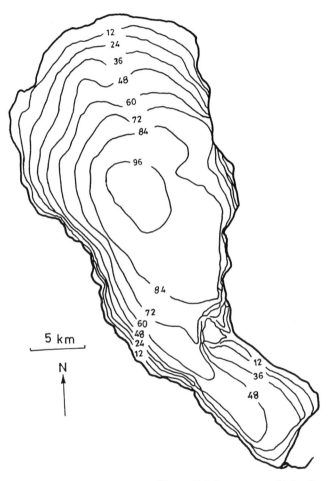

Figure 7.11 Bathymetric map of Pyramid Lake, an area of inland drainage in Nevada, USA. The lake suffered upstream diversions and native fish endangerment that were partially offset by recognition of Native-American reserved water rights since the 1970s. Contours show depth in meters. After ILEC (1994–96); base map from Galat *et al.* (1981).

saline lake in the Americas with a maximum depth of 105 m and a shoreline of 160 km. It has low average annual precipitation of 209 mm, mostly falling in the winter season.

Water transparency ranges between 5 m and 12 m varies between 8 mg/l and 10 mg/l annually at the surface.

The lake waters support two species of submerged macrophyte and four species of photoplankton. Fauna includes six species of zooplankton, seven of benthos, and seven of fish of which one is listed as threatened and one as endangered.

The lake is entirely within the Paiute Indian Reservation, which was established in 1859. Disputes between semi-nomadic Indian tribes and American settlers over land, water, and fishing rights have continued to the present. A dam constructed upstream on the Truckee River in 1905 diverted about half of its annual discharge for agriculture. Lake elevation declined and salinity increased, leading to the formation of a large delta that halted the spawning migrations of two varieties of trout. Efforts are made to cope with the decline of volume and quality of lake water and of recreational fishing, as urban population grows rapidly upstream. In the 1990s, a legal settlement was reached among the tribe, national, state, and local governments to fund lake water quality and wildlife and fish habitat improvements.

Aral Sea, Central Asia

A unique and dramatically complex instance of human alteration of a lake occurred in Central Asia during the twentieth century (Figure 7.12). Early in the century, the Aral Sea was a brackish lake with a surface water area of approximately 65 000–70 000 km^2. Its catchment area was wholly in the Soviet Union, consisting of semiarid and arid lands ranging from flatlands to rough glaciated mountain ranges, drained by the Amu Darya and Syr Darya rivers. It had a large diversity of ecosystems and of social production systems.

By mid century the lowlands were partly irrigated, but by the 1960s a vigorous program of irrigation development to supply export products began to apply more water from the principal rivers to increase cotton and rice production. During the next three to four decades, the lake level was reduced by about two-thirds, the surface area was reduced by one-half, runoff into the lake in some years was reduced to zero, and the salinity of the remaining water body roughly tripled. Fish catch dropped to zero while the number of native species decreased by about two-thirds, and local climatic regimes changed radically.

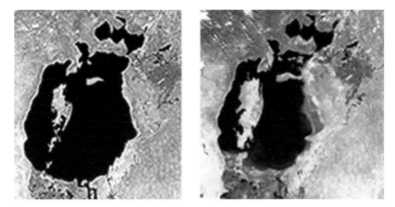

Figure 7.12   Satellite images of the Aral Sea in Central Asia in 1987 (left) and 1997 (right) reveal declining sea surface and increasing island and peninsular land areas. From USGS Earthshots: Satellite Images of Environmental Change. http://edcwww.cr.usgs.gov/earthshots/slow/Aral/ Aral (last visited March 21, 2003).

By the 1990s the Aral Sea for all practical purposes was two separate and different lakes due to continuing drops in water level. The water balance in the Big Aral lake in Kazakhstan and Uzbekistan was negative, with water level continuing to drop and salinity to increase. In the Small Aral in Kazakhstan the water level was increasing and salinity was decreasing. A dam built about 1990 in the Small Aral to maintain increased water level collapsed in 1999, and an effort was started to replace it (Aladin, 2002, p. 3; Dinar *et al.*, 1995, pp. 62–64.)

By the early 1990s the then responsible governments joined in planning to restore some of the environmental and economic deterioration of preceding decades by shifts in agricultural and water practices, and by drastic changes in both land and water policies (Bedford, 1996; Micklin, 1992; Smith, 1994, 1995). The details of the many errors made in managing the lake watershed illustrate the diversity and complications of efforts to change lake ecosystems, and the intricate nature of any efforts to remedy programs leading to basic deterioration of those systems (Dinar *et al.*, 1995). A series of international programs and projects has been launched to remedy various sources of those large-scale regional impacts.

Lake Eyre, Australia

Draining a large area of very dry internal drainage in the Australian continent, Lake Eyre has two sections: the North section is 144 km long

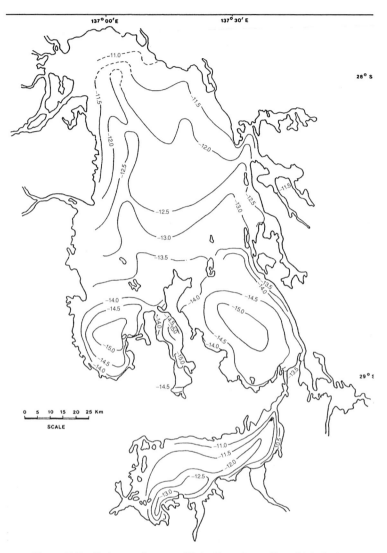

Figure 7.13   Bathymetric map of Lake Eyre, Australia, which drains a
large inland basin, has saline conditions, and episodic floods between its
northern and southern sections. Contours show depth in meters. After
ILEC (1994–96); base map from Kotwicki (1986).

and 77 km wide, and the South 64 km long and 24 km wide. The
lake was once considered dry but had major fillings in 1950, 1974, and
1984 (Figure 7.13). It covers a maximum surface area in the two parts of
9690 km^2 with a total maximum volume of 30×10^9 m^3 and with mean
depths of 3.3 m and 1.9 m. Normal range of unregulated water level

is 2 m. Mean monthly air temperature ranges from 12.4 °C to 29.3 °C, and mean monthly precipitation from 6 mm to 34 mm. Mean monthly water temperature ranges from 13 °C to 33 °C.

Selected measures of mean annual water quality in the North Lake are:

pH   7.7–7.8
SS   50–442 mg/l
DO   7.2–8.2 mg/l
N   0.07–0.19 mg/l

Numbers of distinct species found in the lakes are:

flora   macrophytes   9
fauna   zooplankton   6
         benthos   9
         fish   7

The catchment area is chiefly scattered pasture and sandhill desert, with grass the main crop, and stock raising the only major industry. The total population is 50 000, with almost half in the town of Alice Springs. There is no intense use of lake water and little evidence of problems of toxic contamination, eutrophication, acidification or problems of wastewater. There have been no major development plans according to the World Lakes Database (ILEC, 2002).

LAKE MANAGEMENT

Private and public agencies can exercise a wide variety of measures to manage the quality of lake environment. These management measures include: control of quantity of water inflow and outflow; measures to deal with eutrophication; toxic substance pollution control; management of organic life; control of sedimentation; and planning of use of adjacent lands. Selected standards for environmental maintenance of lakes have been formulated and are variously applied around the world (e.g., De Bernardi and Giussani, 1995). Rarely are all types of action and standards described below exercised or administered by a single agency.

The International Lake Environment Committee (ILEC) in collaboration with the United Nations Environment Program published a series of *Guidelines of Lake Management*. Volume seven of that series for example, focuses on biomanipulation as a means of ameliorating eutrophic water bodies and in some cases enhancing fisheries (ILEC and UNEP, 1995). The World Bank in 1995 published a general review of a comprehensive approach to managing, protecting, and rehabilitating lakes and reservoirs (Dinar *et al.*, 1995). Those included more than a dozen case studies from around the world. An international symposium held at Biwako in late 2001 voiced consensus on the continuing need for a global alliance of citizens, local governments, and international organizations to work more closely together in forming partnerships among all levels in local organization, information flows, and networking to promote integrated approaches to lake management (Aladin, 2002). Such an alliance would promote the aims of the Global World Lake Vision and Action Plan, and would bring together a very wide range of stakeholders in dealing with water flow, eutrophication, plant associations, toxic substance control, organic life, sedimentation, and land-use planning.

Water flow

With many natural lakes, as distinct from man-made reservoirs, the quality of the lake water and life can be very much influenced by the quantity and timing of control of water inflow, outflow, and circulation within the lake. The operation schedule for upstream dams or the design of outlet structures may greatly influence the lake environment, as in Pyramid Lake where the entire character of the lake was altered.

Measures to deal with eutrophication

A common problem is eutrophication as manifest in lakes receiving large quantities of phosphorus and chlorophyll from waste treatment plants and non-point source pollution. Diversion of the waste reduces algal concentration and increases water transparency. A remarkable case of such improvement was Lake Washington, adjoining Seattle, USA, in the late 1960s (Cooke *et al.*, 1993). In the case of Lake Washington, phosphorus concentration declined from an average of 64 mg/l to an average of 21 mg/l, and chlorophyll declined from 36 to 6 µg/l, while transparency increased threefold. This was the result of diverting wastewater from eleven small treatment plants to one large improved offshore facility.

The density of aquatic plants is strongly affected in some lakes by transparency, and thus the control of eutrophication can have a major influence on their vegetative growth and diversity, as does the volume of water withdrawal. But human intervention can drastically change the prevailing plant associations.

Toxic substance control

With the rapidly increasing production of hazardous industrial waste from such materials as pesticides, the danger of accumulation of persistent toxins in lake sediments increases. The effects upon health of both humans and fish can be serious (Dinar *et al.*, 1995) and have only come to be recognized fully in recent decades. Thus, in the Great Lakes of North America, recent research has found relationships between persistent toxic substances such as mercury, lead, DDT, and other man-made chemicals and both physical and mental human health. Their concentrations need to be drastically reduced to stem deleterious health trends.

Management of organic life

Over-fishing and introduction of non-native fish species may have a major effect upon food production from lakes that supply local peoples. Thus, the whole Lake Victoria ecosystem was drastically changed beginning in the late 1950s by the introduction of the non-native Nile Perch (Dinar *et al.*, 1995, pp. 43–45). Measures to deal with eutrophication, for example, may reduce the number or quality of fish for human consumption. Conversion of lands to agricultural production, as in the case of Lake Manzala in northern Egypt, may result in major changes in the proportion of marine versus fresh water fish (Dinar *et al.*, 1995, pp. 51–52.)

Control of sedimentation

In some lakes sediment deposits may increase as a result of upstream agricultural and mining activities. This affects the natural productivity both of the lake and of adjoining wetlands, and may be controlled chiefly by land-use regulations or by dredging which often is costly and very disturbing.

Land-use planning

Local land use regulation and planning in adjacent areas may have a powerful influence on all of the above-mentioned activities and on the quality of the lake environment. The character of use permitted or encouraged in the coastal or shore areas, as well as in the watershed, can have a major effect upon the lake's water quality and organisms.

Although direct effects of waste disposal and aquatic introductions, for example, can be very significant, the consequences of the kind of economic development and environmental activity on the adjoining lands may be even more influential on the life of the lake. This is apparent in such different lakes as Lake Biwa and Lake Nyasa.

The range and variety of lake management practices around the world in the 1990s was reviewed by the World Bank in a policy statement and in description of constructive activity (Dinar *et al.*, 1995). They also are the subject of continuing examination of specific experience by the ILEC (De Bernardi and Giussani, 1995).

The World Bank management policy emphasizes dealing comprehensively with a cross-sectional water resources assessment followed by a detailed water management strategy, with stress on shareholder participation. Examples are cited for such diverse environments as Lake Biwa, Lake Victoria, Lake Titicaca, Lake Manzala, Lake Baikal, the Great lakes, Scandinavian lakes, and the Aral Sea.

The case studies in biomanipulation include experience in small Netherlands lakes, Lake Balaton, and Lake Kinneret. They deal with mechanisms controlling the food chains either from the top down or from the bottom up.

WETLAND MANAGEMENT

To a large degree the management of wetlands around the world is linked with efforts to reconstruct conditions that had existed before economic development for a variety of purposes had changed or entirely eliminated the wetland. It has been roughly estimated that at the beginning of the twenty-first century there were approximately 5.7 million km^2 of relatively natural wetlands. Just how much this had decreased from earlier times is problematic (Ramsar Convention on Wetlands, 2000). Except where a wetland had been specifically designated as a natural preserve by a competent government agency it was likely to have suffered various degrees of alteration. It is thus understandable that in many countries the effort to manage wetlands focuses in large measure on restoration to the earlier state before prevailing human alterations began, insofar as that is known. Where some or all aspects of the earlier state of a wetland in the current climate period is not known with accuracy a major challenge is to determine precisely what conditions of landform, soil, climate, and hydrology prevailed before human alteration began and what is appropriate to changing climatic conditions.

SIGNIFICANT FEATURES OF WETLANDS

Because there is no widely accepted definition of what constitutes a wetland, and because there has been no thorough inventory of what is meant by a wetland in many countries it is impossible to inventory and describe their principal features and magnitude in the same fashion as for natural lakes (Figures 7.14 and 7.15). However, it is practicable to

Figure 7.14   Forested bald cypress swamplands of coastal Louisiana, USA, were extensively logged and drained in the nineteenth and twentieth centuries.

Figure 7.15   Artificial wetlands created by canal seepage and spills near Silt, Colorado, USA, create new wildlife habitat while depleting riparian habitats from which the water is withdrawn.

outline the major efforts to arrive at such an inventory and some of the distinctive characteristics and management programs for some of the world's wetlands, particularly those in the United States.

The first comprehensive effort to examine types of wetland was incorporated in the Convention of Wetlands signed as an intergovernmental treaty in Ramsar, Iran, in 1971. That defined wetlands as "areas of marsh, fen, wetland or water, whether natural or artificial, permanent or temporary, with water that is static or flowing, fresh, brackish or salt, including areas of marine water the depth of which at low tide does not exceed six metres" (Ramsar Convention on Wetlands, 1999). By 2002, the contracting parties had designated more than 1100 separate sites totaling at least 96 million hectares as wetlands deserving of protection and management.

There is no precise estimate of the overall extent of the world's wetlands. The estimate by the World Conservation Monitoring Center placing the total at about 5.7 million km^2 estimated that 30 percent are bogs, 26 percent are fens, 20 percent swamps, and 15 percent floodplains. Mangroves and coral reefs cover large but declining coastal areas that are adversely affected by coastal watershed development (Dubois, 1990). A 1999 estimate by the Conference of the Parties to the Convention on Wetlands placed the wetland total as at least 7.48 million km^2

(Ramsar Convention on Wetlands, 2001). Definitions and estimates still vary widely. Meanwhile, assessment of experience with managing wetlands for the benefit of natural systems has accumulated rapidly.

The Ramsar Conference of the Parties adopted a classification of wetland types for both natural coastal and inland locations and for human-made situations (Table 7.1). This effectively classifies the whole range of wetlands. It is intended to provide only a broad framework for identifying wetland habitats.

Restoration of major wetlands begins with research to specify the particular association and pattern of landform, soil, hydrology, and plant and animal life that existed at the earlier period. This can be facilitated in some instances by comparison with similar lands that have not been altered, but these opportunities are rare, and it may be necessary to examine the relationships of the physical and biological elements through study of similar areas and to carry out experiments to determine precisely what influential factors were at work.

Parallel with research on the workings of the earlier wetland is monitoring of those aspects of the specified landscape as restoration begins and is carried forward. Restoration is not simply a change toward undisturbed soil–climate–plant–animal relations. It is monitored change that builds upon what is found to have been previous undisturbed conditions. It is significant that reports on improved wetlands in the United States typically are entitled "creation and restoration" (Kusler and Kentula, 1990).

Although formal concern with wetlands protection in the United States began principally with the National Environmental Policy Act of 1969, it was not until the 1980s that a series of Federal programs gave more precise directives for action. That included elimination of previous incentives to wetlands destruction and provided support for farmers to maintain wetlands. It also authorized financial incentives for agencies to acquire threatened and impaired wetlands. Section 404 of the Clean Water Act of 1972 (as amended) required permitting of federal actions affecting wetland ecosystems. The 1985 Food Security Act and the Emergency Wetlands Resources Act of 1986 were major advances in that direction. The North American Wetlands Conservation Act of 1989 assured matching funds to state and private agencies for that purpose (Figure 7.16).

Recognizing the tremendous diversity of wetlands reflected in this classification it is clear that the variety of management measures is very large. Basically, they are of three general types: (1) actions to prevent further destruction of wetlands through land use and engineering

Table 7.1 *Ramsar classification of wetlands*

Classification	Includes
Marine Coastal Wetlands	
A – Permanent shallow marine waters	in most cases less than 6 m deep at low tide; includes sea bays and straits
B – Marine subtidal aquatic beds	includes kelp beds, sea-grass beds, tropical marine meadows
C – Coral reefs	
D – Rocky marine shores	includes rocky offshore islands, sea cliffs
E – Sand, shingle or pebble shores	includes sand bars, spits and sandy islets; includes dune systems and humid dune slacks
F – Estuarine waters	permanent water of estuaries and estuarine systems of deltas
G – Intertidal mud, sand or salt flats	
H – Intertidal marshes	includes salt marshes, salt meadows, saltings, raised salt marshes; includes tidal brackish and freshwater marshes
I – Intertidal forested wetlands	includes mangrove swamps, nipah swamps and tidal freshwater swamp forests
J – Coastal brackish/saline lagoons	brackish to saline lagoons with at least one relatively narrow connection to the sea
K – Coastal freshwater lagoons	includes freshwater delta lagoons
Zk(a) – Karst and other subterranean hydrological systems	marine/coastal
Inland Wetlands	
L – Permanent inland deltas	
M – Permanent rivers/streams/creeks	includes waterfalls
N – Season/intermittent/irregular rivers/streams/creeks	
O – Permanent freshwater lakes	over 8 ha; includes large oxbow lakes
P – Seasonal/intermittent freshwater lakes	over 8 ha; includes floodplain lakes
Q – Permanent saline/brackish/alkaline lakes	
R – Seasonal/intermittent saline/brackish/alkaline lakes and flats	

Table 7.1 (*cont.*)

Classification	Includes
Sp – Permanent saline/brackish/alkaline marshes/pools	
Ss – Seasonal/intermittent saline/brackish/alkaline marshes/pools	
Tp – Permanent freshwater marshes/pools	ponds (below 8 ha), marshes and swamps on inorganic soils; with emergent vegetation water-logged for at least most of the growing season
Ts – Seasonal/intermittent freshwater marshes/pools	on inorganic soils; includes sloughs, potholes, seasonally flooded meadows, sedge marshes
U – Non-forested peatlands	includes shrub or open bogs, swamps, fens
Va – Alpine wetlands	includes alpine meadows, temporary waters from snowmelt
Vt – Tundra wetlands	includes tundra pools, temporary waters from snowmelt
W – Shrub-dominated wetlands	shrub swamps, shrub-dominated freshwater marshes, shrub carr, alder thicket on inorganic soils
Xf – Freshwater, tree-dominated wetlands	includes freshwater swamp forests, seasonally flooded forests, wooded swamps on inorganic soils
Xp – Forested peatlands	peatswamp forests
Y – Freshwater springs; oases	
Zg – Geothermal wetlands	
Zk(b) – Karst and other subterranean hydrological systems	inland

Note: "floodplain" is a broad term used to refer to one or more wetland types, which may include examples from the R, Ss, Ts, W, Xf, Xp, or other wetland types. Some examples of floodplain wetlands are seasonally inundated grassland (including natural wet meadows), shrublands, woodlands and forests. Floodplain wetlands are not listed as a specific wetland type.

Human-made Wetlands

1 – Aquaculture ponds	e.g., fish/shrimp
2 – Ponds	includes farm ponds, stock ponds, small tanks; generally below 8 ha

(cont.)

Table 7.1 (*cont.*)

Classification	Includes
3 – Irrigated land	includes irrigation channels and rice fields
4 – Seasonally flooded agricultural land	including intensively managed or grazed wet meadow or pasture
5 – Salt exploitation sites	salt pans, salines, etc.
6 – Water storage areas	reservoirs/barrages/dams/ impoundments; generally over 8 ha
7 – Excavations	gravel/brick/clay pits; borrow pits, mining pools
8 – Wastewater treatment areas	sewage farms, settling ponds, oxidation basins, etc.
9 – Canals and drainage channels, ditches	
Zk(c) – Karst and other subterranean hydrological systems	human-made

Source: Ramsar Convention on Wetlands, 1999.

Figure 7.16 Jointly natural and artificial wetlands in the Tijuana River estuary along the USA–Mexico border, which is a site for wetlands treatment of wastewater from this urbanizing region.

measures serving a variety of economic purposes; (2) measures for restoration and reconstruction of previous wetlands or substitutes for destroyed wetlands; and (3) educational programs to increase public awareness of wetlands value.

As already noted, in the United States the number and type of preventive measures by Federal and state agencies executing public protective policy is substantial. In addition to some of the legal prohibitions of such activities as drainage, channel improvement, mining, and waste disposal, the nation undertook in 1975 a comprehensive inventory of existing wetlands so as to provide a base for identifying areas at risk of further destruction (Tiner, 1989).

Like the types of natural wetlands and the human destructions of them, the classes of restorative measures are large in number. Without attempting to describe all the major classes of such measures, a few examples may be noted of the types that are being practiced. Many are described in the publications of the National Wetlands Policy Forum in 1988 (Kusler and Kentula, 1990) and the symposium of the American Water Resources Association in 1989 (Fisk, 1989). Both publications contained references to earlier studies of specific wetlands.

Sample cases of wetlands management include the following:

- San Diego County, California - creation of 40 vernal pool ecosystems to replace natural pools destroyed by highway construction.
- Southeastern tidal wetlands - creating and restoring large areas of tidal marshlands by elevating sites, controlling erosion and selecting and providing nutrients for reintroduced plant species. Of roughly 565 000 ha, 11 percent are freshwater, 33 percent are brackish, and 56 percent are salt water (Broome, in Kusler and Kentula, 1990, pp. 37-72).
- Riverine wetlands in glaciated northeast United States - assessing the results of efforts to restore wetlands in forested areas covered by the Wisconsin glaciation (Lowry, in Kusler and Kentula, 1990, pp. 267-280).
- Riparian habitat in southwestern arid and semiarid regions - appraising the problems involved in trying to restore natural riparian habitats in arid and semiarid areas (Carothers et al., in Kusler and Kentula, 1990, pp. 351-363).

A review of those and many other efforts in the United States led Kusler and Kentula (1990, pp. xxiii-xxv) to a number of critical observations of wetland efforts. Those included but were not limited to:

(1)   too little is known in many contexts to predict success in restoration or creation

(2)   multidisciplinary expertise is needed;

(3)   site-specific goals are essential;

(4)   site-specific studies of the original system should be made;

(5)   careful attention should be paid to hydrology;

(6)   monitoring and mid-course correction is needed;

(7)   capability for long-term management is required.

For these and other reasons the efforts to restore wetlands and lakes are difficult and often uncertain (for a recent review see Campbell and Ogden, 1999). However, the long history of human ambivalence about economic and environmental values associated with wetlands has particularly slowed their management and restoration, as compared with lakes and rivers.

8

River channels and floodplains

INTRODUCTION

River channels and their floodplains have a long record of human use,
modification, and environmental consequences, e.g., as compared with
groundwater (Figure 8.1). A river channel is defined here as any linear
depression on the earth's surface that regularly conveys surface runoff
from a watershed to a natural outlet in a lake, inland sea, or ocean.
This definition excludes ephemeral rills that range in width from millimeters to centimeters on a hillslope (addressed in Chapter 5 on soil
moisture). It also excludes large tectonic faults that could function as
drainage ways but have not historically done so. However, it does encompass erosion features such as gullies in humid areas and arroyos
or wadis in arid regions, which range in width from meters to tens
of meters and carry intermittent and subsurface flows. This definition
also includes alpine and spring-fed rivulets, creeks and streams in headwater regions that feed straight, meandering, braided, or anastomosing
river channels in downstream alluvial, rock-cut, and gravel-bedded terrain. Ultimately, these channels discharge into oceans, seas, or areas of
inland drainage where their freshwaters mix with salt waters in estuarine and deltaic coastal environments.

The geographer and regional planner Patrick Geddes (1949) described the human importance of these flows from headwaters through
riparian corridors and deltas in a theory known as the "valley section of human civilization." Geddes hypothesized different patterns
of human occupance and resource utilization in the upper, middle
and lower reaches of a river valley, and he argued for coordinating
these upstream–downstream relationships in a regional approach to
planning – an idea subsequently applied by environmental planners
like Ian McHarg in the Potomac, Susquehanna, and Delaware rivers in

Figure 8.1   Ferry across the Ganges (Ganga) River in India, which while considered sacred and pure suffers increasing municipal and industrial pollutant loads.

the eastern USA (Spirn, 2000). Although this chapter recognizes a much greater diversity in river forms, processes, and uses, it shares the continuing concern for coordinating human uses, hazards, and management of rivers and floodplains (Figures 8.2 and 8.3).

CHARACTERISTICS OF RIVER CHANNEL AND FLOODPLAIN ENVIRONMENTS

The basic morphological features of a river channel include its banks, which vary in shape and roughness during high and low flow periods; its bed, which varies in material, form, and slope; and its exposed depositional bars and islands. The water within a channel also varies in flow paths, velocities, suspended sediments, turbidity, chemical characteristics and temperature regimes. These physical factors shape and alter habitats for diverse species of flora and fauna, from the thalweg, or fastest moving current or "thread" of the stream, to habitats at the surface, bed, eddies, backwaters, and banks – all of which contribute to the health of the river ecosystem and its services and values for various human groups.

Figure 8.2   Floodplain settlement along the Ravi River opposite the city of Lahore, Pakistan, before a flood in 1988.

Figure 8.3   Floodplain settlement along the Ravi River after the 1988 flood.

Just as rivers vary in stage (i.e., elevation) and width, so do their adjacent floodplains, which are inundated by flows of different magnitudes and return intervals. These flooding processes shape the landforms of floodplain environments, including their levees, backslopes, widths, and terraces – which in turn affect the frequency, depth, duration, and areal extent of flooding (Ward, 1978). Human beings further modify floodplain landforms, directly through changes in land use and land cover, by construction of artificial levees, sewerage and drainage systems, and by filling of floodplain wetlands; and indirectly through river channel engineering which alters flood processes. The floodplains and adjacent areas are complicated mosaics of land type and land use (Forman, 1995). These apply to river corridors and matrixes of large landscapes.

River channel morphology depends upon hydraulic factors such as the slope, discharge, and flow regime, along with geomorphological factors such as bank, bed, and suspended sediment characteristics. Because these factors interact dynamically, river channel morphologies change continuously and sometimes dramatically, e.g., through channel abandonment and meander cutoffs, in ways that defy simple classification but that are important for human use of and proximity to river channels and floodplains.

At the larger geographic scale of the watershed, river channels give rise to drainage networks that may take dendritic, annular, rectangular and other forms, depending upon the landforms, geologic structure, and climate of a region. Dendritic ("tree-like") patterns are particularly common in alluvial environments, though they vary greatly in network structure and density, while rectangular and other network patterns generally follow larger geologic structures.

HUMAN USE OF RIVER CHANNELS AND FLOODPLAINS

The differences in river and floodplain morphology described above shape a wide array of river uses, hazards, and adjustments – just as human uses transform river channel and floodplain environments. It is useful therefore to survey the range of human functions served, and the types of environmental modification they entail.

River channel functions

The human functions served by natural river channels have ancient origins and continuing significance. They include:

(1)   transportation – navigation in, along, and across river channels;
(2)   fishing – with lines, nets, hatcheries, etc.;
(3)   natural flood and floodplain benefits – e.g., for agricultural soils and riparian habitats;

(4)   milling and run-of-river hydropower generation – through low weirs, diversion channels, penstocks, and mechanical gears or turbines; (see Chapter 9 for larger dams and reservoirs);

(5)   water supply – for all purposes through diversions, flumes, sluices, etc.;

(6)   drainage – and dilution of stormwater, sanitary, and industrial wastewaters;

(7)   recreation and aesthetic functions – from direct body contact through wading, swimming, and bathing to recreational boating of all sorts, and viewing at a distance;

(8)   spiritual and symbolic aspects of rivers – as deities, or homes of deities; as signs of a divinely designed earth; and as media or metaphors of spiritual experience (e.g., Bachelard, 1983; Coomaraswamy, 1993; Dundes, 1988; Eliade, 1963; Feldhaus, 1995; Tuan 1968a).

While some of these functions have little material effect on a channel, others entail major, and continuing, processes of river engineering which may include channel straightening, widening, or deepening through dredging or construction of levees or flood walls; bank stabilization with vegetation or armor stone; waterfront development with piers and quays; and sediment and erosion control with dykes, groins, and jetties.

With this diverse range of functions served by river channels, it comes as no surprise, but a cause of great concern, that there are conflicts among different types of river uses, different approaches to river management, and different environmental values (Adams, 1992). The principal aims of river management include coordinating competing uses of the channel, managing conflicts, and protecting the environmental quality of rivers.

Floodplain functions

The type and extent of measures taken to manage a river channel are in many places influenced by the actual or projected human adjustment to the flood hazard in bordering lands. As indicated in Chapter 4, the flood hazard may be computed in terms of the volume of flow and land area inundated by river discharge of various frequency, from once in two years to once in 500 years, or more. The major types of human use of these floodplain environments comprise:

(1)   using the floodplain in its natural, dynamic condition (e.g., for hunting, gathering, and passive recreation);

(2)   managing the natural woody and herbaceous vegetation and an-
       imal life for timbering and grazing, or for preservation of threat-
       ened species;
(3)   agricultural production of crops and livestock;
(4)   residential, commercial, and industrial use;
(5)   intensive active recreation (e.g., riverfront parks, marinas, sports,
       and fishing.)

In each case, flood processes have produced beneficial and attractive environments for human use, as well as hazards for certain types of use.
While some functions and uses entail relatively little physical and ecological transformation of the floodplain, many if not most floodplains
around the world have experienced escalating human occupance, utilization, and transformation.

In addition to the transformations typical of upland areas, floodplain use also entails human adjustment to the perceived and experienced risks and losses of flood events that create and sustain the
floodplain as an ecosystem. Adjustment may involve any combination
of the following types of measures (White, 1945):

(1)   reduction of the height and frequency of flooding by deepening
       or straightening the stream channel;
(2)   building levees;
(3)   building channel diversions or floodways;
(4)   building dams to reduce the magnitude and frequency of
       flooding;
(5)   organizing flood forecasting networks accompanied by emergency
       measures to reduce flood losses;
(6)   carrying out flood-proofing measures to reduce vulnerability of
       property to flooding;
(7)   providing disaster assistance when a flood occurs;
(8)   facilitating insurance against flood losses;
(9)   enacting community regulations to prevent the construction or
       operation of structures vulnerable to flooding;
(10)   designing recreational and ecological uses of floodplains valued
       by society to replace more hazardous uses.

Depending upon the chosen use and the distinctive local resources and prevailing government policy, if any, the river channel may
be unaffected, or there may be a wide array of measures affecting the
channel. These range from locations where there are no alterations in
the natural channel and adjacent lands to situations where the channel
is completely altered in location and cross-section. The situation may

be even more complex where there are upstream changes in land use and storage affecting the volume and frequency of downstream floods.

The variety of measures taken for river channel management in floodplain environments is immense. Even where the primary or sole use of the land is for preservation of the natural riparian and aquatic ecosystem, it may seem important to adopt minor channel changes to curb bank erosion and the accumulation of debris, or alternatively to plant riparian vegetation and snags that improve fish habitat or spawning conditions. In a highly urbanized floodplain such as in the downtown Pittsburgh junction of the Allegheny and Monongahela rivers, which experienced major losses of life and property in the early twentieth century, the principal instruments of flood loss minimization have shifted in some areas from structural measures for flood control to planning and execution of emergency measures combined with flood-proofing. Thus, in a department store in the central business district where partial flood control measures are in effect there are provisions to move all goods in wheeled display cases to upper floors on a few hours' notice, and the electric and mechanical equipment and glass windows are designed to minimize loss from flooding. The fortified riverfront has also been converted to a park that can withstand flood inundation and even incorporates artistic representations of flood flows (Figure 8.4). These adjustments reduce but do not entirely obviate the

Figure 8.4   Floodplain park in Pittsburgh, Pennsylvania, USA combines armor stone, riparian vegetation, and artistic treatment of waterfront structures.

need for channels that can convey flows without undue obstruction from debris or encroachments.

At the other extreme of land use, such as in designated overland floodways across bends of the lower Mississippi River below Vicksburg, it may be desirable to maintain drainage ways free of obstruction to high flows. The Atchafalaya River floodway in the lower Mississippi River valley partially serves this function on a regional scale, though it has also had major channel engineering and levee construction (Reuss, 1998).

These examples illustrate the close relationship between river channel and floodplain management, in principle. However, comprehensive integration that in practice includes ecological values and functions is rarely achieved. Rather than focus on problems associated with specific river functions, channels, and floodplain types, the remainder of this chapter surveys changing approaches to river channel and floodplain management.

Given the accessibility and utility of rivers, societies have developed a wide range of approaches for managing their resources, hazards, and ecological systems. Those approaches have changed over time, along with broad shifts in the types of river uses, technologies, and values, including "non-use values" (Cameron, 1999). As observed in previous chapters, river resource management is related to but distinct from riparian and floodplain ecosystem management. This chapter focuses on how different approaches to river resource management are related to riparian ecosystem management. This evolution should be considered in the context of broad evolution of water planning in the United States.

These relationships range from finely-tuned human adjustments to natural flood regimes and floodplains to radical river channelization and intensive floodplain development, and to recent efforts to restore and manage complex aquatic, riparian and floodplain ecosystems. Although no single approach operates exclusive of the others, general trends and lessons may be discerned over time and in different regions of the world (Boon et al., 2000).

APPROACHES TO RIVER CHANNEL AND FLOODPLAIN MANAGEMENT

The approaches to management surveyed below are considered in terms of their beneficial and adverse environmental effects, historical relevance, and potential future application – proceeding from the least intensive to the most transformative. Although arranged by degree of human intervention, early historical approaches persist, sometimes generating environmental problems and social conflicts, and at other times suggesting alternatives that could more fully harmonize water and environmental management.

Notwithstanding important differences among approaches, noted in the selections below are some common aims of river channel management: to *enjoy* natural riverine processes; to *improve* upon riverine processes for human purposes; to *protect* riverine processes for multiple purposes; and to *restore* channels disturbed by human and other influences. We begin with processes of natural enjoyment and proceed toward restoration.

Naturalistic river channel and floodplain management

The dominant management approach in prehistory, continuing in increasingly limited river reaches to the present day, involves sophisticated and subtle adjustments to natural flow and flood processes (Figure 8.5). These adjustments included transportation on unmodified rivers; sustained hunting, gathering, and fishing in riparian and aquatic habitats; "flood farming" (harvesting of vegetation after high flows) and recession agriculture (planting and harvesting in the moistened floodplain); and recreational, aesthetic, and spiritual dimensions of management expressed in pictographs and oral tradition.

These low-intensity, generally early uses of river channel environments had few impacts, a high degree of sustainability, and adjustment to variable flood processes. They presumably had less resilience to social pressures of population growth, immigration, and conquest, which brought with them more intensive forms of river channel management.

Run-of-river water management and concentrated floodplain occupance

All of the activities listed above could, and often did, lead to more permanent settlement and intensive use of river channels, accompanied by small scale "improvements" at favored sites and reaches of the channel. The following are some examples of where such management occurs:

- River ports – docks and harbors facilitated trade along a river and its hinterland, servicing vessels, and trans-shipping goods to other modes of transportation.
- River crossings – settlements also rose, and grew, at strategic river fords, ferries, and bridges. If these settlements endured, they

Figure 8.5   Naturalistic river and floodplain reach of the upper
Colorado River in Colorado, USA.

involved increasingly stable engineering of landings, bridge abutments, piers, and banks.

• Water mills – hydropower along small streams and on floating
platforms on larger rivers has been used to mill grain since antiquity, to power industrial mills from the eighteenth century, and
to generate electricity in the late twentieth century. These run-
of-river mills had some impact on fish habitats, and from waste

product disposal, but little compared with those of the later dams and diversions.

- Water-based recreation – settlements on medium-sized streams and islands provided waterfronts for sailing, boating, and swimming. Roman texts describe such recreational areas along the Tiber River.

Environmental impacts from this approach to management commonly include local water quality contamination and habitat degradation. However, as river port and industrial development grew, these environmental consequences could become regional in extent, as in the industrial centers of Lowell, Massachusetts, USA; Manchester, England; Rome, Italy; and many other riverfront cities of Europe and North America.

Systematic river channel engineering

More substantial environmental impacts accompanied channelization (deepening, widening, straightening) to accommodate larger and more numerous cargo vessels and to reduce hazard to floodplain development (Figure 8.6).

- In steeper channel reaches, locks replaced portages.
- In flatter low-lying areas, agricultural intensification of natural levees, e.g., the arpent and long-lot systems of settlement in the

Figure 8.6   Navigation locks and dam along the Ohio River, USA.

lower Mississippi River basin, led to channel engineering to reinforce, drain, and protect the levees.

- Along prosperous urban riverfront areas, e.g., the Pantheon and
  Campus Martius area of Rome, channelization provided some protection against annual floods but not extreme events.
- Drainage of low-lying areas involved channel straightening, concrete lining, and sewerage which amplified flooding and environmental degradation downstream. Settlement of backswamp
  areas often failed due to poor drainage and flooding, but not before damaging natural swampland vegetation, wildlife, and water
  quality.
- In both upland and lowland areas, floodplain settlement reduced
  rainfall interception and infiltration, accelerating runoff, erosion,
  sedimentation, and associated fish habitat and flooding problems.
- Attempts to offset continued flooding by further channelization
  (and construction of artificial levees) reduced short-term risks
  and impacts in local areas, while shifting those short-term risks
  downstream and increasing the risk of low-frequency, high-
  magnitude flood events (e.g., every 500 years) and associated
  system-wide environmental impacts.

River channel engineering of long river reaches and networks has ancient origins from Rome to China, and continues to the present in many
areas.

Systematic management of flood flows with river training works, levees, and detention reservoirs

Management of flood flows shifted from emphasis on channel improvements to include the engineering of levee and reservoir structures to
either control or reduce flows on the floodplain (Figures 8.7 and 8.8).
In the United States, following the disastrous 1928 flood on the lower
Mississippi River, public attention began to focus more explicitly on
building systems of floodways, levees, and detention reservoirs to prevent flooding of floodplains then occupied by intensive agricultural
and urban uses. In addition to heavy outlays for flood relief and levee
construction in the lower Mississippi, authorization was given the US
Army Corps of Engineers to extend its program of river and harbor
improvement for navigation to include the study and construction of
channel, levee, and reservoir structures to prevent or reduce social loss
from floods (Shallat, 1994). The Flood Control Act of 1936 provided that
Federal funds might be used to pay all or part of the cost of such

Figure 8.7   Earth levee with stone cladding along the Arkansas River near the city of Pueblo, Colorado, USA.

Figure 8.8   Channelized reach of the Tijuana River between Mexico and the USA.

structures on specified areas if the estimated reductions in flood losses exceeded the cost of building and operating the structures. Specifications were made as to how local governments of benefiting areas must pay some of the levee costs, with the Federal government assuming the full cost of dams controlling flood flow. Thus, the Federal government accepted major responsibility for controlling flood flows where the estimated benefit–cost ratio was favorable. No provision was made for estimating the environmental costs of any proposed project. The emphasis was wholly on reducing economic damages (narrowly defined) from floods.

In the wake of the Flood Control Acts of 1936 and 1938 a large program of federally-supported construction and engineering works in the United States took shape and continued in subsequent decades. Although federal and private expenditures escalated during the period following federal legislation, the magnitude of reported flood losses continued at about the same monetary level after correcting for changes in the value of the dollar (L. R. Johnston Associates, 1992).

Systematic management of floodplain use

The continuing magnitude of national flood losses in the United States encouraged a number of assessments of what had been happening to the use of floodplains and of possible policies to encourage more socially productive uses. In addition to the statistics on mounting reported damages there were case studies of what had been happening on selected floodplains (White *et al.*, 1958). Those continued to recent years and raised questions both about the full consequences of flood control measures (Montz and Gruntfest, 1986) and about the effectiveness of a variety of alternative approaches to making wise social use of floodplains (ASFPM, 1999, 2000, 2001).

Out of the various assessments there developed a more nearly comprehensive approach to human use of floodplains. This had at least seven major elements: (1) mapping the estimated frequency and magnitude of flooding; (2) planning and regulation of use of vulnerable areas and of areas contributing to flood flows; (3) government support of insurance against flood losses; (4) improvement of flood warning systems and advice and training as to how to respond effectively to warning; (5) research and education as to how to floodproof property against damage; (6) extending the federal program of financial assistance to victims of flood damage, to include support for buying out damaged property to support abandonment of severely affected property and movement to lands beyond the reach of floods; and (7) taking explicit account of the benefits to ecosystems and human recreation of leaving a floodplain completely open to water and silt from natural overflow.

The system of flood insurance offered reduced rates to owners of property below the level of the estimated 100-year flood which had been settled before the Flood Insurance Program was established in 1968, and specified that premiums for new establishments and for property above the 100-year level were to be charged premiums nearer to the calculated market level. As time passed it became increasingly evident that as much as or more than one half of the annual damage suffered was in areas above the elevation of the 100-year flood.

It also became clear that it was possible for occupants of the floodplain to take measures that would increase the flood hazard for other areas, and the Association of State Flood Plain Managers (ASFPM) promoted as part of its effort to achieve wise use of floodplains a policy of "no adverse use." The ASFPM published descriptions of the experience of selected cases of floodplain management with the aim of demonstrating how communities might carry out integrated programs contributing to wise use (ASFPM, 2002).

In 2001 the Federal Emergency Management Agency initiated an appraisal of the effects of the national flood insurance program upon the occupancy of floodplains in the United States and upon the annual volume of flood damages.

The application of their elements in a fashion that was integrated in some areas and independent in other areas was facilitated by a variety of local, state, and national organizations. In addition to the numerous local watershed planning groups described in Chapter 12, some of the more influential national organizations include American Rivers, Association of State Flood Plain Managers, Environmental Defense, River Management Society, River Network, and Trout Unlimited.

The role of river channel management in river basin development

Increasing pressures on river channels, and failings of "channel-only" and "levees-only" approaches led to new paradigms of "comprehensive," "coordinated," and "integrated" river basin development, in principle addressing multiple purposes of river use through multiple means of structural and non-structural human actions. These broader watershed and river basin initiatives are treated more fully in Chapter 12 under the heading of integrative approaches. Here it is simply noted how river channel and floodplain management were increasingly addressed within broader approaches to water resources and environmental management. River basin planning sought to remedy both the narrow approaches of river channel engineering and the environmental impacts of uncoordinated, ad hoc land and water development. While

Figure 8.9   Urban river restoration for commercial, cultural, and passive recreational activities at San Antonio, Texas, USA.

it had some successes, its broader effect, in practice, was to facilitate systems of large-scale hydropower and reservoir development on large rivers, which had perhaps the most devastating environmental consequences of any paradigm, and which are discussed more fully in Chapter 9. But, at the same time, the principles and philosophy of river basin development sowed seeds of more comprehensive and systematic coordination with environmental management that, at the channel scale, has led to programs of river restoration (Figures 8.9 and 8.10).

Figure 8.10   Urban river restoration for active recreational use (kayaking) in Denver, Colorado, USA.

Riparian restoration and ecosystem services

The idea that rivers have restorative and self-restoring properties has ancient origins. Societies observed natural flooding and regenerative processes, from the Nile to the lower Mississippi, and chose to modify those processes knowing that some benefits would be lost. Until very recently, the Ganges River has been regarded by many as inherently pure, no matter what its pollution burden from burning ghats, cities, industries, and agricultural runoff, and has yet to be managed as a sustainable river basin system (Biswas and Uitto, 2001; Chapman and Thompson, 1995; Crow et al., 1995; Dixit, 1994; Gyawali, 2001; Verghese and Iyer, 1993). In many societies, running water, as compared with stagnant water, is regarded as inherently pure for domestic and ritual purposes. "Dilution was the solution to pollution." Even as that view fades in the face of severe degradation, the Ganges and its tributary river goddess the Yamuna, which receives the discharge of Delhi before flowing past the Taj Mahal, indicate that different spiritual, political, and scientific perspectives complicate the challenge of solving regional water quality problems (Alley, 2002; Haberman, 2000).

As the impacts of each of the foregoing approaches became more fully evident, documented, and explained, there arose an emerging science and practice of river restoration, comparable to the programs of wetland restoration mentioned previously and adaptive management, which will be addressed in a later chapter. This section focuses on the stimuli for, and examples of, river restoration. In the USA, the principal driving forces for river restoration include:

- water quality standards, which regulate ambient water pollution levels from all sources in a river reach;
- the Endangered Species Act of 1973, which requires aquatic and riparian species protection and habitat restoration;
- urban stream daylighting and restoration movements by community environmental groups (Gumprecht, 1999; Kondolf, 1995, 1997; Riley, 1998);
- policies to coordinate federal agency riparian restoration efforts.

River channel restoration is an exciting convergence between water and environmental management. Driven by the policies and movements listed above, it has helped support broader scientific organizations for riparian ecology (Malanson, 1993), restoration ecology and ecological restoration, as well as intergovernmental programs that cut across scientific and institutional boundaries.

At the relatively large scale of federal water agencies and major river channels, a federal interagency program was launched in 1998 to develop collaborative multi-disciplinary approaches and projects (Federal Interagency Stream Restoration Working Group, 2001). The interagency manual adopts a clear, and conventional, approach to stream ecology characterized by hydrologic, geomorphic, physical and chemical characteristics and biological characteristics. While the interagency manual articulates concepts of dynamic equilibrium rather than static conditions, it treats human effects as "disturbances" rather than as other important characteristics of stream ecology. Disturbances are classified by water and land use types. By far the largest portion of the manual is devoted to planning and design methods, illustrated by brief case studies of the lower Missouri River, Bluewater Creek in New Mexico, the Chesapeake Bay program, Elwha River dam removal, the Anacostia River in Maryland, the Winooski River watershed in Vermont, the Tennessee Valley, the Green River bank restoration in Washington state, the multi-species riparian buffer system in the Bear Creek watershed in Iowa, Oven Run in Pennsylvania, Big Spring watershed in Montana, and others. This list indicates the different types of restoration underway – from species restoration to habitats and from stream banks to watersheds. For that reason, it is important to focus on a selection of specific initiatives.

Many of the Federal Interagency programs described above involve rural and suburban areas where rural pressures on streams range from livestock damage to streambeds to non-point source runoff from croplands. Although initiated almost a century ago, some rural river channel restoration practices, such as riparian conservation buffers, draw renewed attention. A recent survey of riparian buffer research, which highlighted work at Bear Creek, Iowa, examined a range of methods for protecting stream banks, habitat, and water quality conditions, and emphasized the need to better understand and implement multiple interventions in combination with one another (Lowrance *et al.*, 2002). Specific riparian buffer practices analyzed included:

(1)   riparian forest buffer
(2)   field border
(3)   filter strip
(4)   alley cropping
(5)   contour buffer strip
(6)   vegetative barrier
(7)   shelter belt
(8)   crosswind trap strip
(9)   herbaceous wind barrier

Further research issues include buffer width effects, hydraulic effects, water quality effects, ecological effects, and integrating buffers with stream channel restoration programs (Lowrance *et al.*, 2002, pp. 40a–42a).

In fact, a great deal of practical water resources research has addressed those issues in different local areas around the world. An international conference in 2000 yielded a wealth of papers on "riparian ecology and management in multi-land use watersheds" (Wigington, 2001–02). One trait that distinguishes this emerging work from earlier research on river channel management is its focus on linkages between riparian ecology, stream restoration and related topics, such as watershed management, streambank vegetation dynamics, land use, public involvement, recreation planning, and coastal zone management. A second distinguishing characteristic is recognition of the need to work at multiple scales and with multiple land and water uses.

Another set of experiments that gained momentum in the late twentieth century focused on urban streams that were confined in box culverts or pipes earlier in the century. However, these engineering solutions did not prevent seepage, foundation damage, and building abandonment, not to mention ecological degradation of urban streams such as Mill Creek, Philadelphia, a low-income neighborhood where houses have collapsed over a submerged flood channel through the city (Spirn, 1998, pp. 267–272).

A guide for urban river channels comparable with the Federal Interagency handbook for stream restoration underscores the long-standing concern for urban river quality in waterfront improvement, sanitary commissions, and recreation programs (Riley, 1998, pp. 189–210). Late-twentieth-century initiatives strive to synthesize scientific, citizen, and design approaches. The scientists involved are primarily fluvial geomorphologists, aquatic ecologists, and riparian forest ecologists. Citizen groups have multiple aims of addressing functional problems with aging drainage infrastructure, and rediscovering and re-engaging with local landscape features. Designers help generate plans and construction documents that fulfill these public aims while meeting urban engineering and ecosystem functional needs. Each of these groups has produced specialists in urban stream restoration who meet in national groups with names like Friends of Trashed Rivers, as well as consulting firms (Dreiseitl et al., 2001). In addition, they are part of broader movements for "ecological cities" that link streams with their broader floodplain, watershed, and coastal environments (Platt et al., 1994).

Toward global flood hazards monitoring and response

Flood hazards management and floodplain management are leading in the early twenty-first century toward increasingly global approaches. National programs and agencies, such as the US Army Corps of Engineers and US Geological Survey, have counterparts at the state and local levels. Each state has some agency concerned wholly or in part with the hydrology and effects of flood hazards. As discussed earlier, flood hazards programs attempted in the late twentieth century to move from control to mitigation, defined as prevention, preparedness, and harmonious human adjustment to natural flood benefits and risks. In addition, state officials organized into an Association of State Floodplain Managers to share experiences and support the diffusion of effective innovations.

Beyond these local developments, international flood hazards programs signal an increasing scope of analysis and exchange. The Asian Disaster Preparedness Center in Thailand provides technical support, training, and regional support for flood hazards programs in South and Southeast Asia, from Pakistan to the Philippines. In Europe, a flood hazards center at Middlesex University is linking river-channel flood hazard analysis with sustainable development, environmental policy, and coastal zone management (Penning-Rowsell, 1996). The links between river-channel and coastal flood hazards management, and more broadly between watershed and coastal zone management, is an important theme in a period concerned with sea-level rise and coastal storm damages from hurricanes, tsunamis, and cyclone storm surges (Leatherman, 2002). Finally, a global trend is evident at the Dartmouth Flood Observatory. This website continuously compiles maps and tables on floods around the world. It uses both remote sensing techniques to detect, measure and monitor flood events with international disaster agency reports. These events are mapped at the global, landscape and local scales; and are archived for analysis. Descriptive tables for each flood event identify its location, onset, end, duration, type, magnitude, geographic extent and reported damages. For example, when checked on March 29, 2003 the Dartmouth Observatory had compiled data on 79 large floods during 2003, as compared with 45 floods in the first three months of 2002 (Dartmouth Flood Observatory, 2003).

CONCLUSION

These widening trends in water and environmental management reconnect river channel and floodplain environments. Increasingly, they also address the aims, problems, and adjustments associated with impounded rivers, dam operations, and reservoir management in the following chapters.

9

Impounded rivers and reservoirs

One of the dramatic shifts of modern public opinion with regard to water and environmental policy during the twentieth century involved dams and reservoirs. The technology of dam construction has ancient origins, dating from small brush diversions of water in many regions of the world to the famous large stone dam at Marib, Yemen, which is believed to have been initiated three millennia ago in a region of floodwater farming (Brunner, 2000; Brunner and Haefner, 1986). After reaching a height of about 15 m, length of 720 m, and basal width of 60 m, earthquakes contributed to a catastrophic breach in the early seventh century CE, a disaster ascribed to divine disfavor in the *Qur'an*:

> But they gave no heed. So we unloosed upon them the waters of the dams and replaced their gardens with two others bearing bitter fruit, tamarisks, and a few nettle shrubs (Qur'an 34:17)

The abutments of Marib Dam still stand, as do those of a very large embankment dam at Saad-El-Katara, Egypt, which was begun but apparently not completed in the third millennium BCE (Garbrecht, 1996).

By 2000, the International Commission on Large Dams (ICOLD, 1998) estimated that some 45 000 "large dams" (greater than 15 m high) had been built around the world, almost half of them in China. Some large dams have generated heated public controversy, contributing to a decline in construction, yet thousands more are planned in developing countries for hydroelectric energy supply, flood mitigation, water supply and other purposes (Dreze *et al.*, 1997; Edmonds, 1992; Fisher, 1995; Morse Commission, 1992; WCD, 2000). In some basins the most promising sites for large dams have already been developed or protected from development. For example, in the United States the President's Water

Resources Policy Commission (PWRPC) in 1950 estimated that by 1970 virtually all sites for large dams would be developed, and that was the case for almost all the country by 1980 (PWRPC, 1950).

A few examples remind us that dams and reservoirs vary widely in purpose, size, design, and environmental effects. Some large dams, such as Hoover Dam on the Colorado River and Itaipu in southern Brazil, span narrow channels and rise hundreds of meters high. Others such as the earth- and rock-filled barrages of southern and eastern Asia are relatively low in height but stretch kilometers in length. At the other end of the spectrum, small dams may consist of merely a row of brush, rocks, or earth – such as check dams one meter high and several meters wide that span intermittent streams, impounding their waters for brief periods of time and capturing their fine cultivable sediments. In between these monumental and modest structures are the majority of the world's dams and reservoirs. Most impoundments are earth-filled structures with a cladding of protective stone or vegetation. They are relatively small in height and length, and have been constructed on perennial streams for a range of municipal, industrial, agricultural, flood control, and recreational purposes (Helms, 1992; Person, 1936; US Department of the Interior, 1987).

Reservoirs created by these different types of impoundments also vary in size, volume, purpose, and environmental quality. Reservoir siting decisions give special attention to the volume of water stored relative to surface area evaporation, permeability of soils, and stability of dam foundation and abutment areas. Reservoirs also vary in the volume of water stored in relation to river flow – from "run-of-river" dams that raise the level of the water surface to maintain relatively constant diversions without significantly increasing storage, to large dams capable of storing several times the annual flow of the upstream river basin. Farm ponds may span only tens of meters while the reservoirs behind high dams extend for hundreds of kilometers. The same type of dam will produce different reservoir conditions in different bioclimatic conditions, depending upon their latitudinal, altitudinal, and continental location – as is the case with lakes discussed in Chapter 7. For example, the thermal regime and associated reservoir turbidity, chemistry, flora, and fauna in a cold dry region are subject to frozen surfaces, while those in humid temperate regions are subject to seasonal lake mixing, and those in dry tropical climates to major evaporative losses. Reservoir sedimentation depends upon natural rates of rock weathering and erosion. It is relatively rapid in regions that are either tectonically active or subject to intensive unregulated upland watershed land uses.

While reservoirs resemble lakes in some respects they differ in the processes that create them and the degree to which their inflows and outflows are managed. Most immediately, they inundate upstream floodplains, canyons, and valleys that formerly supported in-stream water uses, terrestrial ecosystems, and associated land uses. Although large areas of major cities are rarely inundated, substantial numbers of smaller cities, towns and villages, and many millions of farmers and pastoralists have been, and in some regions will likely continue to be, displaced by large reservoirs. While some displaced persons or "oustees" are resettled on productive lands, research by international organizations ranging from non-governmental organizations to the World Bank indicates first, that until recently their fate was rarely considered; second, that promises and even detailed resettlement plans are rarely implemented or documented; and third, that whatever their benefits for the regional or national economy, resettlement rarely makes displaced people as well off as they were before dam and reservoir construction. Assumptions that evacuees will be able to make a comparable livelihood from a comparable area of land in a different social and natural environment are rarely supported (WCD, 2000). Riparian wildlife and avifauna likewise suffer diminished habitat and migratory alternatives. Inundated plant and soil communities are simply drowned.

Once constructed and filled, dams trap sediments that would otherwise have been transported downstream, which accelerates erosion as well as depleting sediment supply below the dam. Some dams have devices to release sediments near their base, but the bulk of sedimentation usually occurs far upstream at "deltas" where the reduced velocity of inflows leads to deposition of bedload and coarse suspended sediment. Native fish, especially juveniles, have difficulty navigating these slackwaters, and may face introduced predator species as well. Most small dams have little or no regulation, aside from a spillway to convey excess water safely over the top of or around the dam. Larger dams may have spillways at different elevations, which affect the temperature and chemistry as well as volume of releases. Hydropower dams also alter the chemistry, e.g., dissolved oxygen and nitrogen, which affect fish health, as do the volume and rate of releases. Some dams are equipped with fish ladders to allow return migration of anadromous fish while others are equipped with sonar to try to help guide native fish swimming downstream through the relatively slow-moving waters of a reservoir. Dams may have grates to keep fish from entering turbines, and even trucks to portage them around the dam.

Figure 9.1   Depletion of streamflows downstream of Shoshone Dam on the Colorado River near Glenwood Springs, Colorado, USA.

These modifications of natural river habitat conditions by reservoir construction and operation lead, in turn, to changes in aquatic and riparian conditions (Figure 9.1). In general, native species adapted to natural variability give way to species that tolerate or thrive in the altered pattern of flow variability. When that variability is based on municipal hydropower or irrigation water supply and demand, rather than on hydroclimatic and watershed processes, native species migrate or are displaced by species adapted to human patterns of disturbance. Fluctuating reservoir levels and releases support the invasion of phreatophytes (plants with a combination of deep and shallow roots, tolerant of flooding and desiccation). Invasion of salt cedar (*Tamarix* spp.) in reservoirs and regulated rivers of the southwestern United States is a good example of an exotic species that has spread widely and withstood expensive mechanical, chemical, and biological eradication programs.

Finally, the environmental impacts of dam and reservoir construction are shaped by four major independent variables:

(1)   Watershed land uses affect erosion, sedimentation, eutrophication, and pollution rates, which in turn affect water quality conditions in the reservoir, as well as the life of the reservoir.

(2)   Reservoir surface water and shoreline uses directly affect reservoir conditions through discharge of pollutants (e.g., from

water intake and discharge pipes, boat ballast, toilet and waste products, etc.). Shoreline and surface uses also directly experience environmental changes, such as seasonal reservoir elevation fluctuations that vary in relation to downstream water releases and demand as well as inflows, and that can adversely affect flatwater recreation and marinas.

(3)   Reservoir fisheries policies that purposely stock some commercial and sport fish (e.g., tilapia in tropical reservoirs) that are predators of native species, or purposely strive to eradicate others (e.g., large native minnow eradication programs in the Colorado River in the 1950s).

(4)   Reservoir release policies that affect upstream and downstream environments.

This complex array of environmental and ecological impacts associated with dams and reservoirs contributed to a divergence of water management and environmental policy in the twentieth century (for early influential international reports see Ackermann *et al.*, 1973; Dussart *et al.*, 1972; Lagler, 1969; Lowe-McConnell, 1966; Stanley and Alpers, 1975).

ESCALATING CONFLICT IN THE LATE TWENTIETH CENTURY

Notwithstanding this variety of pattern, purpose, and effects, a division arose as to whether the policies related to impounded rivers were inherently flawed. This view led to the question in some quarters as to whether there could be any such thing as a "good dam." Dam and hydropower organizations responded angrily to these questions and charges, citing environmental as well as economic benefits of dams (ICOLD, IHA, and ICID, 2001). Even so, pressure not to build dams and to decommission existing dams grew, leading to the creation of the World Commission on Dams (WCD) to assemble as much information as possible to shed light on the prospects for future river impoundment, and desirable management of existing impoundments.

As the scale and pace of dam and reservoir construction increased and extended around the world during the twentieth century, so too did concern about and opposition to their environmental benefits and costs (Berkamp *et al.*, 2000; IUCN and World Bank, 1996; WCD, 2000). This analysis therefore tries to survey the prospects for more, fewer, and different kinds of dams and reservoirs in various geographic contexts of the world; and likewise to survey the range of choice in operations, adjustments, and eventual decommissioning of existing dams.

The overarching question asked, at the beginning of the twenty-first century, is whether harmonization of environmental management and dam and reservoir policy is possible? At the beginning of the twentieth century, many believed them inherently compatible, and that the economical effects were worth the environmental impacts. They lauded dams as "wonders of the world."

The voices of displaced or adversely affected indigenous people were raised but rarely heard, for example, in the nineteenth century in the upper Mississippi Valley (Merritt, 1984). However, an increasing number of persons were displaced and impoverished by reservoir impoundments. Outraged by degraded streams, drowned canyons, and endangered species – and unimpressed by the purported benefits of dams and reservoirs – many declared that dams and environment were fundamentally incompatible in the second half of the twentieth century. They gained voice, affected policy, and organized international networks to block new dam construction and call for decommissioning of existing dams (McCully, 1996).

The controversy mounted as many of the more promising sites for river storage were developed. In the United States, for example, the PWRPC in 1950 recognized that there were "only a few suitable dam sites and once they are appropriated the possibilities for multiple-purpose development are very limited. There is a sobering finality in the construction of a river basin development" (PWRPC, 1950, I, p. 18). As the geologically favorable dam sites were developed in the North, dam building shifted to new nations of the South with widening consequences and conflict.

As conflicts mounted, and options narrowed, dam planning processes slowed to decades, cost tens of millions of dollars, and faced mounting evidence and accusation of widening environment and social impacts (PWRPC, 1950, I, p. 385). Although numerous individual studies documented specific impacts, no comprehensive, integrated, cumulative, or long-term evaluations were undertaken to assess the overall benefits and costs of river impoundment. Nor was it clear whether and how the studies that had been conducted were used in planning, designing, operating, and adapting decisions about dams and reservoirs. In the face of this situation, the World Commission on Dams was established to conduct an intensive two-year consultative study to address the question of whether social, environmental and economic aspects of dams, reservoirs, and free-flowing rivers could be harmonized (WCD, 2000).

To understand the trajectory of these events of the twentieth century, this chapter surveys the varied purposes and effects of river impoundment in different regions of the world. It highlights the development of large dams (greater than 15 m high) and reservoirs, plans for further dam construction, and mounting opposition to dams worldwide. It concludes with an assessment of what has, and has not yet, been learned about the cumulative environmental effects of river impoundment in river basins or the possibility of harmonizing river regulation and ecology.

FUNCTIONS, EFFECTS, AND CHANGING CONTEXTS OF RIVER IMPOUNDMENT

Dams and reservoirs vary so widely in purpose, size, and environmental effect that no single text, engineering field, or public policy program covers the full range of phenomena. Thus, this section strives to jointly consider the functions, effects, and changing contexts of river impoundment, starting with natural and small ephemeral features and proceeding toward larger and more complex engineered systems.

Natural impoundments

While the words "dam" and "reservoir" commonly denote human constructions, it is worth noting that at least three types of natural processes can impound rivers for relatively long or short periods of time. Glaciers can block river channels, impounding large bodies of water that, when released in a glacial lake outburst flood, known as a jokulhlaups, can cause damage hundreds of kilometers downstream, as occurred in 1929 and 1958 on the upper Indus River (Hewitt, 1982; Ives, 1986). Landslides in mountainous terrain can also sweep across a valley, impounding for various periods of time the river that drains it. Finally, tectonic uplift, if more rapid than stream incision, can impound rivers in internal lakes. If these lakes subsequently receive massive inflows, e.g., from glacial melt, they may breach the tectonic divide and cut a new channel to the ocean. In many cases, human societies emulate or build upon glaciological, tectonic and erosional processes when impounding rivers for human purposes.

Check dams on ephemeral streams

At the small scale of meters to tens of meters, earth and rock-filled dams, known as check dams, have been constructed on small channels (and wadis in the Middle East), from prehistoric times to the present, particularly in arid, semiarid and mountainous regions (Doolittle, 2000, pp. 309–346). They range in material from temporary brush weirs to enduring earth-fill and stone-armored walls.

These structures impound intermittent flows – and fine sediments – to create favored niches for crop production immediately upstream of the check dam. Those habitats support stands of riparian and mesic vegetation, which provide habitat and food in turn for avian and terrestrial wildlife. Check dams also provide a measure of erosion control and are often linked with water harvesting collection systems along hillslopes to the alluvial fields behind the dam or alluvial fans below it, as in the Negev Desert (Evenari et al., 1971).

Thus, in contrast with large dams, where reservoir sedimentation is viewed as a major problem, these small dams purposely capture sediments as well as moisture for agricultural purposes. Given their small size, rudimentary construction, and provision for continued passage of subsurface flows beneath and often through the structure, their adverse environmental effects on downstream channel environments are generally less significant than their beneficial effects upstream. They require annual maintenance or rebuilding that when discontinued lead to a return to roughly natural stream conditions.

Rural storage dams and reservoirs

More permanent small earthen dams have been constructed in mesic and humid rural watersheds for a wide range of irrigation, flood control, livestock watering, fish farming, and recreational purposes. These dams may have vegetated earth spillways but otherwise limited structural features to control releases. Some are constructed in response to environmental effects of deforestation and cultivation in watersheds where erosion, channel sedimentation, and flooding have been aggravated. They may have the additional consequence of encouraging agricultural intensification and occupance in downstream areas which are perceived by residents to have lower flood risk but which, in fact, become more vulnerable to dam failure and high releases.

Run-of-river, mill dams, and hydropower dams

The purpose of many dams is to regulate the elevation of an upstream river surface rather than to store a significant volume of water. By raising and stabilizing the river surface, these dams help maintain a specific navigation channel depth, divert water into an irrigation canal which returns little water to the stream, or supply a power plant that returns virtually the entire diversion to the stream. As irrigation canals are discussed in Chapter 5, this chapter concentrates on navigation and hydropower dams.

Dams located on steep streams, falls, and escarpments diverted water for milling grain from antiquity to the modern era; and, later, for generating waterpower for various industrial milling purposes (Steinberg, 1991). Conflicts among adjacent mill dam owners helped shape the development of the "riparian doctrine" of water law, which permits and requires "reasonable water use" among landowners adjoining a stream. What is deemed "reasonable" varies with the socioeconomic as well as hydrologic circumstances. It is rarely deemed reasonable to impound or divert the whole flow of a stream. But in the early twentieth century, diversion of scenic waterfalls to a power plant were deemed acceptable, as the aesthetic and ecological values of free-flowing rivers were not yet deemed "beneficial" (*Empire Water and Power* v. *Cascade Town Co.*, 1913). Public and legal recognition of and attitudes toward the beneficial uses of in-stream flows expanded during the middle and late twentieth century. In some sharply dissected regions, such as the fjordlands of Scandinavia, most electric power is still derived from relatively small hydropower dams that have scenic and aquatic impacts, but impound relatively small quantities of water and inundate relatively small areas of land (WCD, 2000).

Weirs and barrages

During the nineteenth and early twentieth centuries, large weirs and barrages, extending tens to hundreds of meters in length, were built across medium to large rivers (Figure 9.2). They raised water levels in order to extend navigation through series of locks and canals. Although low in height, they generally slow the passage of water, increase water temperatures, increase flatwater over whitewater recreation and, in contrast with high dams, may facilitate passage of exotic aquatic species, such as the zebra mussel of North America, or disease vectors for schistosomiasis. In semiarid and plains environments, such as South and Central Asia, large barrages raised water several meters to tens of meters to sustain diversions into major irrigation canals and expand networks of secondary and lateral canals (as mentioned in Chapter 5). These systems were often designed with scouring sluices and diversion works to maintain the canal's "hydraulic regime" of sediment transport. Annual maintenance is required for dam safety, dredging, passage of

Figure 9.2   Barrage on the upper Guggara Canal in Punjab, Pakistan, which is part of the Indus basin, the largest contiguously irrigated area in the world.

flood flows through spillways, and repair of breaches by major flows (Figure 9.3).

High dams

Scientific and technological capacity to dam canyons and valleys hundreds of meters high developed rapidly during the early and mid twentieth century. The International Commission on Large Dams (ICOLD) was formed primarily to share information on technical and financial issues that would promote the construction of large dams around the world and improve dam, power-plant, and reservoir safety and performance, with a focus on the primary purposes for which they were built. ICOLD also dealt with related issues of disease vectors, fisheries, and wildlife management as ancillary aims of dam construction. While their large size and distinctive structural requirements limit the number of sites deemed feasible, their expected benefits led to major site modification investments (e.g., in excavation, grouting, and foundation and abutment design).

Large dams also require substantial and continuing maintenance expenditures and improvements. For example, concrete spillways are subject to cavitation, erosion, and corrosion, especially at their toe or

Figure 9.3 Breached earth-fill dam on the South Fork of the Little Conemaugh River, which destroyed much of Johnstown, Pennsylvania, USA, in 1889 CE.

spillway flip buckets, where gravel churns at high velocities (Figure 9.4). If not repaired and adapted to reduce such damages, steel reinforcement is exposed and structural stability decreased. Dam and abutment foundations are likewise subject to seepage and piping, which must be repaired by periodic grouting, reinforcement, and surface treatment to reduce the risks of dam failure. When dam safety costs exceed the

Figure 9.4   Spillway of Green Mountain Reservoir on the Blue River
of Colorado, USA, which releases water to meet senior water rights
downstream.

social values associated with dam and reservoir use, decommissioning is considered (USBR, 1995). Many small dams are decommissioned
annually. While decommissioning of larger dams has been proposed,
its environmental and social effects have rarely been studied in detail. Recent research on geomorphological and benthological effects of

Table 9.1 *Profile of large dams worldwide*

Number	25 420–48 000
Average height (m)	31
Average reservoir area (km^2)	23
Average reservoir capacity (million m^3)	269
Hydropower potential (TWh/yr)	14 370
Actual hydropower production (TWh/yr)	2643

Source: WCD, 2000, p. 375.

decommissioning a low head dam on the Baraboo River in Wisconsin indicated relatively rapid recovery of invertebrate and aquatic communities (Stanley *et al.*, 2002). Systems of small and large reservoirs entail different types of water management, as their cumulative geographic scale and impacts can affect regional environmental and socioeconomic well-being.

Table 9.1 provides a rough profile of the number and average physical characteristics of large dams worldwide. The vast majority of these dams were constructed after 1950 (WCD, 2000, p. 369). Commissioning of new dams climbed from 913 in the 1940s to 2735 in the 1950s, 4788 in the 1960s, and 5418 in the 1970s. As costs, consequences, and controversies grew in the 1970s, and the majority of dam sites had been developed, commissioning of new dams fell off from the 1980s to the present at roughly the same rate as it had grown. Geographically, the distribution of large dams is concentrated in five countries which contain roughly 77 percent of the large dams: China (45%), USA (14%), India (9%), Japan (6%), and Spain (3%) (WCD, 2000, p. 373). Although several countries with large dams and large controversies, such as Brazil, Turkey, and Canada, contain only 1–2 percent of the world's large dams, they are relatively large in size and located on internationally strategic rivers. Countries with a significant number of large dams currently under construction, or planned for future construction, include India, China, Turkey, South Korea, Japan, and Iran. Not surprisingly, the governments of these countries oppose anti-dam social and environmental movements.

Systems of dams and reservoirs

Large dams have many of the same purposes as small dams – irrigation, power, water supply, flood control, and multiple-purpose – and analogous siting considerations (e.g., in steep gorges, narrow valleys, and shallow stable bedrock conditions). Additionally, in some river and watershed environments, small and large impoundments have been established in combinations and sequences that address regional water demands and have regional environmental consequences. While "river basin development" is discussed elsewhere in this volume, this chapter briefly considers three common combinations of dams and reservoirs:

(1)　A series of large dams and reservoirs sited along a river main stem, managed in coordination as a sequence of pools. The sequence of Tennessee Valley Authority reservoirs managed for hydropower, navigation, health, and recreational uses provides a good example.

(2)　A series of small dams and tanks sited along tributaries, managed and maintained through local and regional organizations. The complex systems of irrigation tanks used largely for rice irrigation in south India and Sri Lanka are a good example (Wallach, 1996). Historical research on these tanks indicates that they are often managed in succession: as some tanks silt up, others are repaired. The prosperity of villages depends upon the degree of local organization, while regional prosperity depends upon the coordination of local efforts.

(3)　Combinations of small upstream dams and larger main-stem dams. This concept was proposed for the Miami River watershed in Ohio in the 1930s but not widely adopted until decades later. Moreover, the relative contributions of small dams, large dams and watershed land use management to water supply and flood damage reduction were for many years disputed (Leopold and Maddock, 1954), and schemes that incorporate multiple approaches are still constrained by fragmented institutional responsibility for different types of river impoundments.

Summary

In each case, the geographic context of dams and reservoirs varies widely in economic, ecological, and technological terms. Although they have similar functions and effects in some contexts, they differ so much in others as to require detailed site-specific analysis of impacts and a range of approaches to harmonizing their social and environmental purposes and effects.

The geographic context of dams also changes over time as, for example, when runoff farming and industrial milling expands or declines,

Figure 9.5   Reservoir above the Karakum Canal in Turkmenistan,
choked with sediment and abandoned in the late twentieth century.

or when reservoirs fill with sediments, or when reservoir use changes
from water storage to recreational purposes, and as older dams become dangerous – as has occurred in many places over the past century
(Figure 9.5).

It is important to keep in mind these similarities, differences,
and changes when considering the alternatives available for harmonizing impounded river management in different geographic situations.
Before discussing the alternatives to dams, it is useful to review the
recently published work of the World Commission on Dams on the environmental performance of large dams, the state-of-the-art in ex-post
evaluation, and the prospects for harmonization.

ENVIRONMENTAL EFFECTS OF LARGE DAMS

A vast body of scientific research has focused on various environmental
impacts of large dams (Goldsmith and Hildyard, 1984, 1986a, 1986b).
Much of this literature deals with specific impacts at specific dams, and
much of it focuses on the expected vis-à-vis actual impacts of proposed
dams. An estimated 45 000 dams have been constructed that are over
15 m high, (Figure 9.6) and thousands more are planned, primarily in
Asia but also in Africa and South America (ICOLD, 1998). Escalating
environmental and social conflict over large dams led to formation
of the World Commission on Dams, and in November 2000, the WCD

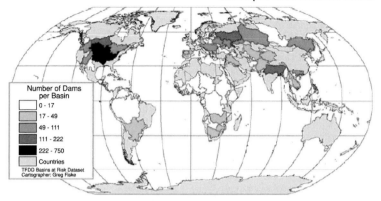

Figure 9.6   Number of large dams per international basin in 1998.
Darker areas have higher rates of river impoundment. From Fiske and
Yoffe (2002).

released its report *Dams and Development: a New Framework for Decision-Making* (WCD, 2000).

The WCD created a knowledge base of seven detailed dam case studies, a survey of 125 dams in 52 countries, a series of regional consultations over a two-year period, and some 130 papers commissioned to prepare 17 thematic reviews on different aspects of large dam performance. Studies focused on environmental performance are listed in Table 9.2.

The seven focal dam case studies provide the most thorough information on large dams to that date (they were preceded by brief comparative surveys of 50 dams by the World Bank, 1996, whose data remain unpublished). WCD summarized the costs and benefits of dams under several broad categories of performance:

- technical, financial and economic performance (i.e., the project purpose)
- environmental performance
- social performance
- alternatives to large dams
- decision-making and institutional performance

Given the wide range of dam purposes and contexts, it proved difficult to develop reliable quantitative measures of performance across either the focal case studies or cross-check survey. However, Table 9.3 lists key characteristics of the focal dams, which vary in purpose, height, size, cost, and effects.

Table 9.2 *WCD studies of the environmental performance of large dams*

Detailed case studies (focal dams)
   Aslantas Dam, Ceyhan River, Turkey
   Glomma and Laagen Basin (40 dams), Norway
   Grand Coulee Dam, Columbia River, USA/Canada
   Kariba Dam, Zambezi River, Zambia/Zimbabwe
   Pak Mun Dam, Mun-Mekong River, Thailand
   Tarbela Dam, Indus River, Pakistan
   Tucurui Dam, Tocantins River, Brazil

Thematic Reviews
   II.1 Dams, ecosystem functions and environmental restoration
   II.2 Dams and global change
   V.2 Environmental and Social Assessment for large dams

Papers Contributed to Thematic Review II.1
   Managed flood releases from reservoirs: issues and guidance – Mike Acreman
   Capacity and information base requirements for effective management of
      fish biodiversity, fish stocks and fisheries threatened or affected by
      dams during the project cycle – Garry Bernacsek
   International mechanisms for avoiding, mitigating and compensating the
      impacts of large dams on aquatic and related ecosystems and
      species – John R. Bizere
   Large dams and freshwater fish biodiversity – John Craig
   Biodiversity impacts of large dams: waterbirds – Nick Davidson and Simon
      Delany
   The influence of dams on river fisheries – Donald Jackson and Gerd
      Marmulla
   Definition and implementation of instream inflows – Jackie King, Rebecca
      Tharme, and Cate Brown
   Information needs for appraisal and monitoring of ecosystem
      impacts – Jackie King and Cate Brown
   Dams and fish migration – Michel Larinier
   Biodiversity impacts of large dams – Don McAllister, John Craig, Nick
      Davidson, Diane Murray, and Mary Seddon
   Ecosystem impacts of large dams – M. P. McCartney, C. Sullivan and M. C.
      Acreman
   A review of guidance and criteria for managing reservoir and associated
      riverine environments to benefit fish and fisheries – Steve Miranda
   Report on hydrological and geochemical processes in large scale river
      basins, 15–19 November 1999, Manaus, Brazil – Leonard Sklar
   Molluscan biodiversity and the impact of large dams – Mary Seddon

Source: WCD, 2000, and http://www.dams.org.

Table 9.3 *Focal dam characteristics*

	Date	Height (m)	Reservoir area km²	Irrigated area (ha)	Hydropower capacity (MW)	Resettlement (households)	Cost 1998
Aslantas	1984	78	49	84 000	138	5000	$1.3 bn
Glomma and Laagen	40 dams	varies	varies	–	2165	–	$0.8 bn
Grand Coulee	1941	170	260	200 000	6809	6000	$9.2 bn
Kariba	1960	128	5577	–	1266	57 000	$1.5 bn
Pak Mun	1994	17	60	–	136	700	$0.29 bn
Tarbela	1976	148	240	18 000 000 (system)	3478	96 000	$8.8 bn
Tucurui	1986	78	2430	–	4000	25–30 000	$5.5 bn

Source: WCD, 2002.

The WCD considered the "environmental performance" of dams, a term that has a more balanced connotation than "impacts." Following a common ecological practice, WCD differentiated between first-order effects on physical river qualities, second-order effects on primary biological productivity, and third-order effects on fauna (WCD, 2000, p. 74). While this classification of effects is well established, it has been worthwhile to compare it with alternative approaches in different regions, ecosystems, and culture groups (e.g., Brosius *et al.*, 1998). The stakeholder group for the Glen Canyon Dam adaptive management program, for example, has numerous public agencies, tribes, and nongovernmental organizations, all of whom define and value environmental resources in different ways (Jacobs and Wescoat, 2002; Wilkinson, 2000).

The WCD analysis yielded eight main categories of environmental performance, both in its knowledge base and for application in future studies:

(1)   Terrestrial ecosystems and biodiversity (affected by reservoir inundation). The WCD reported that wildlife relocation efforts at Kariba and Tucurui dams had not been successful, and that forest replanting policies in India were only partially implemented and maintained (WCD, 2000, p. 75).

(2)   Greenhouse gas emissions (mainly carbon dioxide and methane). Although emissions vary greatly over time and regions, greenhouse gases from large shallow reservoirs in tropical regions, e.g. Tucurui in Brazil, may exceed emissions from alternative power generation methods (WCD, 2000, p. 77).

(3)   Downstream aquatic ecosystems and biodiversity (e.g., trapping sediments and nutrients, decreasing temperatures, altering flows and chemical characteristics, and disrupting migration of aquatic fauna). By one analogy, constructing a dam transforms that reach of a river into a headwaters-type stream that has cold temperatures, low nutrients and sediments, and relatively low biodiversity (Ward and Stanford, 1995). Reducing streamflow variability favors disturbance species, and blocking river passage further reduces native biodiversity. Interannual climate variability further complicates river restoration efforts on regulated rivers (Pulwarty and Redmond, 1997). While structural measures have been taken to facilitate fish passage, from ladders to trucking, these measures failed to prevent decline of endangered salmon stocks, which led

in turn to calls for decommissioning large upstream dams on the Snake River and to intense conflict in the late 1990s.

(4)   Floodplain ecosystems (inundation upstream, and channel incision and floodplain desiccation downstream). Although many large dams have flood control as one of their objectives, impoundment and flood flow reduction degrade floodplain environments. Controlled flood experiments are under way at Manantali Dam in Mali and Senegal, Pongolapoort Dam in South Africa, Glen Canyon Dam in the USA, and the Tana River in Kenya (WCD, 2000, p. 84).

(5)   Fisheries (transformation of river to lake habitat upstream; and from warm-water, sediment-laden habitat to clear cold water downstream). Fisheries impacts are one of the best-documented aspects of dam and reservoir construction. However, the impacts are complex. At Tucurui reservoir, the number of species decreased but productivity of remaining species increased. Downstream sport fisheries have sometimes increased in tailwater reaches below dams. Impact evaluation is further confused by fish stocking (e.g., of tilapia in many tropical reservoirs, bass species in US reservoirs, and salmonids and trout in tailwater reaches), which alters competition and predation in reservoirs. The WCD (2000, p. 85) documents a tendency to overestimate the projected fisheries benefits of large dams.

(6)   Ecosystem enhancement (e.g., increased shoreline and wetland habitat). Although reservoir construction increases some habitat types and conditions, the WCD knowledge base found relatively low biodiversity in these habitats, in part due to reservoir operations and resulting unnatural variability in both downstream releases and reservoir levels.

(7)   Cumulative impacts (from systems of dams and associated water and land uses). As large dams became part of comprehensive river basin development programs, their cumulative impacts on river flows, quality, and biodiversity escalated in complex ways. Cumulative diversions for irrigation reduced Aral Sea inflows so dramatically as to lose 75 percent of its average annual volume, leading to fish extinction, airborne transport of polluted shoreline sediments, and hazardous levels of water pollution. Development of large dams and associated diversions and uses from the Colorado River has cumulatively increased salinity conditions in the lower basin and delta environments.

Measurement and analysis of cumulative impacts is extremely difficult.

(8)   Anticipating and responding to ecosystem impacts (through planning and ex-post evaluation). The WCD (2000, p. 89) reports that "almost 60% of the impacts identified were unanticipated prior to project construction." The report notes increasing attention to potential impacts between the 1950s and 1990s, and increasingly sophisticated environmental impact planning, mitigation, and compensation practices. What the WCD does not stress in that discussion of environmental performance (though it is mentioned elsewhere) is that even fewer projects have been the focus of detailed ex-post evaluations of the actual environmental impacts of completed projects over the decadal time periods that are needed both to predict future impacts more accurately and to mitigate current impacts.

EX-POST EVALUATION OF THE ENVIRONMENTAL EFFECTS OF LARGE DAMS

Although there have been many environmental assessments of proposed dams and reservoirs, there are surprisingly few detailed assessments of actual consequences for the environments and social groups affected. This section returns to the theme of ex-post evaluation, introduced in Chapter 1. After recalling the criteria for detailed ex-post evaluation, it summarizes the results of a survey of published research on environmental effects of dams and reservoirs in different regions of the world (Wescoat and Halvorson, 2000), and compares those findings with results of other studies undertaken by the WCD.

Conceptual framework for ex-post evaluation

As outlined in Chapter 1, a detailed ex-post evaluation has five characteristics: comprehensiveness (environmental, social and institutional effects); integration (of those effects); cumulative effects; long-term monitoring and research; and adaptive response to monitoring results.

WCD focal dam case studies

The seven detailed case studies commissioned by the WCD fulfill the first three of these criteria, but few had a long-term record of monitoring or adaptive management to assess. Tarbela Dam in Pakistan, for

Figure 9.7   Spillway and dam for Tarbela reservoir on the Indus River in Pakistan, the main impoundment of the Indus Basin Development Programme.

example, had published monitoring of technical conditions, government monitoring of resettlement programs, but little ecological monitoring (Figure 9.7) (though see Ortolano *et al.*, 2000).

WCD cross-check survey

Of the 125 dams surveyed, 60% identified unanticipated environmental impacts, based presumably on ex-post evaluation. However, the WCD found that many of the reported impacts were based on qualitative information, and a large proportion lacked ex-post environmental data.

WCD national studies

The national studies of dams in India and China did not cite studies of ex-post evaluation and gave little project-specific data on the environmental performance of large dams.

WCD thematic reviews

While the thematic reviews were based on literature reviews and data from many dam and reservoir sites around the world, they were compiled from contributing papers that likewise have in some cases very detailed ex-post evaluation data but in most cases lack comprehensive,

Figure 9.8   Glen Canyon Dam on the Colorado River in Arizona, USA, just above the Grand Canyon and now the focus of an adaptive management program.

integrated or cumulative impact assessments. Still, the thematic reviews and their contributing papers are a rich source of actual impact data on specific issues.

Ex-post evaluation of dams review

One report commissioned by the WCD compiled references to ex-post evaluations of dams (Wescoat and Halvorson, 2000). As underscored in this volume, ex-post evaluation is essential in all water sectors to reliably identify lessons learned and good practices. The report to the WCD concluded that "broad evaluations of completed projects appear to be few in number, narrow in scope, poorly integrated across impact categories and scales, and inadequately linked with dam operations decisions" (Wescoat and Halvorson, 2000, p. 5). There is no lack of evaluation frameworks and methods, or planning studies. Instead, it is detailed implementation and monitoring that rarely occur. Important exceptions include the Glen Canyon Dam adaptive management program on the Colorado River (Figure 9.8), the Lesotho Highlands Project, the Kariba Dam on the Zambezi River, the Xiaolangi and Ertan II projects in China, Arun III in Nepal, the lower Kihansi project in Tanzania, and now the WCD case studies.

A related problem is that the evaluations that do occur are often unpublished reports that are rarely accessible and poorly archived. Again, the WCD's electronic archiving, continued by the UNEP Dams and Development Project website, represent important steps forward (see websites for this chapter in the appendix).

PROSPECTS FOR HARMONIZING DAMS, RESERVOIRS AND ENVIRONMENTAL MANAGEMENT

In charting a way forward for impounded river management, the World Commission on Dams developed a "New Framework" consisting of seven strategic priorities and five decision points. The first principle of the new framework is titled "Human Development through Rights, Risk Management, and Negotiated Outcomes." As in other recent global forums, the WCD concluded both that "humans come first" and that "sustainable human development" could provide the basis for a new and effective approach. The key components of human development – rights, risk management, and negotiated outcomes – are elaborated as the following strategic priorities:

(1) Gaining public acceptance (of shared water management issues, rather than the need for a dam or other specific solution at the outset).

(2) Comprehensive options assessment (i.e., broadening the range of choice to include demand management, ecosystem management, and the full array of water supply and power options as well as dams).

(3) Existing dams. Special attention will be needed in the decades ahead to manage, maintain, modify, and in some cases decommission existing dams. The vast majority of the world's large dams were built in the 1950s to 1990s, and many of these will require major attention in the decades ahead.

(4) Sustaining rivers and livelihoods. The WCD process presented a broader perspective on rivers and their relation to sustaining human livelihoods, e.g., through fishing and recreation as well as impoundments.

(5) Recognizing entitlements and sharing benefits. The WCD drew attention to the injustices imposed on displaced peoples and the inequitable distribution of project benefits locally and regionally. It stopped short of recognizing entitlements and benefits for non-human species, communities, and ecosystems – notwithstanding

the presentations of indigenous and mainstream culture groups who do recognize them.

(6)   Ensuring compliance. This requires substantially greater investment in baseline assessment, and continuing monitoring and evaluation following project construction.

(7)   Sharing rivers for peace, development, and security. The WCD further recognized the increasing significance of river use and development in cooperative international relations.

These seven strategic priorities are to be advanced throughout the project cycle, or what WCD referred to as five "decision points": (1) needs assessment, (2) selecting alternatives, (3) project preparation, (4) project implementation, and (5) project operation (which includes monitoring and ex-post evaluation). These recommendations and strategies reflect the collective judgment of many, but not all, involved in dam and reservoir management. Thus it is important also to consider the reception and follow-up to the WCD process in 2001 and beyond.

Reception of the WCD report

To its credit, the WCD (2002) electronically compiled and posted the reactions to its process and report, as well as the reports themselves. From those documents the following major points may be discerned:

(1)   Reception by international professional hydropower organizations. Although represented as commissioners and contributors to the WCD process, some hydropower utility and construction organizations did not feel adequately included in procedures for writing the final report, while others stated that relatively limited attention was given to pressing technical issues, economic benefits of dams, and the need for future dams.

(2)   Reception by environmental organizations. Environmental organizations involved in the WCD generally received the final report favorably, though some sought to summarize its findings to advance an anti-dam agenda. An independent review of the WCD process by the World Resources Institute and other organizations (Dubash et al., 2001) critically examines the stakeholder processes, politics, conclusions, and reception of the WCD.

(3)   Reception by development organizations. Multilateral sponsors of the WCD process and reports, such as the World Bank, gave it a generally favorable reception, and felt it would help guide their project preparation, investment, and subsequent evaluation processes.

(4)   Differences in reception by national groups. Notwithstanding the general responses stated above, individual country organizations (governmental, non-governmental, and professional) varied enormously. For example, while professional engineering organizations in North America gave a generally positive response, their counterparts in South Asia gave strident criticism and in some cases completely dismissed the report.

As chairman Kader Asmal stated, the WCD officially ended after submitting its report, so it will be up to the diverse organizations listed above and others to carry forward and adjust the process initiated by the World Commission on Dams.

Follow-on studies

Each contributing organization to the WCD process, from the International Hydropower Association (IHA) and ICOLD to the IUCN and the International Rivers Network pursued its own agenda following the WCD. In addition, the WCD staff budgeted over a year to disseminate its results in several regions, languages, and forums around the world. Fortunately, in February 2001, the UN Environment Programme developed a two-year Dams and Development Project to continue several key initiatives that could not be completed in the two-year time frame of WCD:

(1)   Stakeholder consultation and dialogue – through continuing regional forums, a newsletter titled *Confluence,* and a website to maintain the WCD archive and more recent postings.
(2)   A work programme – of promoting dialogue, furthering the WCD information network, disseminating results, and facilitating exchange of ideas on good practice.
(3)   Follow-on processes – that to date include initiatives in South Africa, Pakistan, Lesotho, Poland, the United Kingdom and Germany (Toepfer, 2002).

Given the large-scale investments and consequences involved in impounding rivers, there is little doubt that proposed projects will receive continuing international attention. Whether ex-post evaluation of dams and reservoir effects advances in systematic and informative ways, and whether such evaluations and consultative processes explored by the WCD actually lead to better dams, more sustainable development, and improving livelihoods for humans and other species – these would seem to be key questions and challenges for the twenty-first century.

10

Domestic and industrial water management

This chapter appraises the range of methods employed to provide water for domestic and industrial water use and to dispose of their wastes. It considers the effects that each method has on the related ecosystem, and looks ahead toward improved means of coordinating domestic, industrial, and aquatic environmental management.

The focus is on intersections among domestic, industrial, and environmental water management, which may be outlined as follows:

(1)   environmental quality, protection, and treatment of source waters for domestic and industrial use;
(2)   environmental effects of domestic and industrial withdrawals (e.g., stream and aquifer depletion), taking into account the different effects of consumptive and non-consumptive uses;
(3)   environmental effects of domestic and industrial waste discharges (pollution);
(4)   environmental value of non-consumptive use, wastewater reuse, and harmonization of domestic, industrial, and environmental water management.

The first step in addressing these themes is to survey the current range of domestic and industrial water uses, followed by illustrative case studies in the USA and Africa.

Definitions and data problems

Although often grouped together under the heading of municipal and industrial water use, the types, scales, and effects of these

Table 10.1 *Estimated population supplied with safe drinking water and adequate sanitary facilities by country*

	Percentage of population with access to safe drinking water			Percentage with access to adequate sanitary facilities			
	Year	Total	Urban	Rural	Year	Total	Urban	Rural
USA	1984	100	100	100	1980	98	?	?
France	1983	98	–	–	1980	85	?	?
India	1983	54	80	47	1983	8	30	10
Tanzania	1984	52	85	47	1984	78	91	76
Kenya	1983	27	61	21	1983	44	75	39
Uganda	1983	16	45	12	1983	13	40	10

Source: Gleick, 2002.

non-agricultural uses vary enormously. Domestic water use includes rural as well as municipal users. It refers to uses most immediately associated with basic human needs for drinking, bathing, and washing – and associated household uses for irrigating gardens, washing vehicles, and providing for animals. Domestic water sources range from natural, sometimes ephemeral, water bodies to cisterns, dug wells, and drilled wells for individual households, to small water systems for villages and towns, and to metropolitan and regional water utilities that supply millions of urban, suburban, and industrial customers.

The prevailing conditions of domestic water use around the world are often described by government estimates of the populations believed to have access to safe drinking water and adequate sanitary facilities. A selection of such estimates for diverse countries is given in Table 10.1 and mapped in Figures 10.1 and 10.2.

These estimates, compiled by the World Health Organization from national reports, do not apply the same criteria for every nation. Country data are self-reported as percentages of urban and rural populations with access to what are defined by the reporting agency as safe water supplies and adequate sanitation services. Although guidance is provided to estimate these figures, sampling and aggregation of data remain crude (see Gleick, 1998b, 2000a for discussion of data limitations).

Definitions of "safety," "adequacy," and "access" vary across cities as well as countries (UNCHS, 1996a, 2001). Data are not comparable over time, there is no independent collection or verification of data quality, and the sample design for estimating national levels of access is unclear (Gleick, 1998b). Jonsson and Satterthwaite (2000) argue

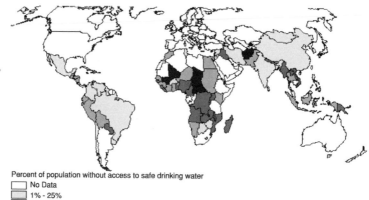

Percent of population without access to safe drinking water
- ☐ No Data
- ☐ 1% - 25%
- ☐ 26% - 50%
- ☐ 51% - 75%
- ■ 76% - 100%

Figure 10.1   Percentage of national populations without access to safe drinking water. From Gleick (1998b, p. 41).

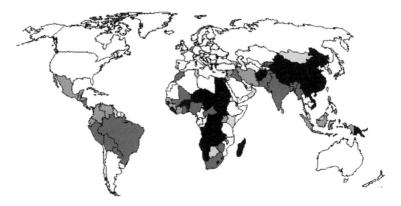

Percent of population without access to sanitation services, 1994
- ☐ No Data
- ☐ 1% - 25%
- ☐ 26% - 50%
- ☐ 51% - 75%
- ■ 76% - 100%

Figure 10.2   Percentage of national populations without access to adequate sanitation. From Gleick (1998b, p. 41).

that international data seriously, and perhaps increasingly, overestimate urban access to safe water supplies and sanitation.

A surprising number of countries, including the USA, report 100 percent access to safe water and sanitation. The judgment that 100 percent of a population has access to "safe drinking water" assumes all public and private facilities are effectively designed and are managed efficiently. A more detailed sample in the *American Housing Survey*

Table 10.2 *Inadequate water by social groups in the USA, 1999*

	Total	African-Americans	Hispanic	Elderly	Indian reservations[a]
Total sample	115 253	12 936	9041	21 423	–
Lack plumbing (%)	2.2	1.9	2.2	1.8	20.2
No toilet (%)	0.8	0.5	0.2	0.3	–
Unsafe water (%)	9.3	12.1	23.4	5.5	–

[a]US 1990 Decennial Census, 1995.
Sources: USHUD, 2000.

reports significant numbers of homes that lack indoor plumbing, safe water supplies, and basic sanitation (USHUD, 1999). For example, some 2.2 percent of households in the USA in 1999 lacked adequate plumbing (defined as lacking hot water, indoor bath, or indoor toilet). Of these, the majority were in rural areas, followed by central city areas, and then suburbs. More disturbingly, an estimated 9.3 percent of households reported that their water was unsafe to drink (USHUD, 2000). These problems also vary by region and socioeconomic group (Table 10.2). A disproportionate number of American Indians on reservations lack basic plumbing facilities. Reservation plumbing conditions in 1990 approximated those in the rest of the southwestern USA in 1950. The percentage of reported unsafe drinking water for the USA as a whole and for disadvantaged groups is also surprisingly high. And those data do not include homeless persons or temporary migrant worker housing, where water scarcity is often linked with environmental health and contamination problems.

Patterns and trends in US domestic water use

Estimates by the US Geological Survey of domestic freshwater consumption are subject to similar variations in accuracy as those in other parts of the world. Keeping these data problems in mind, it is still important to try to discern broad patterns and trends in domestic water use. The average daily residential use in public systems in the United States includes a wide range of indoor and outdoor uses (Table 10.3). Although the three largest uses are for bathing, toilets and lawn watering, and drinking water is one of the lowest daily uses, all uses are supplied with water treated to potable standards.

The Water Resources Council (1986) estimated that the average daily water withdrawal for a family of four in the United States was of the order of 325 liters per capita per day (lpcd). However, that average

Table 10.3 *Typical urban water use by a family of four in the USA (assuming no water delivery losses)*

Type of use	Daily use per family of four		
	Liters	Percent	Liters per capita
Drinking and kitchen	30	2%	7.6
Dishwasher (3 loads per day)	57	4%	14.2
Toilet (16 flushes)	363	28%	90.8
Bathing (4 baths or showers)	303	23%	75.7
Laundering (6 loads per week)	129	10%	32.2
Automobile washing (2 per month)	38	3%	9.5
Lawn watering and swimming pools (180 hours per year)	379	29%	94.6
Garbage disposal (1% of above)	11	1%	2.8
Total	1310	100%	327.4

Source: US Water Resources Council, 1975–2000 (figures converted to SI units).

Figure 10.3   Lavish use of water at a resort hotel in Las Vegas, Nevada, USA, a desert city.

masks variations ranging from lows of 90 lpcd in the Virgin Islands and 150 lpcd in Alaska to highs of 495 lpcd in Arizona and 575 lpcd in Florida. Grandiose water displays occur in arid zones, along with advances in residential water conservation and recycling in places like Las Vegas, Nevada (Figure 10.3).

Table 10.4 *Estimated domestic and industrial water use in the USA, 1995*

Population in millions = 267.1	Quantity used in 1995 (m³/day)	% change, 1990–95
Off-stream use		
Total withdrawals	520 000	−2
Public supply	151 000	4
Rural domestic, livestock.	33 700	13
Average domestic per capita use	0.3	−
Industrial		
Thermoelectric power use	719 000	−3
Other industrial use	110 000	−3
Source of water		
Ground		
Fresh	289 000	−4
Saline	4160	−9
Surface		
Fresh	999 000	2
Saline	226 000	−12
Reclaimed wastewater	3785	36
In-stream use		
Hydroelectric power	120 00 000	−4

Source: Solley *et al.*, 1998 (figures converted to SI units and rounded to three significant digits).

In the USA, public domestic water supplies are about 10 percent of total annual withdrawals and have increased 4 percent over the past five years (Table 10.4). Although rural domestic and livestock water uses are much smaller, in combination they have a higher per capita water use, and they increased during the 1990s. Wastewater reuse had the largest percentage increase, while saline surface-water and groundwater uses declined. Over the past half-century, it is interesting to observe that domestic water use has grown slowly but steadily (Figure 10.4).

A basic factor affecting domestic water use is the cost of construction, operation and maintenance. In 1984 the average cost in US dollars per 1000 gallons in 368 reporting utilities ranged from $0.28 in Delaware and $0.60 in Nebraska to $2.50 in Vermont (Van der Leeden, Table 5–18, pp. 326–327). In computing charges it is also important to recognize the proportion of water in the public system that is unaccounted for. This has ranged from roughly 5 percent to 15 percent over various regions in the USA (Grigg, 1988).

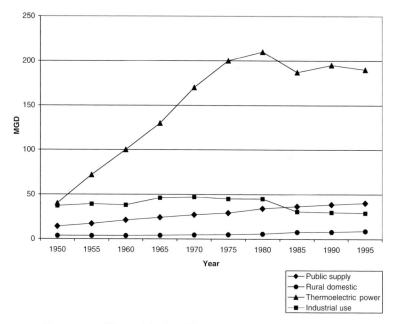

Figure 10.4   US municipal and industrial water-use trends, 1950–95.
From Solley *et al.* (1998).

Drawers of water: long-term East African case studies

Among the most detailed long-term studies of domestic water use to
date is a set of case studies conducted initially in the 1960s in East Africa
(White *et al.*, 1972). Although these case studies illustrate the difficulties
noted earlier of comparing data in different countries and local situations, they also shed new light on domestic water use. One concept that
gained attention from the *Drawers of Water* study was that of recognizing
the major ways in which domestic water supply is related to individual human health. Bradley classified the four principal routes though
which water use affects disease (Thompson and Cairncross, 2002). The
categories are (1) waterborne, e.g., typhoid fever, (2) water-washed, e.g.,
trachoma and shigella dysentery, (3) water-based, e.g., schistosomiasis
and guinea worm, and (4) water-related biting or breeding insects, e.g.,
Gambian sleeping sickness and onchocerciasis. Each class indicates an
appropriate type of intervention in water use that may be effective in
reducing the incidence of disease. The control of each disease type also
requires a different type of behavior related to water use.

In 1967 sites were selected to represent a range of environmental
conditions from semiarid to rain forest, demographic conditions from

agricultural villages to urban slums and high-income residences, and piped and unpiped water supply systems. Study methods consisted of intensive household observations and interviews. In 1998, thirty-three of these areas were resurveyed to understand how domestic water use had changed over the previous three decades. The 33 sites are not statistically valid samples of each nation, but are representative of different landscapes and settlement patterns. Of the population in the 33 areas, 40 percent were rural and 60 percent were urban. The urban sites included a high-income city residential area, a slum in the same city, and towns of various sizes. In 1998 roughly half of the selected households had piped water sources and half were unpiped and went outside the household daily for their water (Thompson *et al.*, 2001). Table 10.5 ranks the 33 settlements by rates of piped and unpiped water use in 1967, which facilitates comparison both with 1998 data and with different environmental and settlement conditions.

In 1967, average daily per capita water use varied from 4.4 liters for rural unpiped households to 243.9 liters for urban piped households (this upper value is comparable to average US water use). Interestingly, drinking water ran between 3 and 4 liters daily in most households while the water used for hygiene purposes such as bathing, washing, and toilet flushing varied on the average from 10 liters in many rural households to 40 liters and more in urban households – which accounts for a large proportion of the difference in water use among settlements.

In 1967, all but one piped water system provided much more water than all of the unpiped settlements. While there were differences in total consumption related to local conditions, the most powerful correlation was between mean per capita water use and the type of water delivery, in which the unpiped sites consistently had far less use than piped sites. In addition, per capita water use varied inversely with the density and directly with the income level of the population (see Table 10.5; Thompson *et al.*, 2001, p. 149).

However, in all three countries over the 30-year period of study the per capita daily use from piped supplies declined substantially while the per capita use from unpiped supplies increased markedly. This trend reflected in part the deterioration of many public water supplies that suffered from lack of proper maintenance and, in some cases, population growth and increased demand exceeding supply. It also reflects increasing volumes of water used for domestic animals, brewing drinks, house construction, watering crops, and other productive purposes by rural households. These increases have been facilitated by the greater availability of piped water to rural households. Although piped systems

Table 10.5 *Mean daily per capita domestic water use in 33 East African field sites, 1967 and 1998 (ranked by water use in 1967)*

Environmental type – community and density	Mean per capita use (liters)	
	1998	1967
Piped		
Kamull, Uganda — small town, mixed density	32.4	16.2
Nairobi, Kenya — urban, high density	41.6	26.3
Karuri, Kenya — small town, medium-low density	28.4	28.3
Dodoma, Tanzania — urban, medium-low to high density	62.1	72.1
Iganga, Uganda — small town, mixed density	34.2	78.7
Tororo, Uganda — urban, medium-high density	27.8	100.1
Moshi, Tanzania — urban, medium-low to high density	40.7	108.2
Dar es Salaam, Tanzania — urban, high density	64.4	153.5
Dar es Salaam, Tanzania — urban, medium-low density	*n.a.*	157.7
Dar es Salaam, Tanzania — urban, medium-high density	43.7	161.1
Nairobi, Kenya — urban, medium-high density	52.9	167.3
Tororo, Uganda — urban, low density	140.7	160.9
Nairobi, Kenya — urban, medium-low density	60.9	176.9
Dar es Salaam, Tanzania — urban, low density	164.3	243.9
Unpiped		
Mwisi, Uganda — rural, hilly, dense	9.1	4.4
Hoeys Bridge, Kenya — rural, commercial farming	45.3	6.0
Masii, Kenya — rural, hilly, cool	12.0	6.9
Mutwot, Kenya — rural, scattered settlement	20.5	7.7
Mkaa, Kenya — rural, hilly, dense	20.5	7.8
Mukaa, Kenya — rural, hilly, cool	9.3	8.2
Kasangati, Uganda — rural, wet, scattered	19.5	8.9
Karuri, Kenya — small town, medium-low density	22.3	9.3
Manyata, Kenya — rural, hilly, mixed farming	29.8	10.4
Kiambaa, Kenya — rural, dense	24.6	11.1
Mathaei, Kenya — urban, high density	29.8	11.4
Iganga, Uganda — rural, wet, scattered	15.5	12.7
Kipanga, Tanzania — rural, dry, very dispersed	16.6	12.7
Mulago, Uganda — urban, hilly, medium-high density	21.6	13.1
Moshi, Tanzania — urban, mixed density	19.3	13.3
Iganga, Uganda — urban, mixed	22.2	13.8
Kamuli, Uganda — urban, mixed	25.8	16.1
Alemi, Uganda — rural, dry, scattered	15.7	17.6
Dodoma, Tanzania — urban, mixed density	28.3	20.8

Source: Thompson *et al.*, 2001, pp. 109–110.

still deliver more water than unpiped systems, this could change in some areas in the decades ahead. These changes are only a few of those conditions revealed by detailed analysis of sample households as contrasted with summary national statistics.

International domestic water initiatives

To put these case studies in a broader international perspective, it is useful to trace the recent history and debates of domestic water use in international water forums. The first major international program emerged from the Mar del Plata Conference on Water in 1977, which helped launch the UN International Water Supply and Sanitation Decade (1980–90). Although the Decade did not achieve its aims of providing safe drinking water and adequate sanitation for all, it did help establish a knowledge base, multilateral programs, and nongovernmental organizations that continue to advance these aims. The International Conference on Water and Environment in Dublin in 1992, which prepared water-sector reports for the UN Conference on Environment and Development in Rio de Janeiro later that year, presented principles central to domestic water management (ICWE, 1992, p. 4):

(1)   Water is a finite and vulnerable resource, essential to sustain life, development and the environment.
(2)   Water development and management should be based on a participatory approach ... [in which] decisions are taken at the lowest appropriate level.
(3)   Women play a central role in the provision, management and safeguarding of water;
(4)   Water has an economic value in all its competing uses and should be recognized as an economic good ... Within this principle, it is vital to recognize first the basic right of all human beings to have access to clean water and sanitation at an affordable price.

Although the Dublin and Rio conferences helped maintain international concern about freshwater resources, they did not yield international programs comparable with the UN Decade.

To articulate a plan of action, the Second World Water Forum was held at The Hague in the Netherlands in 2000. It included a domestic water vision statement titled *A Shared Vision for Hygiene, Sanitation, and Water Supply, and A Framework for Mobilisation of Action* (Water Supply and Sanitation Collaborative Council, 1999). Instead of reproducing national data tables on the *percentages* of populations *with* access to water, this report produced graphs of the *numbers* of people *without* access to water and sanitation. Although subject to the reservations mentioned above, these graphs suggest that the number of people without safe drinking water increased in Africa but declined significantly in Asia and the Pacific and in the world overall between 1980 and 1994. However, the number of people without adequate sanitation appears to have increased worldwide between 1980 and 1994 to almost three billion. The report discussed problems with those data and went on to present a qualitative discussion of the issues. It made thirteen points ranging from the assertion of a human right to water (comparable to claims for a human right to housing) to increased emphasis on hygiene and sanitation, gender, and institutions (Boot and Cairncross, 1997; El-Katsha and White, 1989).

The disproportionate burden on poor women to haul water, wash food and clothes, and care for family members with water-related diseases has led to the mobilization of local, national and international water and gender programs (Halvorson, 2000). Women's organizations link water issues with health, food, and labor reforms. By 2000, the emphasis had expanded from improving women's traditional water and sanitation roles to "mainstreaming" gender considerations and empowering women in all water and related environmental programs.

The Second World Water Forum set targets for 2015 and 2025 and for improving monitoring strategies, as did subsequent conferences on sustainable development in Johannesburg in 2002 and Kyoto in 2003 (discussed in Chapter 2). In each case ministerial and non-governmental delegates questioned whether sufficient emphasis was being given to the priorities for "action" while at the same time disagreeing on the principles that should guide action, as evidenced in the three debates discussed below.

Minimum water needs and human rights

It has been argued for a long time in highly diverse ways and media that all human beings have "an inherent right to water in quantities and of a quality necessary to meet their basic needs" (Gleick, 2000a). Peter H. Gleick, a principal recent spokesperson for that right, has outlined its significance for human health and welfare, and its varying recognition at public levels over the years. He recommended that basic needs would be met at a minimum by the provision of 50 liters person per day for the following purposes (Gleick, 1996, pp. 487–503):

drinking water   5
sanitation service   20
bathing   15
food preparation   10
total   50

While water economists sought to treat water as an economic good as a way to increase investment in and access to water (e.g., through marginal cost pricing and privatization of water utilities), other water policy analysts and advocates advanced the concept of water as a "human right." Although the UN Committee on Economic, Cultural and Social Rights endorsed that view in 2002, it has yet to be shown what difference these legal norms can make for water and sanitation conditions in practice (UN Economic and Social Council, 2002).

From water supply to sanitation

A major problem in assessing the costs and benefits of supplying water for domestic use is assigning values to effects on human health among consumers. For a long time, water-related diseases were associated primarily with: (1) spread through water supply such as typhoid and infectious hepatitis; (2) lack of household water for personal hygiene; (3) spread through an aquatic invertebrate host, such as guinea worm; and (4) spread through insects depending upon water, such as onchocerciasis.

The classic initiation of this approach was in Snow's analysis of cholera cases in relation to water sources, and the consequent historic action to close down a public hydrant in London because of its role in infecting water (Snow, 1855). The emphasis was primarily upon the quality of public supply.

This view emphasizes the specific role of water. It does not stress the role of human behavior in methods of using or not using the available water. The broader problem was illustrated by the effects of the national Egyptian policy to require that every Egyptian village should be supplied with high-quality drinking water from public hydrants. The hydrants were installed by the Egyptian Department of Public Works, but a follow-up review of public health statistics showed that the incidence of typhoid and some other waterborne diseases had not declined significantly in those villages. As a result, studies were undertaken of households in such areas. Out of those and similar studies elsewhere there emerged an emphasis upon the importance of modifying household behavior so as to minimize disease transmission in the home. Thus, attention was directed to the training of children who by unsanitary practices in the home could transmit infections even though quality of water entering the household was excellent. There also was attention to various methods of counseling family members about cleanliness and incidence of disease transmission (El-Katsha and White, 1989). The lesson from the experience in Egypt and elsewhere is that it may be misleading to assume that the provision of water of good quality alone will eliminate water-related disease threats unless the affected households follow or are trained to follow practices that minimize disease transmission.

By the conclusion of the Third World Water Forum in Kyoto, Japan, in 2003 international agencies seemed poised to shift from the historic emphasis on water supply to environmental sanitation and health behavior.

Privatization, regulation and governance

Far less consensus has been achieved on political and economic dimensions of domestic water management. Protestors at the Second World Water Forum at The Hague focused on the trend toward privatization of water utilities in Europe and developing countries. Protests turned violent in Cochabamba, Bolivia, in April 2000. Case study research has yielded strikingly different findings and inferences (e.g., Barlow, 1999; Bauer, 1998; Baumann et al., 1998; Briscoe, 1997; Dinar and Subramaniam, 1997; Swyngedouw, 1995), leading some analysts to conclude that good governance and equitable pricing were more important than either the precise calculation of efficient prices or the presumed virtues of public, private, and community ownership (NRC, 2002). Conflicts over the industrial organization of municipal water supplies have occurred throughout history and reflect deeper struggles for good governance and economic justice.

Industrial water use

Domestic and industrial water use intersect in several important respects. Many public and private utilities are operated as industries, and water is sold as a commodity as well as a public service. For example, consumption of bottled water grew rapidly during the later part of the twentieth century. In the USA total sales, including non-sparkling, sparkling, and imported water, amounted to 1.382 billion gallons

(5.23 billion liters) in 1986, an annual consumption of about 5.7 gallons (21.6 liters) per capita. By 2000, this figure had increased to approximately 5 billion gallons (18.9 billion liters) (Beverage Marketing Corporation, 2000; Van der Leeden *et al.*, 1990, p. 339). In a number of high-income countries an interesting development of recent decades was the growth in purchase of bottled water by urban dwellers. This reflected a willingness to pay for the convenience and assured quality of drinking water even though bottled-water quality is not highly regulated. Discarded plastic water bottles are an increasingly prevalent solid-waste problem.

Although irrigation agriculture is also increasingly industrial, as are dams that produce hydropower for industrial development, the industrial water sector is more commonly associated with manufacturing and production processes. Interestingly, total off-stream industrial water use in the USA, the bulk of which is used for thermoelectric power production, and most of that in cooling processes, is more than four times the volume of domestic water use. Figure 10.4 indicates that industrial uses for manufacturing have actually declined with increased water recycling and reduced water demand, and that thermoelectric power uses, which increased sharply from 1950 to 1980, subsequently leveled off and slightly declined, again with technological improvements. In-stream hydropower use remains the single largest water use in the USA – if one does not count water left in the stream for ecosystem uses and services, as the US Geological Survey has not to date. Reclaimed wastewater use is increasing, especially in the industrial sectors, but in 1995 it still amounted to only 3800 m^3 per day, less than saline groundwater use.

Industries are classified in many ways, e.g., from extraction to consumption. Primary-production industries include farming, forestry, fishing and mining. Other industries process these raw materials and fabricate durable and non-durable goods. Distributive industries ship wholesale and retail goods, which are consumed, and ultimately treated by waste and recycling industries. The International Standard Industrial Classification (ISIC) system subdivides these uses into the following major categories (UN Statistics Division, 2003):

- Mining and quarrying
  - mining of coal and lignite; extraction of peat
  - extraction of crude petroleum and natural gas; service activities incidental to oil and gas extraction, excluding surveying

- mining of uranium and thorium ores
- mining of metal ores
- other mining and quarrying
- Manufacturing
  - manufacture of food products and beverages
  - manufacture of tobacco products
  - manufacture of textiles
  - manufacture of wearing apparel; dressing and dyeing of fur
  - tanning and dressing of leather; manufacture of luggage, hand-bags, saddlery, harness and footwear
  - manufacture of wood and of products of wood and cork, except furniture; manufacture of articles of straw and plaiting materials
  - manufacture of paper and paper products
  - publishing, printing and reproduction of recorded media
  - manufacture of coke, refined petroleum products and nuclear fuel
  - manufacture of chemicals and chemical products
  - manufacture of rubber and plastics products
  - manufacture of other non-metallic mineral products
  - manufacture of basic metals
  - manufacture of fabricated metal products, except machinery and equipment
  - manufacture of machinery and equipment
  - manufacture of office, accounting and computing machinery
  - manufacture of electrical machinery and apparatus
  - manufacture of radio, television and communication equipment and apparatus
  - manufacture of medical, precision and optical instruments, watches and clocks
  - manufacture of motor vehicles, trailers and semi-trailers
  - manufacture of other transport equipment
  - manufacture of furniture
  - recycling

Water use in these industries ranges from hydraulic extraction processes (e.g., quarrying, hydraulic mining and leaching, oil and gas extraction) to cleaning, processing, cooling, and waste disposal.

While water use and treatment data exist for individual industries by country, international data by industry are rare. Industrial water-treatment processes include cooling, ion exchange, coagulation, emulsion breaking, aeration, adsorption (Kemmer, 1998). Many finished products include water. All incorporate "virtual water," which is the amount of water required to produce them, which can be measured as imports and exports of water between producing and consuming regions (Allan, 1997).

Industrial water processes have undergone in recent years substantial technological change, including reuse and containment of wastewater streams, and industrial pretreatment before discharge to a public wastewater treatment plant. At the same time, some new industries such as semi-conductor production are contributing untreated toxic waste streams to urban sewers. It seems likely that future industrial invention and population growth will involve new types of industrial water use, new wastewater loading, and also new forms of wastewater treatment.

With this extraordinary variety of domestic and industrial uses – from rural to urban users, groundwater to surface water supplies, and production inputs to finished outputs – few broad generalizations would seem to apply. However, there are some typical combinations of quantity and quality of withdrawals that can help clarify our grasp of their environmental effects.

ENVIRONMENTAL EFFECTS OF DOMESTIC AND
INDUSTRIAL WITHDRAWALS

As indicated above, most self-supplied domestic and industrial uses involve withdrawals from a surface or ground water source. But before turning to those cases, it is important to recall the types of domestic and industrial uses that are either "in-stream" or "run-of-river." In-stream water uses range from simple bathing in a stream to booming water-related recreational industries associated with boating. Although simple drinking and bathing have few environmental impacts, water-front waste disposal and motorized water transport and recreation can pose serious water-quality problems on streams and lakes. Industrial waterways face more severe environmental threats from spills, accidents, warehousing of commodities along the waterfront, and waste disposal in a water body.

Most uses involve "withdrawals" of water, even if only by bucket from a stream, pond, or handpump. A key difference, for local environmental purposes, is whether those withdrawals are consumptive or non-consumptive.

Consumptive use refers to the evaporation or transpiration of water withdrawn from a stream. Although the water is subsequently available somewhere else in the world, it is no longer available to local or downstream users. Irrigation of crops or lawns has relatively high rates of consumptive use, while those for industrial use vary from negligible amounts for run-of-river hydropower production to 100 percent for hazardous chemical production processes.

In some texts, water polluted beyond any capacity for subsequent reuse is regarded as "consumed." For practical purposes, water diverted from one basin to another, is also deemed "consumed" from the source-basin perspective. However, these views confuse the prevailing definition of consumption as evapotranspiration.

Non-consumptive uses are therefore those that return, soon or later, by surface runoff, drainage, or subsurface return flows to the stream–aquifer system from which they were withdrawn. As mentioned above, domestic (and other animal) drinking water use is largely non-consumptive. However, as will be shown below, the environmental impacts of non-consumptive uses vary with a number of key variables:

- place of withdrawal, relative to existing flows
- place of use, relative to location of withdrawal
- duration of withdrawal
- timing, path, and location of return flows

In addition to the proportion that is evapotranspired these differences in amounts of withdrawals and return flows, the quality of withdrawals, their effects on water quality, and quality of return flows are key factors affecting environmental quality.

The quantity and quality of consumptive and non-consumptive withdrawals, and the environmental effects of those depletions, differ in a wide range of circumstances. For example, according to the volume of consumptive withdrawals the progressive depletions may differ greatly downstream and the contaminated return flows may be either reduced or concentrated. Consumptive withdrawals may lead, for example, to (1) urban river depletion and degradation in return flows downstream; and (2) seasonal depletions during peak-demand months. However, non-consumptive uses may also lead to increased return flows and base flows (e.g., in South Platte summer flows).

Gaps between water infrastructure and environmental management

Water and sanitation have often been viewed as "infrastructure and services" programs, while broader links with and implications for urban ecosystems are neglected. Urban withdrawals from streams and aquifers have long-term consequences for sustaining human benefits from natural hydrologic, aquatic, and riparian ecosystems. Even well-sewered cities can discharge untreated wastes into urban watercourses, polluting drinking, bathing, washing, and fishing waters.

It is encouraging that the Istanbul+5 *Guidelines for Country Reporting* address several water and sanitation indicators under the heading of "Environmental Management": indicator 13, water consumption; indicator 14, price of water; indicator 16, wastewater treated; along with urban population, transportation, air pollution, solid waste disposal, and natural hazards mitigation (UNCHS, 2003).

However, the relationships among these environmental indicators are not entirely clear. Some research has sought to link water-supply and sanitation variables to measures of "ecosystem services" and "ecosystem health," which are, in turn, related to economic and human health benefits (Costanza *et al.*, 1992). Other projects have employed concepts of "sustainability" or "carrying capacity" from environmental management to address issues in infrastructure planning (e.g., Joardar, 1998; McGranahan and Kjellen, 1997).

More immediately pertinent to the water and sanitation sector are emerging programs in "ecological sanitation" (Esrey *et al.*, 1998). Ecological sanitation employs biological methods of waste treatment, disposal, and reuse (e.g., wastewater lagoon and ponding systems) and seeks to link infrastructural development with environmental restoration (WHO, 1989). In Japan the UNEP International Environmental Technology Center is focusing on urban water supply in ways that reduce eutrophication in lakes (UNEP/IETC, 1999). Ecological sanitation encompasses broad linkages between water use, land use, wastewater management, and urban agriculture (Smit and Nasr, 1992). In a related vein, some organizations have sought to rediscover and adapt traditional water management systems to new urban and rural settlement situations. An outstanding example is the Centre for Science and Environment study titled *Dying Wisdom: Rise, Fall and Potential of India's Traditional Water Harvesting Systems* (Agarwal and Narain, 1997).

Urban environmental hazards have implications, often under-examined, for water supply and sanitation. UN disaster information briefs often cite disruptions of, and need for, emergency freshwater supplies and infrastructure restoration. The World Bank has recently sought to link project lending with disaster mitigation.

IDRC has launched a water demand management program for cities in North Africa and the Middle East (Brooks *et al.*, 1997; Rached *et al.*, 1996; cf. in Asia, Esrey *et al.*, 1998). It funds programs to manage demand and water system losses.

To be effective over the long term, these efforts must be linked with urban ecosystem processes, including those most closely related to water supply and sanitation. Cities should begin to monitor key ecological variables along waterfronts, river corridors, riparian habitats, wetlands, and floodplains. Urban riverfront restoration programs, which are increasingly promoted, e.g., on the Sabarmati River in Ahmedabad, India (Environmental Planning Collaborative, 1998) should include baseline measurement and monitoring to assess their actual, in contrast to, planned, environmental benefits.

It is useful to examine the relations of those environmental benefits and costs at the following locations: (1) the water source, (2) the place of use, and (3) downstream locations. Individual and collective choices are presumably influenced by the location as well as by type of environmental contamination.

Water quality and environmental protection

Unprecedented policy attention was directed toward water quality protection during the late twentieth century. It is important to remember that probably all societies have had norms protecting water against various types of pollution by humans and other animals. Similarly, all societies have valued what they regard as clean water for drinking and healthy water for therapeutic purposes, and have discounted what they regard as impure or poisonous waters. The ancient Greek theory of *miasma*, vapors emanating from wet surfaces believed to cause disease, persisted in much of the world through the eighteenth century, and in some places to the present day. And, indeed, stagnant water (from the Latin *stagnum* for pond) does provide habitat for the vectors of some disease like malaria, river blindness, and guinea worm. At the same time, all societies have used water for washing and waste disposal, assuming, to varying extents, that "dilution is the solution to pollution." They recognize that different water qualities are needed for different water uses. Generally speaking, societies strive to store water where and when it falls for drinking purposes and to successively reuse it for other domestic and manufacturing needs as it becomes less pure. Important exceptions include high-quality fossil groundwater for drinking purposes, and high-quality water needed for certain industrial purposes such as bottling and computer manufacturing.

This section focuses on emerging efforts to coordinate domestic and industrial water uses with environmental protection. In some cases, these efforts involve rediscovery of traditional technologies, such as dual domestic water supply systems that deliver high-quality drinking water to the tap and lower-quality water for other domestic uses, and separate domestic wastewater systems for sanitary, sullage, and stormwaters. Although increasingly common in some countries, such as Australia, the early principle of separating water supply and waste streams encounters public health, financial, and legal constraints elsewhere. In addition to this interior household example that has exterior environmental implications, five main themes stand out:

(1)   source-water protection (springs, wellheads, and watersheds);
(2)   water treatment for domestic and industrial use;
(3)   wastewater production and return flows;
(4)   water quality standards;
(5)   downstream disposal effects, treatment methods, and environmental remediation.

After examining these challenges, the chapter identifies innovative programs that strive to encompass most or all of them.

Source-water protection (springs, wellheads, municipal watersheds)

Although source-water protection has ancient origins in cults of sacred springs and prohibitions against pollution or poisoning of wells (a capital offense in some societies), local standards vary enormously from virtually no control in some headwaters and wellhead locations to continuous policing and monitoring (Figure 10.5). In some societies, running water is regarded as inherently clean. However, most societies now require some protection of municipal reservoirs. Some reservoirs are covered or fenced off against all human use, with violations punishable by fines. Other municipal reservoirs allow boating, fishing, and even motorized transport that discharge hydrocarbons and other wastes into the drinking water supply. The degree of headwaters protection varies from the reservoir at a minimum to its entire watershed upstream. In some areas of Nepal intensifying upstream grazing and cultivation increase sediment, nutrient, and animal waste loading to municipal water supplies. Stall-feeding animals and terracing reduce some of these impacts, but economic, demographic, and political pressures to increase headwaters uses are intense (Pereira, 1989).

Figure 10.5   Toxic mine drainage waters in holding pond near Leadville, Colorado, USA.

Over time, societies have established standards for potable water that range from color, taste, and odor to parts per trillion of toxic organic and inorganic compounds. Health concerns vary from communicable diarrheal diseases and parasites to carcinogenicity (cancer-causing) and mutagenicity (genetic defects) risks. Over time, there has been a convergence of drinking-water standards for inorganic, organic, radionuclide, and microbial contaminants across jurisdictions, though some variations remain (Table 10.6).

Each type of domestic water source has different natural water quality conditions and protection requirements and challenges. For example, wellhead protection poses difficulties because aquifer flow paths are difficult to measure: one often learns of an aquifer problem long after it occurs. Advances in hydrogeology and aquifer contaminant transfer have reduced these uncertainties and resulting rules of thumb about, for example, minimum distance between a well and a septic field. Watershed protection involves forestry regulations while groundwater source protection requires field crop regulations. In each case, potential sources of contamination must be identified, risks of their entering drinking-water supply estimated, uncertainties described, and contingency plans developed. Some common sources of domestic water contamination (USEPA, 2002b) include:

Table 10.6 *Selected contaminant regulations for drinking water by jurisdiction*

Contaminant	Maximum permitted level			
	USA (EPA)	Canada	WHO	EU
Inorganics				
Arsenic (mg/l)	0.05	0.025	0.05	0.05
Cadmium (mg/l)	0.005	0.005	0.005	0.005
Chromium (mg/l)	0.1	0.05	0.05	0.05
Fluoride (mg/l)	4.0	1.5	1.5	1.5
Organics				
Aldicarb (µg/l)	3	9	*n.a.*	*n.a.*
Lindane (µg/l)	0.2	4	3	*n.a.*
Toxaphene (µg/l)	3	*n.a.*	*n.a.*	*n.a.*
2,4-D (µg/l)	70	100	100	*n.a.*
Radium 226 (Bq/l)	0.19	1	*n.a.*	*n.a.*
Microbial coliforms (per 100 ml)	0	0	10	0

With the exception of the EPA standards, these figures are now dated. Even EPA has announced a change in its Arsenic standard to 0.01 mg/l effective 26 January 2006. The International Organization for Standardization has addressed a wide range of water quality testing methods and standards. Nevertheless, the figures illustrate a general conformity between Canada and the EU and different standards in both the USA and World Health Organization.
Sources: Gleick, 1993, 225–230; Cotruvo and Vogt, 1990; USEPA, 2003.

- storm-water runoff
- pet and wildlife waste
- septic systems
- agricultural fertilizer
- above-ground storage tanks
- underground storage tanks
- turfgrass and garden fertilizer application
- large-scale application of pesticides
- vehicle washing
- small-scale application of pesticides
- livestock, poultry, and horse waste
- sanitary sewer overflows and combined sewer overflows

While it is unlikely that a single community faces all of these potential contaminants, monitoring even a few of them carefully requires

substantial investment both in protecting existing supplies and in reducing treatment costs. In addition, new types of contamination, e.g.,
hormones in animal feed and pollen from transgenic species, that enter
the waste stream pose new measurement and regulatory challenges.

Increasing recognition of long-distance aerial transport and deposition of contaminants is one of the most challenging source-water
protection problems for the twenty-first century. An early attempt at
national and international regulation involved acid rain (weak concentrations of carbonic acid that contribute to the acidification of surface
and groundwaters in northern temperate and taiga regions). However,
wet and dry deposition of other chemicals and radionuclides (e.g.,
nitrogen from automobile exhaust) in formerly pristine headwaters
poses a jointly scientific, environmental quality, and transboundary
policy challenge.

Typical methods of domestic and industrial water treatment

Most small systems around the world have no water treatment. Thus, it
is not surprising that water-related disease is a chief cause of death for
children under five years old (Figure 10.6). Typical methods of treating
available drinking water supplies, from simple to complex technologies,
are:

- sedimentation – allowing solids to settle out in stilling basins and
  jars by gravity;
- aeration – through increased water movement to increase dissolved oxygen;
- filtration – passing water by gravity or under pressure through
  porous media (e.g., sand, charcoal, membranes) that trap coarse
  and fine particles;
- coagulation or flocculation to aggregate and remove small solids
  and colloids;
- ion exchange to remove cations such as calcium and magnesium;
- adsorption of organic compounds (e.g., on resins);
- disinfection with chorine or ozonation;
- fluoridation for dental health (or fluoride removal to prevent bone
  disease).

When combined together, these processes are referred to as advanced
wastewater treatment. Water treatment plants require relatively little
land and have high reliability under conditions of reliable energy supply and maintenance. In addition to their wastewater stream, which is

Figure 10.6   Turbid tap water in Karachi, Pakistan.

often returned directly to a natural water body, these processes yield biosolids that may have nutrient value as a soil amendment (Milwaukee sludge has been sold for decades as "Milorganite") but may also pose windborne health hazards, residual contaminant levels, and aesthetic problems for residents and soil ecosystems.

Where land is available, a less expensive less energy-intensive option is to use advanced ponding systems, which pass wastewater through a series of lagoons with different algal combinations that

Figure 10.7   Oil refinery plant that has point- and non-point-source discharge into Sand Creek and the South Platte River and their alluvial aquifers near Denver, Colorado, USA.

digest and/or absorb organic and inorganic pollutants. These plants have proven effective in warm climates, e.g., central and southern California, India, and Australia, where ponds do not freeze and where there is a relatively regular flow of wastewater through the system. They generally require less maintenance and energy input and can achieve secondary treatment standards. As with advanced wastewater treatment plants, advanced ponding systems require pretreatment of industrial wastes that kill the algae and bacteria that are vital to the treatment process.

Industrial water treatment shares some of the traits listed above but must usually deal with two additional problems (Figure 10.7). First, manufacturing processes often produce much higher concentrations of toxic pollutants than domestic systems, and these must be pretreated before wastewater can be sent to a public water treatment plant. This has led many industries to recycle their process water until it is unusable, then store it in membrane-lined evaporation ponds, which reduces the liquid fraction but leaves a highly concentrated solid waste. Increasing regulation of industrial waste disposal has led to reduced water demand and increased reuse and recycling in manufacturing processes.

A second common challenge in industrial water management involves water cooling processes. Increased water temperatures from coolant effluents alter stream and lake habitats, in generally adverse ways for native and endangered species, which has led to temperature regulation. An interesting twist on this problem occurs at large dams that release cold water from intakes below their reservoir surfaces, which is harmful to native warm-water species and has led to installation and experimentation with temperature control devices, e.g., at Flaming Gorge Dam on the Green River, a tributary of the Colorado.

Wastewater return flow management

The foregoing discussion of domestic and industrial uses indicates the varied sources of water pollution. Increased regulation in the late twentieth century led to a greater recognition of the different pathways of wastewater return flows and transport of contaminants. Four main types of water and pollutant paths may be distinguished:

(1) Point-source return flows are discharged from a place of use or treatment through a pipe or channel to a natural water body. The environmental impacts of untreated waste at the point of discharge can be visible and traumatic, but they are also relatively easy to measure, regulate, and physically control. Many regions of the world have made progress toward point-source pollution control, with two important exceptions: developing countries where urban wastewater is collected but not treated before being discharged into a river (e.g., Delhi and Agra on the Yamuna River in India); and transitional or economically declining countries that invested in advanced treatment facilities that are not maintained (e.g., countries of the former Soviet Union where wastewater treatment plants that lack chemicals, spare parts, and paid professional staff no longer operate). Although surface water bodies have some assimilative capacity (dilution), the complexity of pollutant transport and uptake in aquatic ecosystems is a major scientific and policy challenge.

(2) Non-point-source return flows can return to wetlands, lakes and streams through diffuse surface runoff. Storm events suspend pollutants deposited on roads, industrial work sites, and cultivated fields. Diffuse polluted runoff is more difficult to control than piped flows. Two common stormwater control practices can address or aggravate environmental quality problems. Construction of stormwater detention ponds and wetlands traps polluted water and sediment, preventing their direct discharge into surface water bodies and enhancing soil filtration and plant uptake. However, if the pollutants in these detention ponds contaminate plants and soils, aquatic and avian wildlife may suffer, as occurs

Figure 10.8   Open sewer subject to overflow in the Old City of Lahore, Pakistan.

at selenium-contaminated drainage sinks in the western USA. And if the pollutants migrate to underlying aquifers, the treatment problems become more difficult. A second treatment strategy involves stormwater collection in sewerage systems: if those stormwaters are discharged into a stream, as is common, they become a point-source pollution problem; if they are combined with sanitary wastewater, they increase the size and variability of wastewater flows, which can lead to combined sewer overflows that exceed treatment plant capacity and are bypassed directly to natural water bodies during severe storm events (Figures 10.8 and 10.9). Creative examples of non-point-source pollution control are discussed in several chapters, including sections of Chapter 5 on soil water management, Chapter 6 on constructed wetlands, and Chapter 8 on riparian buffers.

(3)   Non-point-source return flows seep into the soil, enter aquifers, and eventually return to a surface water body or the ocean. These domestic and industrial waste streams pose difficult scientific, technical, and policy problems. The physics and chemistry of contaminant transport in groundwater flows and residence times in aquifers are difficult to measure, monitor, and model. Remediation of contaminated groundwater and aquifer formations may involve water treatment, microbial technologies, or isolation of contaminated aquifer areas.

Figure 10.9   Water infrastructure and cultural heritage upgrading
project in Lahore, Pakistan, covers open sewers within the traditional
street network.

(4)   Finally, some wastes (e.g., brines) are injected by deep wells
      into rock strata that are believed to have little or no connec-
      tion to other uses. Deep-well injection of industrial wastewater
      requires permits and monitoring designed to reduce the risk of
      contaminant migration to other usable aquifers and water bod-
      ies. Injection wells are also used in coastal areas experiencing
      salt-water intrusion to create a pressure barrier that protects in-
      land municipal water supplies from increased salinity.

Managing water quality in natural water bodies

Ultimately, the goal is to harmonize water uses and waste disposal with the water quality in rivers, lakes, and aquifers; and by extension to maintain their quality for sustained ecosystem services, both for humans and other species. This goal entails managing the water quality in those natural water bodies, in conjunction with protecting and treating waters withdrawn for human use and returned as waste flows.

Water quality standards vary naturally with the type, location, and source waters of a stream, as discussed in Chapter 4. From an ecosystem services standpoint, they also vary with the types of uses anticipated for different reaches and areas of a water body. As those uses change over time, and standards of usability also change, water quality standards will also vary by place, time, and culture group.

Notwithstanding these variations, national water quality programs strive to identify minimum criteria and procedures for determining acceptable variations and, in addition, the pollutant loadings by specific sources and areas that will enable those standards to be met. In general, water quality standards include biological criteria (aquatic life), nutrient criteria (to reduce eutrophication), and sediment criteria (contaminated and uncontaminated) (USEPA, 1994). As of 1999, the US Environmental Protection Agency (USEPA) had published recommended water quality criteria for 157 pollutants in three categories: priority toxic pollutants, non-priority pollutants, pollutants with organoleptic effect (e.g., taste and odor).

To meet such standards, criteria must also be established for pollutant loading. Because pollution incidents are time-dependent, i.e., their effects depend upon concentrations over a given period of time, wastewater permits increasingly specify a time period, e.g., total maximum daily load, for an industrial or domestic user (USEPA, 1997). Again, the scientific and policy challenges of setting waste loads that will meet environmental water quality standards are difficult to calculate, finance, implement, and enforce even in wealthy areas. The affordability of new drinking water standards for simple compounds such as copper and lead, let alone the testing and treatment costs for more complex synthetic organic compounds, is beyond the reach of many small rural communities in the USA and most communities worldwide. Thus, a global perspective on domestic and industrial water management requires innovative, practicable approaches for managing environmental quality (Figures 10.10 and 10.11).

Figure 10.10   Protected uplands and intensive urbanization along the waterfront of Hong Kong, China.

SUMMATION OF INDIVIDUAL, COLLECTIVE AND ENVIRONMENTAL EFFECTS

This chapter and others have mentioned adaptation of low-cost traditional technologies for domestic and industrial use, such as rainwater harvesting and ecological sanitation. Coordination of urban, peri-urban, suburban and rural water uses to facilitate successive reuse of water from pristine supplies to increasingly degraded wastewaters – and to treat those wastes as "wealth in the wrong place" to be recaptured and reused as sources of nutrients or raw materials for other industrial processes – is one of the greatest institutional as much as technical or financial challenges of the twenty-first century.

Fortunately, the UN Commission on Human Settlements has begun compiling a Best Practices Database of municipal water management around the world, examples of which are listed in Table 10.7. Although some case studies are new and have yet to sustain themselves and prove they can adjust to natural and social variability and change, these case studies deserve continuing attention and ex-post evaluation of the sort described in Chapter 9 on impounded reservoirs. Detailed long-term monitoring has occurred in selected cases, such as the Orangi Pilot Project in Karachi, Pakistan (Hasan, 1993, 1997; Khan, 1994). While some peri-urban projects have succeeded admirably in improving

Figure 10.11   Interior housing block with outdoor clothes-washing in less wealthy area of Hong Kong, China.

sanitation, sewerage, and environmental conditions within squatter settlements, they need to go the next step to treat collected wastes before they are discharged into the nearby river and contaminate human and ecological habitats downstream.

Additionally, as globalization leads to industrialization in areas with limited regulatory capacity, new environmental products and

Table 10.7 *Water management examples from the UNCHS Best Practices Database, 1998*

Australia – Southwell Park Wastewater Recycling Pilot Scheme
Australia – Western Australia Sewerage and Wastewater Quality Program
Austria – Sewer construction/the Viennese Approach
Columbia – The Community as Drinking Water Provider in a Low Income Area
Egypt – National Public Scheme for Conservation of Drinking Water
Egypt – The Aqueduct Area Project: urban environmental management
Honduras – Empowering Poor Communities in Tegucigalpa: water supply
Japan – Fukuoka: Water Conservation Conscious City
Kenya – Maina Village Community Water and Sanitation Project
Kenya – Water for Work Project
Malawi – Piped Supplies for Small Communities in Malawi
Papua New Guinea – Building of Water Tank and House Using Indigenous Materials
Romania – New Technologies for the Water Treatment Plant in Slobozia
Senegal – Community Based Environmental Sanitation and Hygiene Project
Senegal – Women Run Waste Management and Recycling Programme
Spain – Navarra, Water and Waste Management
Spain – Zaragoza: A City Saving Water
Sudan – Rural Towns Water Supply Project in South Darfur State
Sudan – Upgrading of the Water Supply System in Nyala and El Geneina
Tanzania – The Health through Sanitation and Water (HESAWA) Programme
USA – Integrated Watershed Management: government and NGO partnership

Source: UNCHS, 1998.

processing methods are needed for both pollution prevention and waste recycling (McDonough and Braungart, 2002). The concrete industry, for example, is making innovative use of waste products, such as fly ash, in aggregate mixes. Earlier cases of recycling uranium tailings in concrete mixes underscore the need for caution, and a comprehensive environmental systems perspective.

11

Decision processes

INTRODUCTION

Water is managed in highly diverse ways by decisions made in local areas as well as in national capitals, and international river basin negotiations. This chapter reviews the various types of participants – individual and collective – in many of those decisions and their modes of interaction in deciding how water will be used or controlled. The future character of water management will be profoundly affected by the kinds of organization, scientific findings, and evaluative criteria that are employed in specific situations. The resulting modes of decision making will, in effect, strongly influence how the resources of water are used and how the related environment is affected.

VARIETIES OF DECISION MAKING

The most elementary decisions about water are made by individuals or corporations that draw upon or manage an available source for a single purpose without directly collaborating with others and without being subject to guidance or regulation by other individuals under prevailing social policy. Decisions become more complex when they start to involve collaboration with other managers, or when they are subject to some kind of influence by a public agency or other organization, affecting the criteria used in the decision process. According to the number and diversity of the other users and of social organizations, the complexity of the basic decisions varies enormously. The range in complexity of the decision process is thus from a single family as the sole user of one water source to a highly diverse population of individuals, corporations, and public agencies over an entire international river basin using and altering water in ways subject to standards and regulations set by a variety of public agencies in competing areas with differing standards of water quality use and cost sharing. Contrasting examples from around the world were described in more detail in Chapter 10. It is important to recognize that official reports on the proportion of the population served by public supply may describe a wide variety in quality of service.

A single, isolated farm family of two adults and three children in a part of eastern Kenya draws its water supply from a spring at an average distance of 160 m to which the mother and the eldest daughter walk with pots on their heads every day. The mother has chosen to use that particular spring after considering alternative sources. They have selected that spring rather than a somewhat nearer stream subject to seasonal fluctuation and crowding at that place. They carry a total of about 35 l each day, and there always is enough flow in the spring to supply them and the other families using it. Their cost is in (a) calories to transport the water and (b) time spent in either carrying or waiting at the source. They are not limited by law as to the amounts they can withdraw, and there is no public supervision of either the quantity or quality of their supply or of their disposal of household waste in the privy or on the ground around their farmstead.

At another extreme, a family of five living in a third-floor apartment in a city of the eastern or midwestern United States draws all its daily water supply of 1250 l from pipes in the building connected to a city-wide supply system operated by a private utility that is regulated by municipal ordinance and that draws from a nearby reservoir (Figure 11.1). They feel that they have choice only in the volume and timing of water they draw from the taps each day. The monetary unit cost is fixed. The city itself operates a sewer and waste-disposal system. The quality and cost of water supplied and of effluent from the sewage-treatment plant is subject to standards set by the State and Federal health agencies. In the extremely rare event that supply is interrupted the family has no emergency plan.

In between, a family in a low-income section of Nairobi, Kenya or Lahore, Pakistan has a choice of walking to a public standpipe at a distance of 100 m to carry 70 l each day, or of paying to have that amount delivered to its door by a private porter (Figure 11.2). The expenditure of the time and calories for carrying varies greatly with the time of day, and the fee to a porter also varies. The quality of water meets city standards. If the standpipe shuts down they can find another that is functioning.

The eastern Kenya family has to decide where to go for water and how much to draw daily, taking into account what it will cost

Figure 11.1 Apartments and office complexes along the Chicago River, Illinois, USA, served by water intake structures several kilometers offshore in Lake Michigan.

them in time and calories. The Nairobi family has to decide how much water to either carry or pay a porter to deliver. The eastern United States family has to decide how much water to use from the piped supply at the established rates. The rates it pays and the quality of water it uses are set by private and public agencies. Increasingly, it may consider the environmental effects of municipal water development

Figure 11.2   Peri-urban area of Lahore, Pakistan, served by wells, standpipes, and the Ravi River.

and conservation, along with water rates that may or may not reflect those impacts, when deciding how much water to use.

The decision process in drawing potable water for one family is relatively simple by comparison with the collective choices made by public agencies in a medium-sized river basin. There, all the domestic and industrial water users draw from supplies provided by municipal agencies subject to public decisions as to rates charged for supply and waste disposal, but also to policies affecting the supply and quality standards, the volumes of water that may be withdrawn from various sources, the volume of river flow that must be assured for navigation or other public purposes, the operation of dams to store water for electric power generation, and for flood management for the entire basin (Figure 11.3). Changes made in knowledge, criteria, or organization by any one of the agencies may have powerful effects upon quantity, quality, availability, and cost of water for individual users.

The complexity of planning and operation decisions for a populated basin is large under systems of powerful central governments but is more intricate where there are also significant private organizations, and it is even greater where more than one nation or state is involved. Some understanding of the complexities is suggested by the number and diversity of groups involved in the process of planning and execution of programs for further management of water supply and related resources for metropolitan New York City. The landmark

Figure 11.3   Laundry washers' (*dhobi*) settlement in an area with scarce water supplies, severe wastewater contamination, and flood hazards in Karachi, Pakistan.

1997 Memorandum of Agreement (MOA) governing the management of the watersheds supplying water for the New York metropolitan region included New York City, New York State, EPA, the Coalition of Watershed Towns, 40 watershed communities, and five conservation organizations. The MOA covers about 1000 pages and provisions for water quality monitoring, public health monitoring, water quality protection, land acquisition and planning, wastewater treatment upgrades, setbacks and buffers along reservoirs and tributaries, management to control non-point-source pollution, watershed partnership programs, dual approaches to design of new facilities, and cooperative investigations. The character and precise details of a plan for further management of the water and associated natural resources of the area would be influenced in significant ways by the policy positions of one or more of those groups.

In the literature about water resources it is common to find reference to the effects upon water management of prevailing public policies, and the possible consequences of changing those policies in various ways. Those changes may be as simple as setting the financial charges for sale of domestic water, or as complex as requiring that any action affecting water consumption or disposal be contingent upon satisfying a range of standards including legal rights to water supply or anticipated effects upon the quality of vegetation and fauna. In each of the decisions that must be made for the change in policy there is involved some consideration – direct or implied – of the decision process by the individuals or institutions involved.

The remainder of this chapter summarizes the major types of participants in water management around the world, how some of them make their decisions, and the types of criteria they use as reflected in an array of decision situations, including the broad number of environmental criteria that may apply to any management choice.

PARTICIPANTS IN THE PROCESS

The major classes of participants around the world in decisions as to water management range from individual users to large private and public enterprises and to public regulation agencies. The actual costs and benefits to be anticipated by a major project for water management usually are estimated by an engineering team that attempts to design a new project or the revision of an old project, taking into account the full array of probable impacts on social and environmental welfare as estimated by different participants using a variety of criteria for evaluation of probable costs and benefits. These often are incorporated in a comprehensive decision support system that seeks to combine diverse lines of action and accompanying criteria into a single, mutually consistent plan of action to either revise existing systems or undertake new programs for water management.

The number and variety of such plans of action at any one time is immense when account is taken of the number and type of participants and the range of criteria that they choose or are obliged to apply to decisions in evaluating possible future action. Those are summarized for a range of possible United States participants in management decisions in Table 11.1. The types of decisions and criteria may differ more widely in some other parts of the world.

In addition to the "basic right" to water for human consumption, three of the major issues relating to water management in many areas have to do with other rights to water (Gleick, 2000a, pp. 2–15). One relates to the right to withdraw and use water from specified sources. A second relates to the right to degrade the quality of water at a source. A third relates to the right to alter a natural environment by the withdrawal or degradation of a source. Increasingly, rights for in-stream flows are acquired for environmental protection and restoration. Each of these has important political, economic, and environmental implications, and they may be joined in some places (Figures 11.4 and 11.5).

Table 11.1 *Participants in and major types of water management decisions in the USA*

Participant	Type of decision	Selected criteria used
Domestic water consumer		
Self-supplied from un-regulated source	Carry and consume water	Convenience and cost in time and money
Self-supplied from approved source	Carry and consume water	Quality essential to health
Piped system – private	Purchase and consume water	Cost of purchase
Public supplier	Reliability and quality of supply	Minimum quality for health; liquidity of investment
Public health agency	Regulate minimum water standards for public source	Quality essential to health
Industrial water supply		
Self-supplied industry	Install supply	Cost and reliability
Piped system purchase	Purchase and consume	Cost of purchase
Self-managed disposal	Type of disposal	Cost of disposal
Sewered waste disposal	Type of disposal	Effects on public health
Public health agency	Minimum treatment standards	Effects on public health and ecosystem
Irrigation		
Self-supplied farmer	Install supply and distribution system	Cost and reliability; water right
Public water rights agency	Allocation of volume and timing of supply	Water right equity
Federal environmental agency – reservoir	Maintenance of natural system	Effect on ecosystem
Power production		
Mechanical run-of-river enterprise	Build weir and generating equipment	Cost and reliability; liquidity of investment
Electricity using storage enterprise	Build weir and generating and distribution equipment	Liquidity of investment; effect on ecosystem
Public water rights agency	Allocation of volume and timing of supply	Water right equity
Public water agency	Permission to alter channel	Benefit and costs of altering channel
Federal environmental agency	Maintenance of national or regional system	Effect on ecosystem

Figure 11.4   Homeless settlement along the South Platte River in Denver, Colorado, USA, faces water and sanitation decision-making problems comparable to those faced by poor urban residents in developing countries, but with additional harassment from public officials. There is at this time no human right to water in the USA.

Figure 11.5   Although unevenly recognized and implemented, there is a natural right to water for both humans and animals in Muslim societies.

In the western United States there developed after 1855 a complex body of State laws administered by State agencies that authorized the assignment to individual owners of the right to withdraw specified volumes of water from specified surface or ground sources over specified times (*Irwin* v. *Phillips*, 5 Cal. 140, 1855). An immense body of statutory and judicial law developed over the authority and administration of those water rights. Irrigation of agricultural land in the western States today cannot be practiced without ownership of a legal "property right" to the necessary water. While the details of water-right laws differ significantly among the states, the general principle is widely applied (Getches, 1996). Once granted to a qualified applicant in most states, a water right can be sold or transferred independently of the land for which it first was used for irrigation or other purposes (*Coffin* v. *Lefthand Ditch*, 6 Colo. 443, 1882).

Not all states or nation-states grant a property right in perpetuity. Many countries issue permits or licenses for water allocations, wastewater discharge, or water use (Burchi, 1994). Some licenses are limited to a fixed period of use, after which they must be renewed. If conditions, regulations or public values have changed the license may be modified or denied. These institutional dimensions of decision making, which vary over time and space, have played an important role in facilitating or constraining the incorporation of environmental protection in water use, as well as the overall harmonization of water management and environmental policy. The European Union passed a Water Framework Directive in 2000 that strives to integrate water quality and water use planning through a river-basin approach, pricing, and public participation (Chave, 2001; European Environment Agency, 2001). In addition, Muslim societies recognize, in varying ways and degrees, animals' "right" of access to water, comparable to recent arguments for a "human right" to water (Caponera, 1973; Faruqui *et al.*, 2001; Gleick, 2000a; Wescoat, 1995b).

In recent years the decision process in water management became more complicated and challenging for a combination of reasons that are reviewed in the preceding chapters. These are more than the continuing growth of human population in many sectors of the globe while the natural supply of fresh water has changed very little, important as that is. Social organization has been increasing in complexity and in its capacity to try to apply enlarged concepts of both human and environmental health. Scientific findings as to the intricacy and the fragility of those systems has mounted, while the number of technological options to both enhance and deteriorate the ecosystems also has enlarged. Socially acceptable criteria for judging the health of both human and environmental systems have been changing. Those and other changes affecting the decision process at local, national, and regional scales must be taken into account in assessing the global water outlook and ways of altering it.

The criteria for evaluating the effects of any measure to manage water are as diverse as the combination of responsible agencies and social organization involved, as noted in preceding chapters. For a long time in the United States there was unqualified use of the economic criteria early formulated for Federal agencies in the Flood Control Act of 1936. By the late 1960s there began to be legislation and executive orders that specified the need to take into account possible broader social costs of changes in water flow and of costs and benefits to ecosystem health (WRC, 1973). Other nations have responded differently in a variety of ways.

The social right to alter the natural environment by water management has been the most intricate and controversial criterion. It is applied in the decision process, if at all, quite differently from one region to another. Part of the difficulty is in the lack of sound scientific evidence of the precise environmental effects of a given management measure. Another part of the difficulty is in finding appropriate means of comparing the values and costs to various types of peoples in contrast to community costs and benefits. For example, it may be difficult to devise mutually agreeable methods of estimating the benefits of restoring salmon fishing and the benefits of improving river navigation.

Two instances of recent controversy are illuminating. The effects of a river discharge management program for rivers in part of the Columbia Basin in Washington State upon previous runs of salmon led to abandonment of several reservoirs that had been considered economically justified in the original analysis (H. John Heinz III Center for Science, Economics and Environment, 2002). Studies of the consequences of land drainage upon the diversity and health of native vegetation and fauna led to drastic curbs upon further drainage distribution in portions of the Florida Everglades (NRC, 2001).

The social right to degrade water quality, coupled with the obligation to restore that quality in some degree, varies greatly among different social and political groups. In many societies, such as those in parts of East Africa, there is no formal constraint upon what is done with waste from a household that carries its own supply of fresh water or collects it from the roof. In a nearby city, however, there may be public requirement that all liquid human waste be discharged into a sewer and that the community output be treated physically and chemically to a prescribed level of quality. Some communities discharge their raw, untreated waste into streams. Others, like several Shenandoah Valley communities, treat their waste by means that make it useful for crop irrigation without endangering human health (Sheaffer, 2000).

Of increasingly recognized importance in water planning are efforts to calculate the full social impacts of the proposed decision. There are well-established criteria for judging the economic feasibility of an irrigation water storage project in terms of the direct costs and benefits to the farmers using the water, but it may be far more difficult to assess the full social costs to people and environment of constructing the reservoir. As described by the World Commission on Dams, the social costs of displacing and relocating the population that had been living in selected reservoir areas may be very large. Large dams in China displaced at least ten million people between 1950 and 1990, and in India large dams displaced 16–38 million people in that period (WCD, 2000, p. 104). From a review of experience in selected basins, the World Commission on Dams concluded that for most areas the number of displaced people was under-counted, that they were not properly compensated or resettled, and that indigenous, low-income peoples and women were especially affected adversely. Its review shows that the true economic profitability of large dam projects remains elusive as the environmental and social costs of large dams were poorly accounted for in economic terms (WCD, 2000, pp. 129–130).

Taking a broad view of the world water picture, the minimum number of participants principally involved over the long run in decisions about the future course and character of water management may be very roughly estimated as shown in Table 11.2. These figures do not count the numbers of people, such as the persons forced to change their location, who are directly affected by the management project and the decisions made by others. The figures are for only the magnitude of numbers of people who may participate in a decision as to the design or operating policy of a water management system, and does not include individuals who simply use the product without being able to discriminate as to cost and quality. An irrigation farmer may determine how much water to apply to a given crop at a given time, while a city resident may buy household water at whatever price and quality is set by supplying and regulatory agencies.

Table 11.2 *Types and approximate numbers of participants in water management decision in the world*

Types of participants	Approximate number of participants
Individual households that satisfy domestic needs by directly bringing water into the household daily	billions
Individual farmers that apply their allocations of water in volumes and at times they may choose to the irrigation of their fields during each annual crop season	millions
Community and private water supply and distribution systems that serve billions of domestic households and industrial customers every day	millions
Irrigation districts that provide water to individual farmers annually	hundreds of thousands
Public and private hydroelectric power generation agencies	tens of thousands
Community and private sewage and waste disposal systems that treat and dispose of municipal and industrial waste	hundreds of thousands
National government agencies that set standards for the treatment of community domestic or industrial water supply and waste disposal	thousands
National government agencies that set standards for human alteration of supply and quality of water and for alteration of groundwater and wetlands	thousands

VARIETIES OF PROCESS

To better understand some of the problems involved in making decisions about water management and environmental quality it is helpful to outline a few of the more common varieties of decisions.

Engineering design

For many forms of management an initial and highly influential process is the preliminary design of specific engineering measures to help achieve the aims of management in a fashion that would be reliable in performance in the face of physical, biological, and social uncertainties

Figure 11.6 Engineering decision-making processes guided construction of Glen Canyon Dam on the Colorado River in the USA, and operations within the control room of the dam today.

(Figure 11.6). This often involves the specification of the hydrologic and hydraulic systems involved, and the quantity and quality of proposed measures – such as channels, levees, reservoirs, treatment plants, and operating schedules – to deal with them. This always requires some description of the criteria employed in the design and of the criteria to be employed in judging the certainty of performances. Simulation and stochastic methods may be required (Maass, 1962). A wide variety of analytic tools may be employed for programming (Cohon, 1978). The elements of uncertainty and risk always enter into any tentative design and may not always be quantified (Haimes *et al.*, 1994). The results of the engineering design often are presented for decision without specifying the extent of uncertainty and risk.

Economic valuation

In some plans for construction of an engineering project the prospective economic costs and benefits of the proposed measure may be presented without specific reference to the reliability or comprehensiveness of the measures used. In addition to some of the frequently employed measures of cost and benefits, there is a wide range of possible methods of estimating non-market costs and benefits, of using market mechanisms to estimate values, and of programming the management of demand (Baumann *et al.*, 1998). Often, a slight difference in the method

Figure 11.7   Socioeconomic decision-making processes have guided diarrhaeal disease control programs in Bangladesh.

of estimating costs and benefits can have a profound effect upon the preliminary choice of a possible engineering measure.

There has been dramatic growth in the economic analysis of environmental benefits and costs of water management options. From the early development of benefit–cost analysis as a means of rejecting financially infeasible (but sometimes politically favored) projects to more recent efforts to estimate the benefits for future generations and different species, research on economic valuation has made major theoretical, methodological, and practical contributions (Figures 11.7 and 11.8). Cameron (1999) has surveyed the literature on environmental valuation relevant to water resources under two broad headings: (1) types of environmental value; and (2) methods of valuation. Research on types of values ranges from direct water resources use (e.g., for recreational rafting, fishing, hiking, and viewing) to ecosystem benefits of biodiversity, endangered species protection, water quality, cultural heritage values associated with environmental protection, and what are sometimes called the "non-use values" of people at a distance who economically value environmental benefits that they may not physically experience. Economic valuation methods have expanded from the compilation of market costs and benefits to include non-market methods, such as hedonic pricing (the implicit value of environmental benefits in housing or labor markets), travel cost methods (the amount of time and

Figure 11.8 Economic decision processes are shaped by political processes in which water has symbolic as well as material significance as, for example, at the Bangladesh Parliament Building, Dhaka.

money spent to experience the environment), health cost methods (lost work days or years and medical costs), and contingent valuation (statistical surveys of willingness to pay for environmental benefits). More recent methods include "conjoint analysis," "stated preferences," and "choice experiments," which shed increasing light on the roles of information, communication, substitute environmental benefits, problems of double counting, and combining stated preference data with actual behavioral data (Cameron, 1999, pp. 210–212). Although in some ways controversial (e.g., monetization of values), these economic methods can be compared and contrasted with other methods of valuing the environmental benefits of water, e.g., in ethical, political, and aesthetic terms (Feldman, 1991; Litton *et al.*, 1974).

Environmental evaluation

The procedures for estimating environmental costs and benefits are even less refined and reliable than for traditional economic effects, but they have great and growing public salience (Figure 11.9). Although in the United States there were somewhat arbitrary standards for evaluation of certain measures such as wetland restoration, some of the methods are highly speculative while others are creatively insightful. Only at the end of the twentieth century, for example, did the Corps of Engineers launch highly systematic methods of estimating the social value of protecting a natural ecosystem in a floodplain (Stakhiv, 2002).

THE RANGE OF CHOICE IN DECISION MAKING

A basic element in the preparation of any evaluation of a proposal for a decision as to next steps in any water management is the range of choice involved in the proposal. This aspect may not be mentioned in the proposal but it may have a powerful influence on whatever action is taken. A proposal for additional supply of domestic water, for example, may not examine an alternative of reducing existing wasteful use. An irrigation project proposal may not consider the possible alternative of enhancing agriculture in the area by innovative improvements in dry farming. A plan to build flood protection works for a given stream reach may not appraise the costs and benefits of readjusting land use and structures to make them less vulnerable to damage. Recent research on the range of choice has in some cases shown how an effort to expand one set of alternatives (e.g., "reasonable and prudent" measures for endangered species habitat protection) is linked with a contraction of other options (e.g., species "jeopardy" decisions and "no action" alternatives) (Gosnell, 2001). Other studies have shown how difficult, yet common, it is to compare alternatives at different geographic scales of water

Figure 11.9   Environmental decision processes strive to estimate the
ecosystem services and inherent (i.e., aesthetic, biocentric, and
intergenerational) values of unique water courses such as the Black
Canyon of the Gunnison River in Colorado, USA.

management, e.g., comparing wastewater treatment plant options with
urban, watershed, and international wastewater policies (Michel, 2000).
The whole process of engineering and economic evaluation may be basically affected by the decision as to range and integration of choice to
be examined.

THE EXPANDING SCOPE OF DECISION MAKING

Integrated decision making with respect to all aspects of water management and its environmental impacts has long been a theoretical challenge but was slow to enter into practical operations of communities and national government agencies. Local watershed management groups in the United States, for example, began to be organized in the mid 1900s but were slow to exercise major influence upon decisions taken by Federal and State agencies. A review in 2002 of the experience with the then widespread watershed management groups recognized the problems encountered in integrated modeling, methods of evaluating social and environmental impacts, and effective methods of combining the work and techniques of diverse groups and agencies (Bosch, 2002). The roles of local stakeholders and different levels of government in research, planning, and execution varied greatly among the hundreds of watershed groups surveyed.

Some of the major problems encountered in decisions on water management are identified in the 2000 report of the World Commission on Dams, in which the Commission recommends a policy framework for future decisions about dam construction or maintenance (WCD, 2000, pp. xxxiv–xxxv). It proposed that future decisions take account of:

(1) gaining public acceptance of key decisions;
(2) exploring comprehensively all options;
(3) addressing the problems encountered by existing dams;
(4) protecting and restoring river basin ecosystems;
(5) recognizing entitlements that improve livelihoods and quality of life for affected people;
(6) ensuring public trust in dam sponsors meeting all commitments; and
(7) sharing water of transboundary rivers through directing contracting parties to constructive cooperation.

The same considerations apply to many other objects of water management. Final decisions need to be carefully taken with those considerations in mind, and in many instances the consequences of previous decisions need to be re-examined with broader criteria than those used in evaluating the prior action.

Integrative approaches

Previous chapters have given examples of where water and environmental decisions have been made independently of one another, with unanticipated consequences both for environmental quality and human water use. Each chapter has also examined responses that sought to harmonize specific aspects of water management and environmental policy – in different types of water bodies, such as lakes, rivers, and aquifers; and in different types of human action, such as agricultural, domestic, and industrial water use. In several places it is noted how these responses have sought to "integrate" previously separate water uses, management systems, and environmental impacts.

This final chapter reflects more broadly upon integrative approaches to water management and environmental policy, discusses three current examples in watershed management, adaptive environmental management, and global environmental change; and speculates on the prospects for further integration.

In so doing, it builds upon and draws together the findings from earlier chapters. It builds, for example, upon observations in the third chapter about the unfolding recognition of environmental effects of water use, by recalling where and how recognition has contributed to the development of integrative approaches, such as the progression from single purpose/single means to multiple purpose/multiple means water development. Historic experiments with integrated approaches include selected examples of watershed, metropolitan, river basin, and national planning.

The previous chapter on decision making examined how individual and collective processes of choice have addressed increasingly complex situations. It has been demonstrated that some emerging water and environmental problems are exceedingly complex. For example, Chapter 8 showed how impoundment of rivers disturbs hydrologic regimes, trapping sediments and warm waters upstream and eroding channels and decreasing temperatures downstream. These effects, along with other management interventions, accelerated the extinction of some native species and the invasion of other exotic fish and plants, such as salt cedar (*Tamarix* spp). While exotic phreatophytes consume more water and outcompete native riparian species, some of them also provide new habitat for endangered avian species, and stabilize river channel banks in hydrologically disturbed rivers in ways that native vegetation could not. Thus, attempts to remove exotic vegetation – by chaining, burning, and biological control – can threaten native bird habitats and riverbank erosion.

Proposals to change dam operations to provide for environmental management gained momentum in the 1990s only to be followed by energy shortages that led to economic and political pressure to increase hydropower production. Decommissioning of dams promised to integrate hydrologic and ecological processes, while reducing coordination among some human uses such as for water supply, flood management, and some types of recreation. It is sobering to recall that "integrated river basin development" provided the conceptual framework for building multi-purpose dams in many parts of the world that had adverse effects on riparian, aquatic, and local human communities.

Other chapters offered similar examples. Many water managers in the 1890s and 1930s hoped that reclamation of "wastelands" would harmonize the aspirations of small farmers with local natural resources and regional economic development – but this was at the cost of extensive wetland, riparian, and desert ecosystems. At the scale of the individual farm, lining irrigation ditches to improve physical efficiency may eliminate wetlands created by seepage waters. Transfer of water from agricultural to urban uses may lead to deficit irrigation and increase soil salinity in some remaining irrigated areas, or to wind erosion and revegetation problems in the case of dried-up lands. Some methods of promoting urban water conservation (e.g., by increasing water rates) could improve in-stream flows while decreasing water affordable to the urban poor.

In river channel management, water engineers planned flood control projects that entailed hydraulically coordinated modifications (i.e., levees, dikes, armoring, dredging and straightening), which destroyed riparian ecosystems and contributed to escalating flood damages. Even in the scientific decision-making arena, discussed in the previous chapter, water managers in the 1950s relied on the guidance of optimization models to make comprehensive river basin investments that failed to include the benefits of aquatic ecosystem services or costs of ecosystem degradation.

In each of these, there were occasional critical voices and consideration of alternative approaches and practices. For example, in the United States:

- In the nineteenth century, some criticized US Army Corps of Engineers projects in the upper Mississippi River that adversely affected the environment and Native American tribes (Merritt, 1984).
- In the twentieth century, Native American lawyers and supporters advanced tribal claims both for in-stream flows for fishing and for water rights allocations based on practicably irrigable acreage on their reservations.
- In the mid 1930s, proposals were made to zone against further land use occupation of specially hazardous floodplains proposed for protection by dams and levees in California.
- Following the severe power shortages in the early 1970s, there were policy proposals to adopt a zero energy growth scenario rather than to build more generating plants.
- In the wake of the 1993 floods on the upper Mississippi River, there was a shift in policy in some areas from structural protections to buy-outs and relocation of floodplain occupants.
- As a substitute for more urban wastewater treatment plants in the Shenandoah Valley, a method was adopted to aerate waste and use the effluent to irrigate farms and floodplains.

Are the critics always right? Probably not, but it is hard to know without continuing ex-post evaluation and monitoring. Ex-post evaluation of the High Aswan dam in Egypt has produced mixed findings, at odds with at least some criticisms (Abu Zeid and El Shibini, 1997; White, 1988b). Ex-post evaluation of the Columbia Basin Project in the northwestern USA reveals changing benefits, costs, and summary assessments over the past four decades (Macinko, 1963, 1975; Ortolano et al., 2000). Water fluoridation had strident critics, but it has dramatically decreased dental caries for most. Water chlorination contributed to dramatic reduction of waterborne disease in the early twentieth century, only to be followed by increasing concern about carcinogenic effects of disinfection by-products such as trihalomethanes (THMs) in humans and aquatic species.

Upon reflection, the complexity of individual and collective decision making about water, environmental, and human systems makes the achievement of integration difficult if not elusive. Partial achievements have been offset by adverse human and environmental impacts. That is why this chapter refers to "integrative" approaches, knowing that they must expand with new knowledge about the relations among water, environmental, and social systems. This chapter thus begins by revisiting the central themes of this book – conflict and harmony – as they shaped explicit historical attempts to achieve "integrated water management." It examines the changing aims, scope and logic of those efforts.

The chapter uses this perspective to assess in more detail three current integrative approaches – first, watershed management, which has a long and highly varied history with renewed vitality; second, adaptive environmental management, which operates at a larger scale with decision support systems and large databases but less well-tested concepts and methods; and third, water resources management in the context of global environmental change. The final section of the chapter, and of the book, raises questions about how these emerging integrative approaches might be harmonized with one another, and what further integrative approaches might be discovered and encouraged in the future.

AN HISTORICAL-GEOGRAPHIC PERSPECTIVE ON INTEGRATED MANAGEMENT

Modern concepts of integrated water and environmental management probably have ancient roots in practices of local resource use. Ellen Churchill Semple (1911) noted communities whose lands conformed with watershed boundaries, as in mountain environments of the Alps and Atlas mountains. In less well defined physiographic provinces, and many montane environments as well, human settlements and resource uses follow other geographic boundaries and ecological niches that cross river-basin boundaries. In both situations, age-old practices of co-operative local water and environmental management deserve greater attention than often occurs. Recent studies in the upper Indus River basin, for example, document water systems that involve local and long-distance water use coordinated by centuries-old conflict resolution methods over environmental as well as water resources impacts of development (Kreutzmann, 2000). Similarly, Lansing (1991) documents the efficacy of traditional Hindu temple water management in Indonesia for crop pest management as well as crop water requirements. At the same time, traditional systems should not be romanticized as inherently integrative. At best, they are integrative at the community level and coordinated at small regional scales. At worst, they may fail locally or regionally. Modern scientific systems developed in part to address larger-scale impacts and conflicts that could not be understood or resolved at the local community scale.

Scientific integration of water and related environmental management has relatively recent scientific origins compared with river channel hydraulics and engineering (Wescoat, 2000). The complex history of harmony and conflict between modern water and environmental sciences is well illustrated by developments in France over the past three- and-a-half centuries. Longstanding debates about the origins of springs led in seventeenth-century France to experimental studies of rainfall–runoff relations, which yielded scientific principles of watershed hydrology (Biswas, 1970). Eighteenth-century French geographers such as Philippe Buache regarded *bassins* as the primary physiographic units for research, both on the continents and in the oceans. While others sought to extend that scientific method to regional administration and planning, those efforts encountered some of the logical and political obstacles that persist to the present day (e.g., rejection of river basin governance proposals advocated by the Western Water Policy Review Advisory Commission, 1998).

French studies were institutionalized at the École des Ponts et Chausées, which has trained civil, topographical, and military engineers for almost three centuries, and influenced other nation's water engineering institutions, e.g., the US Army Corps of Engineers, (Shallat, 1994). The dual role of these engineers – preparing hydrographic surveys at a comprehensive basin scale and engineering plans for less comprehensive river channel works – helps explain approaches toward integrated water and environmental management in the nineteenth and twentieth centuries. While Joseph Nicollet prepared a hydrographic map of the entire upper Mississippi River basin, the US Army Corps of Engineers began its program of dredging, draining, and reclaiming floodplains through specific levees and river channel engineering. The unfavorable reception of proposals to use a river basin framework for managing settlement and resource use in the western USA was predictable.

Concurrently during the nineteenth century, but at a generally smaller watershed scale, urban commissions were established to survey, acquire, and protect watersheds that provided drinking water supplies.

Figure 12.1   In its early years the Tennessee Valley Authority (TVA) in the USA sought to combine land use planning, affordable planned housing, and comprehensive water resources management.

In the USA, the progressive conservation movement led urban sanitary commissions to form fragile coalitions with new scientific forestry organizations and irrigation organizations with the aim of coordinating timber management, its effects on watershed hydrology, erosion and sedimentation; and urban water management (Wescoat, 2000). These efforts were followed by comprehensive flood control efforts on a watershed and basin framework in the first decades of the twentieth century, e.g., by the Miami River Conservancy District. In the western USA, several basin development programs sought to link water resources development with land use planning, community planning, transportation, and some factors that would later be regarded as environmental impacts (USBR, 1941–47). Although inspiring for their foresight, they were not widely practiced nor did they encompass a full range of environmental variables.

Flooding, combined with expanding commercial interest in navigation and hydropower development, led to plans for "comprehensive" surveys and plans for use of navigable (i.e., public) waters. However, these plans were redirected toward problems of economic recovery, culminating in the Tennessee Valley Authority in the USA (Figure 12.1). Related experiments in Sri Lanka (Ceylon), Colombia, India and elsewhere, and major multilateral integrated river basin development programs, were undertaken in the United Nations family, beginning with its first conference on natural resources at Lake Success in 1948.

Concurrently, rural and urban agencies and their constituencies renewed the smaller-scale watershed tradition of integrative management in a document titled *Little Waters* (Person, 1936), with plans administered by the Soil Conservation Service and Rural Electrification Administration. State Planning Offices in states such as California and Michigan undertook their own "unified" watershed and water policy studies (California in 1915, Michigan in 1936). As in earlier eras, coordination of federal, state, and local river-basin and watershed planning efforts proved difficult.

The rise and fall of TVA and rural watershed planning in the USA and elsewhere, and of subsequent integrated river basin development efforts of the twentieth century, have received detailed attention (Creese, 1990; Wescoat, 2000; White, 1957, 1997) (Figure 12.2). In light of the diverse historical experiments regarded as "integrated," "comprehensive," or "unified," it seems useful to shift attention to examples of the frameworks that were developed to interpret and build upon these experiments.

INTERNATIONAL APPROACHES: FROM LAKE SUCCESS TO KYOTO, 1948–2003

At the international scale, the first United Nations conference on natural resources at Lake Success in 1948 gave special attention to river basin development (Figure 12.3). Complex river basin development also received support from United Nations development agencies that, along with the World Bank and bilateral development organizations, funded early planning and development programs in the Mekong, Damodar, Gal Oya, Indus, Helmand, Nile, Niger, Zambezi, Rhone, Plate, and Cauca basins – to name a few. Based upon these early experiences, and to guide and coordinate future planning efforts, the UN prepared a volume on *Integrated River Development* (United Nations, 1957). At about the same time, the central ideas in river basin development were summarized as including multiple purpose storage, basinwide scope, and comprehensive regional development (White *et al.*, 1958). Associated ideas that were passionately voiced but less fully realized included coordinating land and water management, and unified administration.

Environmental concerns rose soon after, especially in reservoirs associated with multiple-purpose dams. Again, UN organizations such

Figure 12.2   By the 1990s, TVA had shed many ancillary social and environmental programs to focus primarily on electric energy production and marketing.

as the Food and Agriculture Organization and UN Environment Programme sponsored studies of environmental and social impacts of reservoirs in Africa (see Chapter 9). A revised edition of *Integrated River Development* (White *et al.*, 1971) drew attention to some of these consequences, with the aim of integrating them into planning practice. By

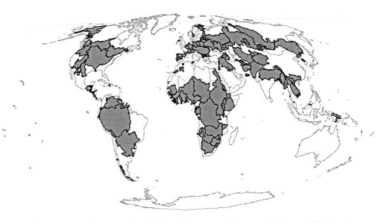

Figure 12.3   International river basins of the world. From Wolf *et al.* (1999).

the 1970s, the term "integrated river basin development" denoted the following trends:

(1)   shift from single-purpose single-means to multiple-purpose multiple-means;
(2)   shift from river channels to river basins;
(3)   shift toward large scale public infrastructure investment for regional economic development;
(4)   integration of water resources and land use planning;
(5)   unified basin administration;
(6)   negotiation of international and interstate agreements;
(7)   trend toward public involvement and behavioral sciences research in water and environmental planning.

Advances in mathematical hydrology, operations research, and computer engineering facilitated integration.

Another influential effort to combine scientific and technological advances with policy analysis (especially water resources economics and public administration) was the Harvard Water Project, launched in the 1950s (Maass, 1962). Some key components of this initiative were advances in:

(1)   statistical hydrology, including analysis of historical hydroclimatological records; generation of synthetic streamflows of hundreds of years with a range of statistical characteristics that could help anticipate plausible but unrecorded runoff scenarios; and advances in theorizing and testing statistical attributes and distributions of extreme flood and drought events;

(2)   esconomic optimization, which involved algorithms for minimizing net costs or maximizing net benefits of river-basin development alternatives that involve large numbers of water use production functions and constraints;

(3)   public administration, Maass's own field of expertise, which recognized the importance of bureaucratic organization, rationality, behavior, and reform in water resources management, either as preconditions for or as constraints on optimization of water resources systems;

(4)   computer models, which incorporated each of these hydrologic, economic, and administrative variables, to varying degrees, but gave limited initial emphasis to the environmental values and benefits of water resources; these were initially treated as regulatory constraints rather than objectives or benefits in their own right.

Each of these advances continued to develop during the late twentieth century, to the point where specialized fields of statistical hydrology, water resources economics, water policy analysis, and water systems analysis were recognized in their respective disciplines. Statistical hydrologists developed mathematical approaches to risk, uncertainty, and spatial scale. Water resources economists gave increased attention to non-market valuation of environmental benefits using hedonic pricing, contingent valuation, and travel cost methods (Cameron, 1999; Howe, 1997). Policy analysts shed light on power relations in government, social movements, legal disputes, and policy formulation. And a new technology of decision support systems, designed to use and provide real-time data and evaluate "what if" scenarios, was developed to assist (rather than optimize) water systems from the scale of individual structures on an hourly time scale to complex river basin systems on long-term planning time scales.

Full integration of environmental and water resources management in the United States proved elusive. An early attempt was made in the 1970s with the *Principles and Standards for Planning Water and Related Land Resources* (WRC, 1973), which provided for four "accounts" or criteria for evaluating federal actions:

(1)   National Economic Development (NED), the main criterion;

(2)   Regional Economic Development (RED), only to be employed in special cases of underdeveloped regions;

(3)   Environmental Assessment (EA), to be employed on every project but in a more descriptive or qualitative way than the economic analysis;

(4)   Other Social Effects (OSE), ranging from demographic to cultural impacts, which were also to be evaluated independently of the others.

This multiple-criteria approach was applied at the national, river basin, and project scales, up until its repeal for largely political reasons in 1983.

However, progress along these lines resumed at the international scale during the 1990s and beyond (Jacobs, 1995). The United Nations sponsored an International Conference on Water and Environment in Dublin, which helped define the freshwater section of Agenda 21 at the UN Conference on Environment and Development (UNCED, 1992) at Rio de Janeiro (ICWE, 1992). Integrated water planning was a major theme in the Dublin conference and statement. Progress toward Agenda 21 was reviewed in Johannesburg in 2002, both in a document submitted by the Prince of Orange (2002) and in a parallel conference called the "Waterdome." The former listed seven challenges that collectively constitute a crisis. The Food and Agriculture Organization prepared a series of reports on integrating land and water management that incorporated environmental protection (FAO, 1995a, 1995b). The Stockholm International Water Institute launched an annual world water conference devoted to water management, which includes science, policy, and children's water programs.

These initiatives led to the second and third World Water Forums in The Hague and Japan and to a written *World Water Vision* (Cosgrove and Rijsberman, 2000). While some of the most heated debates of those meetings involved social issues, such as privatization of water utilities, gender equity, and arguments for a human right to water, several of the World Water Vision preparatory documents focused on environmental management. Privatization and pricing of water infrastructure and service has many potential links with environmental quality, including different levels of water quality for different customer groups and ecosystems (Barlow, 1999; Bauer, 1998; Briscoe, 1997; Dinar and Subramaniam, 1997; Swyngedouw, 1995). Interestingly, the World Water Vision addresses environmental issues under two broad headings: Water for Nature and Water in Rivers. The first of these reports emphasized the need for protecting wetlands, lakes, and wildlife habitat while the second focused on riparian ecosystems. The third World Water Forum in Japan in 2003 also featured environmental concerns. It seems fair to state that while consensus is emerging about some goals and strategies it seems more integrative in social than environmental terms. Social integration is evidenced in increasing commitments to inclusivity, transparency, and shared governance, which are prerequisites for environmental as well as social benefits in international water programs.

A promising example is under way in the *Dialogue on Water, Food and Environment*, founded by ten international development organizations and convened by the International Water Management Institute in Sri Lanka to help bridge the gap between agricultural and environmental water management programs (Galbraith *et al.*, 2001; IWMI, 2001). The *Dialogue* entails three main activities (IWMI, 2001):

(1) A true cross-sectoral dialogue process among the stakeholders, primarily at national and local levels, that is open, clear, transparent, inclusive, and solution-oriented. A large number of national-level dialogues or roundtables would form the heart of the dialogue. River-basin and local-level dialogues would complement these to exchange information and address issues affecting users directly. Special efforts would be made to connect to the local level, where the key challenge is to involve the real water users – the man or the woman "at the pump."

(2) An enhanced knowledge base to feed the dialogue and establish credible and authoritative knowledge accepted by both agricultural and environmental constituencies. The knowledge base would focus on achieving food and environmental security and on the impacts of past development as well as on evaluation of options for future development. It would focus on creating and implementing linkages and interactions among the ongoing and new key activities that fit the overall framework (but are funded and managed independently).

(3) Networking for local- and basin-level action-oriented projects focused on testing and evaluating innovative approaches that enhance sustainable water security for agriculture and the environment. This would essentially be a platform for information exchange leading to identification of "best practices."

The commitment to developing a knowledge base to guide decisions is yet another reminder of the importance of conducting detailed ex-post evaluations and developing explicit strategies and policies for actually using the information compiled.

Concurrent with these water management initiatives, the United Nations International Law Commission drafted a Convention on the Law of the Non-Navigational Uses of International Watercourses that

was passed by the General Assembly after two decades of deliber-
ation (United Nations, 1997). Its application to "watercourses" was
a compromise between customary river channel treaties and more comprehensive river basin agreements, which bears comparison with "prob-
lemshed" approaches that combine watercourse, river basin, and trans-
basin contexts for planning (Michel, 2000; Weatherford, 2000). Although
the Convention does not focus on environmental issues or agreements,
as such, it does emphasize joint resource planning, data sharing, and
mutual obligations of riparian states (Wescoat, 1995c).

What is less clear about these initiatives is how well they have
performed over the years in environmental and social terms. Detailed
ex-post evaluation of integrated water management programs, as with
other types of water projects, is rarely undertaken. It is also challenging as it entails multiple purposes and multiple means of water management and cumulative impacts of development. An "integrated" ex-
post evaluation examines the linkages among environmental, socioeconomic, and institutional impacts. In addition to integration, ex-post
evaluations should also strive to be comprehensive, long-term, cumulative, and adaptive (Wescoat and Halvorson, 2000). Although relatively
few studies meet these criteria, several river-basin development programs, such as the Tennessee Valley Authority, Aswan High Dam, and
Columbia Basin Project have received detailed examination. One recent
study called for an international program of designing, monitoring,
archiving, analyzing, and applying the results of ex-post evaluation both
to advance specific types of water projects and to contribute towards
greater integration of water and environmental management (Wescoat
and Halvorson, 2000). Three examples of where progress towards these
ends is occurring are discussed below.

THREE EXAMPLES OF INTEGRATION: WATERSHED MANAGEMENT, ADAPTIVE ENVIRONMENTAL MANAGEMENT & GLOBAL ENVIRONMENTAL MANAGEMENT

The foregoing discussion indicates a diversity of approaches to integrating water and environmental management, both historically and geographically. At the start of the twenty-first century, three movements
seemed particularly promising. Although by no means new, watershed
management, adaptive management, and water resources management
in the context of global environmental change seem to have renewed
energy.

(1) Watershed movements and management

By some accounts, modern watershed management dates to the seventeenth century when French scientists discovered that the volume of precipitation over small catchments was more than sufficient to account for discharge from the catchment, and that land cover and land use in the catchment affected the timing and volume of that discharge (Biswas, 1970). Since that time, there have been many efforts to integrate the control of river channels with their headwaters and land uses. The 1990s witnessed rapid expansion of local civic and governmental watershed initiatives both in the USA and internationally.

Local watershed movements in the United States

Interestingly, a significant proportion of recent watershed movements in the USA arise from grassroots concerns about water supply, water quality, local landscape identity, and related issues. To be sure, some of these movements stemmed from crises, such as pollutant spills, or problems of complying with federal environmental regulations, but many of them had local origins. School teachers sought a local laboratory for their science classes; environmentalists sought a clearly discernable context for local protection initiatives; and local leaders became interested in local approaches to sustainable and healthy community development.

These varied local origins enabled "100 flowers to bloom," as some groups formed discussion groups, others created rich websites of local information and others organized restoration projects (e.g., Boulder Creek Watershed Initiative, 2003; Boulder Area Sustainability Information Network, 2003). School groups created electronic and paper atlases, databases, and websites. Table 12.1 indicates the wealth of information compiled.

These movements grew so rapidly that some local river protection groups, riparian habitat restoration groups, and urban environmental groups became members of the new watershed coalitions. As the number of coalitions proliferated, consortia were formed at the state level (e.g., Colorado Watershed Assembly, Colorado Watershed Network, Watershed Management Council California, etc.). Some of these organizations have dozens of members, others hundreds. National databases, which are clearly incomplete, list thousands of members.

It is still an open question what these local organizations and consortia can and will achieve. Skeptics fear they may lose momentum

Table 12.1 *Examples of data compiled by a community watershed organization – Boulder Creek Watershed, Boulder, Colorado, USA*

Natural systems
  Weather and climate
  Streamflow
  Water quality

Waterworks
  Drinking water
  Waste water
  Hydropower

Close to home
  Making a difference
  Personal actions
  Public policy
  BASIN quiz

About BASIN
  History of BASIN project
  Invitation for participation
  Timeline of BASIN project

Watershed
  Boulder Creek and tributaries
  Flash flood data and maps
  Neighborhoods and school

History
  History of water development
  Timeline and origin of local names

Gallery
  Historic photographs from the Denver Public Library
  Local artists
  Maps and visualizations

Learning
  BASIN Learning and Service Community

BASIN news
  Local and global water and environment news
  BASIN project updates

BASIN recreation
  Information, ethics and impact

BASIN discussion forum
  Online discussion of issues and concerns relating to the
    Boulder area community

Sources: Boulder Creek Watershed Initiative, 2003; Boulder Area Sustainability Information Network, 2003.

or lack sufficient resources to achieve and sustain tangible environmental benefits, along with their facilitation of civil communication (Kenney, 1997). Numerous practical guides have been published to help groups benefit from experience and avoid pitfalls (Western Governors' Association, 1997). For that reason, some argue that government is an essential partner (Natural Resources Law Center, 2000).

United States government watershed management programs

Interestingly, with a few important exceptions, state governments have been less involved in watershed management programs than the federal agencies. Some federal programs date back almost a century, e.g., to watershed soil-conservation programs, while others have followed the most recent wave of public interest. Among federal programs, two agencies stand out. The USDA Natural Resources Conservation Service, formerly the Soil Conservation Service, provided cost sharing and technical assistance for land-use practices that would reduce erosion, sedimentation, and rural flooding. Their projects included small dams, tillage practices, fallowing and rotation practices, vegetated swales, and other rural watershed land use management (NRCS, 1998; see also US watershed websites listed in the appendix). Given the age of some of these facilities, NRCS has given increasing attention to maintenance and safety (e.g., NRCS, 2000).

The USEPA, by comparison, was created more recently with a primary concern for water quality. It has funded limited watershed area water quality plans; non-point-source pollution control programs and, more recently, regulatory establishment of total maximum daily loads of selected pollutants. While EPA's regulation of non-point-source pollution remains relatively weak, the electronic tools it has developed to monitor and assess watershed conditions and overall health are impressive, including Surf Your Watershed and the Index of Watershed Indicators (details in the appendix). Like NRCS, it has also developed educational programs for students and practitioners (e.g., the Watershed Academy). In hundreds of drainage basins around the nation, networks of observations and measurements were established by local groups that reported and communicated their findings to local and state groups.

As an increasing number of agencies become involved in supporting, collaborating with, or mandating watershed management, the federal government has been moving toward coordination at its own level. The Clean Water Action program (2000) strives to define a "unified federal policy for a watershed approach to federal land and resource management." It has also organized an Interagency Watershed Training Cooperative to help administer and coordinate federal watershed management programs.

International watershed programs

Less well known in the USA are the many and varied watershed initiatives in other parts of the world (Mitchell, 1990). For decades, the UN Food and Agriculture Organization and other development agencies have promoted watershed management in tropical rural areas, for example, in Southeast Asia (Easter *et al.*, 1986) and eastern Africa (Pereira, 1989). Another body of work focused on mountain watershed management in the Himalayan and Andean regions (Bochet, 1986). These efforts of development organizations have been so numerous, and evaluations of their effectiveness so extensive, that a World Bank technical study (Doolette and Magrath, 1990) assessed the relative efficacy of different watershed management techniques ranging from grazing limitations and feeding alternatives to cultivation techniques (Table 12.2). While these variables differ from those associated with the community and EPA watershed programs, they bear comparison with those of other national agricultural agencies (e.g., the NRCS).

By the 1990s, watershed management in Asia had shifted from its emphasis on physical interventions to participatory approaches, institution-building, and institutional coordination – all of which had limited the success of earlier efforts (FAO, 1993, 1996a, 1996b; Ostiani and Patrizio, 1996; Sharma, 1995, 1996; Sharma and Wagley, 1996a, 1996b) (Table 12.3). Once again, monitoring and ex-post evaluation has proven a weak link (Becerra, 1995).

It is important to underscore that different social groups and individuals within a community may participate in different ways, such that a community has a participatory "profile" rather than a single "type." Participation of women, indigenous tribes, and non-agricultural-occupation groups in the benefits of watershed management has increasing salience in international programs (Farrington *et al.*, 1999, pp. 118–158).

But, according to some, the flaws in international watershed management programs are deeper. While promising on paper, or in principle, the obstacles to truly inclusive participation across multi-ethnic and socioeconomic boundaries are only rarely overcome and require long-term sustained political as well as economic and technological

Table 12.2 *Types and measures of watershed management in Asia*

Problems
Loss of productivity
  reduced infiltration and
    moisture-holding capacity
  reduced topsoil depth
  soil surface impairment
Increased sedimentation
  on farmlands
  of aquatic habitat
Flooding
Decreased low flows

Actions
On-farm cropland
  contour farming
  vegetative contouring
  furrowing, ridging
  tillage practices
  vegetative cover
  grass cover
  agroforestry
  terracing
  land leveling
Non-arable land
  vegetative barriers
  earth/rock barriers
  reduced grazing,
  stall feeding
  area closure
  pasture improvement
  buffer zones
  trail and road treatments
Drainage lines
  gully control
  check dams; silt traps
  diversion drains
  vegetated swales
  stream bank protection

(*cont.*)

Table 12.2 (*cont.*)

Off-site treatments
  Drainage lines (as above)
  Compacted areas
  Settlement planning

Expected Benefits
Soil moisture
Surface runoff
Reduced erosion
Reduced sedimentation
Increased yield
Increased productivity

Source: Doolette and
  Magrath, 1990, pp. 36–39.

Table 12.3 *Participatory watershed management in Asia*

Aims and benefits of participatory management
Help form and strengthen farmers' organization networks for watershed
  management at village, district, and national levels
Facilitate exchange of experiences at all levels, i.e., farmers, extentionists,
  educators, as well as technicians and professionals within a member
  country and in the region
Facilitate exchange of information between member countries through
  regional/national workshops and training/seminars and dissemination of
  literature
Strengthen a movement of the government, non-government, people's or
  farmers' organizations for sustainable natural resource management of
  the fragile watersheds in the Asian region
Publish a quarterly regional newsletter of Asian WATMANET to strengthen
  people's participation in watershed management and fill the gap in
  participatory watershed management literature by publishing other field
  documents and training aids

Typology of participation
Passive participation (e.g., meeting attendance)
Information giving (in response to questions)
Consultation
Material resource contributions (e.g., labor, cash)
Functional group participation (e.g., group formation)
Interactive participation (e.g., joint analysis)
Self-mobilization (independent of external organizations)

Sources: Sharma, 1995; Farrington *et al.*, 1999, p. 5.

intervention (Farrington *et al.*, 1999). Some observers note the geographic clustering of "successes" near experiment stations and accessible roads while poor remote areas are neglected, and still others underscore the uneven distribution of watershed management program benefits. Each of these problems is likely more widespread than in the region where it has been observed, and much could be gained from detailed comparison of successes and problems in the new generation of watershed management experiments around the world.

(2) Adaptive management of water and environmental systems

At a larger scale of complex regional ecosystems, other than river basins, another set of integrative experiments is under way, under the rubric of Adaptive Environmental Assessment and Management or "adaptive management" for short. Adaptive management originated in work at the International Institute for Applied Systems Analysis (Holling, 1978; Walters, 1986) to address environmental problems in regional ecosystems that are so large and complex that they cannot be reliably modeled in laboratories or on computer systems. In some complex regional ecosystems, modeling of existing management practices is possible, but alternative management practices lie beyond the boundaries of the model.

Adaptive management encourages quasi-experimental "learning by doing" (Walters and Holling, 1990). This approach involves detailed documentation of benchmark conditions and monitoring of ecosystem changes; it also involves willingness to undertake significant management adjustments as "experiments," monitoring their impacts and altering the experiment in ways that are more flexible and yet also more scientifically based than current environmental policies allow. Recent theoretical and methodological works include Anderson (1998), Clark and Dickson (2001), Gunderson (1999), Gunderson *et al.* (1995), Haney and Power (1996), Iles (1996), Johnson (1999), Lee (1999), Sit and Taylor (1998), Walters (1997).

Adaptive management in North America

Adaptive management experiments were initiated in forest and aquatic ecosystems of British Columbia and Nova Scotia in the 1980s, followed by comparable efforts in the Columbia River basin (Lee, 1993).

Based on these early experiences, a second round of experiments gave greater emphasis to participatory approaches, including

Figure 12.4   Researchers investigate the effects of experimental flood releases and flow regimes downstream of Glen Canyon Dam on the Colorado River, USA.

stakeholder decision-making, and to the social learning that can occur as new data are produced and new experiments devised (Parson and Clark, 1995). This second generation of studies includes dam operations at Glen Canyon Dam on the Colorado River (NRC, 1999b; Webb *et al.*, 1999); the California–Federal program in the Sacramento–San Joaquin River delta; an environmental restoration program in the Everglades of Florida – to name a few that are funded at the level of millions of dollars per year (Figure 12.4).

It can reasonably be asked whether such experiments in some of the most complex and politically contested ecosystems lend themselves to effective collaboration. Surprisingly little social research has addressed the dynamics of stakeholder based ecosystem management (Jacobs and Wescoat, 2002). Thus, a third generation initiative has organized an adaptive management practitioners' network to share experiences and approaches and adjustments based on those experiences (Adaptive Management Practitioners' Network, 2002). Participants in the network in 2002 include:

- American Rivers
- CALFED Bay–Delta Program
- Comprehensive Everglades Restoration Plan
- Earth-Tech Watershed Programs

- Ecosystem Management Initiative, University of Michigan School of Natural Resources and Environment
- Grand Canyon Monitoring and Research Center
- Institute for Agriculture and Trade Policy
- Institute for Environment and Natural Resources, University of Wyoming
- International Institute of Applied Systems Analysis
- Kissimmee River Restoration
- Lower Colorado River Multi-Species Program
- Mississippi River Basin Alliance
- Missouri River Adaptive Management Ecosystem Science Committee
- National Audubon Society Upper Mississippi River Campaign
- National Research Council, Water Science and Technology Board, Committees on Everglades Restoration and Missouri River Adaptive Management
- Platte River Endangered Species Partnership: Nebraska, Wyoming, Colorado, and the US Department of the Interior
- Resilience Alliance
- Resilience Network Research at Emory University Environmental Studies Department
- Science and Environmental Health Network
- TNC Freshwater Initiative
- Upper Mississippi Basin Stakeholder Network

While this forum constitutes a further step away from formal hypothesis-testing, it is an important contribution to qualitative assessment of adaptive management experiments.

The list of stakeholders reflects the array of adaptive management experiments that remain active. While it is too early to assess their long-term ecosystem effects, most of them have accomplished four major goals of adaptive management: (1) convening sustained meetings of stakeholders concerned with water and environmental management who were in some cases in conflict with one another; (2) articulation of management objectives and information needs for science-based decision-making; (3) mobilization of resources to fund research, database development, and stakeholder processes; and (4) varying degrees of hypothesis-driven resource management experiments. This last accomplishment is to date the most difficult to advance but will ultimately determine the material success or failure of adaptive management.

Adaptive management outside North America

As noted above, adaptive management was initially formulated in Europe by an international team of scientists. The Landcare program also employs an adaptive management framework for environmental systems in Australia, though not with an emphasis on water (Curtis and DeLacy, 1996; Gilmour *et al.*, 1999). Several projects of the Global Environmental Facility (GEF), e.g., in the Danube and Black Sea basins, have sought to incorporate similar approaches. Although the GEF program is formally incorporating adaptive management goals in its program, and has also developed stakeholder processes, its adaptive management projects are at an early stage of scientific development (i.e., hypothesis formulation, database protocols, and management experimentation).

However, research sponsored by the Australian Centre for International Agricultural Research tested adaptive management approaches in the upper Chao Phraya basin in Thailand and an area of sugarcane cultivation in Fiji. That study concluded that all stakeholders "will probably have to change their behavior to allow for the planning, research, and implementation of management strategies across traditional and legislatively mandated roles and disciplinary biases" (Lal *et al.*, 2001), findings consistent with those in North America.

Conceptually, the Beijer International Institute in Sweden has extended these efforts with an emphasis on issues of ecological and societal "resilience," which it defines as the likelihood of recovery from unanticipated disruptive events or disturbance (Gunderson and Holling, 2001). As some of the most uncertain disturbances of concern in the late twentieth century involved global environmental change, which were also pursued in independent research and management programs, it is to those programs that we now turn.

(3) Global environmental management

Previous chapters have cited international scientific programs on global hydrologic processes, ranging from single variables such as precipitation and temperature to complex land–atmosphere interactions, sea-level change, and snow and ice hydrology (Figure 12.5). Some of the impetus behind these global environmental research programs has been growing concern about global environmental changes that are jointly natural and anthropogenic in their origins and that may have profound consequences for human beings, water resources, and environmental quality.

In addition to scientific programs of the International Geosphere–Biosphere Programme (IGBP) that have been discussed,

Figure 12.5   Global warming has raised concerns about accelerated melting of alpine glaciers and snowfields in the Rocky Mountain region, ranging from single climatic variables such as precipitation and temperature to complex land–atmosphere interactions, sea-level change, snow and ice hydrology.

several international initiatives have begun to focus on relationships between global environmental science and policy. Early studies of climate change were undertaken by SCOPE. These were followed by continuing investigation and reporting by the Intergovernmental Panel on Climate Change (IPCC), which produces volumes on human impacts and adjustments as well as reviews of climate science. Although freshwater resources are deemed an essential resource and given some attention, IPCC reports in 2001 did not give detailed attention either to water resources or to linkages between water and related environmental consequences of climate variability. The IPCC Working Group II on Impacts, Adaptation and Vulnerability stated that "there is high confidence that observations of widespread glacial retreat and shifts in the timing of streamflow from spring to winter in many areas are associated with observed increases in temperature" (IPCC, 2001b, pp. 28–30). Other IPCC volumes and special reports on land use, forestry, regional vulnerability, and technological options for mitigating climate impacts briefly mention water resources impacts.

However, other organizations and scientists are examining these impacts, linkages, and potential regional adjustments to global hydroclimatic change. Gleick (2000b) edited a report on water resources vulnerability in the USA. Riebsame et al. (1995) compared results from the

Mekong, Indus, Nile, Zambezi, and La Plata basins, which indicated that in addition to widely varied hydroclimatic scenarios, each basin had distinctly different patterns and processes of vulnerability and adaptability to climate variability. Some of the most integrated studies have occurred in the Mackenzie basin in Canada where relationships between climate, water, fisheries, and livelihoods have been studied. A limited amount of research has examined links between climate variability, water resources, and disease ecology. Other work addresses the impacts of climate warming on aquatic ecosystems, e.g., in lakes, rivers, and wetlands. But it seems fair to say that as of the early twenty-first century no comprehensive or broadly integrative perspective had been developed on hydroclimatic variability, water resources, and environmental management.

FUTURE PROSPECTS FOR INTEGRATION

There are many fascinating, yet still nascent, prospects for integrated water management and environmental policy For example, one line of integration would establish closer links between water policy and environmental design (Cosgrove and Petts, 1990; Mathur and da Cunha, 2001) (Figure 12.6). Creative examples of wetland restoration, urban

Figure 12.6   In light of global environmental variability and competition for scare water resources, many municipal utilities have constructed experimental low-water-use landscape design demonstration gardens (Boulder, Colorado, USA).

stream restoration, water harvesting, and suburban stormwater management have been mentioned in this book, but the potential extensions are far greater. A volume on *Sustainable Landscape Design in Arid Climates* described water-sensitive housing developments in the western USA, recreational parks in Cairo and Tehran, new towns, university campuses, and diplomatic compounds in the Middle East, and rural landscape conservation in northern Sudan (O'Reilly, 1999). A *Handbook on Water-Sensitive Landscape Planning and Design* (France, 2002) describes the expanding array of environmental and engineering design experiments in the USA, Europe, and other regions (Johnston, 2003).

During the 1990s, scholars and water managers from a broad range of disciplines examined the theme of "security" in international water resources cooperation, environmental security or sustainability, and political sustainability (Amery and Wolf, 2000; NRC, 1999d; SIWI, 2000; Wolf, 1995, 1999a, 1999b). A consortium based at Oregon State University has compiled databases of US interstate water compacts, international water treaties, and an *Atlas of International Freshwater Agreements* (Wolf, 2002). Many of these studies focused on Middle Eastern water resources. Yet while one study succeeded in convening four national academies of science in the Middle East and the USA, obtaining their approval of a final report on the basic facts, and concrete proposals for cooperation, these achievements were at least temporarily eclipsed and suspended by escalating violence in the region in 2002 (NRC, 2000b). Terrorist attacks in the USA in 2001 also led to renewed concern about "security" of local water supplies and water quality (Haestad Methods, 2002).

These sobering, and distressing, events were balanced to some extent by increasing involvement of religious communities in environmental conservation. Religion and ecology conferences were organized at Harvard's center for the study of world religions. An electronic Encyclopedia on Religion and Nature includes a wide range of articles on the spiritual bases of harmony between water, environment, and cultures around the world. And a new field of "sustainability science" strives to cross science and policy boundaries in ways that have drawn the attention of the world's national academies of science (Kates *et al.*, 2001). Even if these specific efforts seem nascent or ephemeral, they testify to continuing creativity and desire for harmonious relations between human individuals, societies and cultures – and the waters and ecosystems that people need and love.

Appendix: Guide to Internet resources on water and environment

The information revolution in the late twentieth century transformed the procedures to compile, analyze, and distribute environmental information on the availability and quality of water. In the mid twentieth century, hydrologic and water use records were increasingly archived on computer tapes for use by an expanding range of water scientists and agencies. By the 1990s, however, new Internet technologies merged to create the World Wide Web. This pivotal development vastly increased the amount of information available electronically, as well as the ease of access and extent and sophistication of public information use. At the time of this publication, the types of electronic information being made available include:

- water and environmental organization websites, which describe the organization's aims, programs, publications, and calendar of activities;
- electronic portal and links pages, which provide connections to hundreds of related web pages, which in turn facilitate contact and information exchange via electronic mail (email);
- websites and file transfer protocol (ftp) sites that archive climatic data, hydrologic data, water quality data, water rights records, and water use records;
- remote sensing websites, which compile satellite images and air photos of water and related environmental phenomena;
- geographic information system (GIS) websites, which contain base maps, map layers, and interactive mapping tools;
- legal and regulatory websites, which facilitate complex searching of court cases, regulations, and treaties;
- websites that release real-time weather, water and environmental data, animations, and video images;

- project and university websites, which compile many of the types of information above on specialized topics, e.g., wetlands restoration, ecological sanitation, glaciology, and environmental engineering;
- general and specialized library catalogs, which enable searching of and, to some extent, borrowing from remote libraries around the world;
- water and environmental abstracts and full-text publications.

It is extraordinary to realize that *none* of these resources was available to the general public in 1980, and that the amount and sophistication of available information has increased exponentially, rendering many types of published material obsolete or unnecessary.

However, there are some important caveats. The geographic and temporal coverage of electronic information varies enormously. Some agencies provide most of their information online, others little, and still others have little data to provide. While wealthy institutions and individuals tend to have full access to Internet resources, the very poor have none. Increasingly sophisticated tools require regular upgrading of software, hardware, and electronic connections. While some resources are publicly available, others, including most comprehensive and specialized research library catalogs, are only available by subscription. Moreover, as previous publications have cautioned, the quality of information varies widely; website addresses change; some websites are maintained daily, others casually, and still others are abandoned; some search tools are precise, while others are inefficient and ineffective (Gleick, 2000a, p. 192).

This appendix offers a guide to Internet resources on water and environmental management (Gleick, 2000a, pp. 193–196). Previous publications, and web tools themselves, have provided extensive lists of available information and links. While those lists could be comprehended by an individual student or researcher in the early 1990s, by the year 2000 the sheer number and complexity of content of online resources exceeded the ability of most individuals. While students in the twentieth century were effectively limited to information in local libraries and sites, students and resource managers in the twenty-first century will have to make full and responsible use of the myriad resources that are becoming available. Although web designers have responded increasingly with lists and descriptions of websites – searchable in some cases by region, sector, and types of organization – the challenges of using these resources have mounted to the point where it is no longer feasible simply to browse for information.

Basic principles for Internet searches

This guide thus strives to provide useful strategies for navigating emerging information technologies and resources, along with a broad survey of sites relevant to the 12 chapters in this book. Although information technologies are changing rapidly, the following principles may have enduring value:

(1)   *Plan your search* – Formulate search objectives; estimate the amount of time required, and the different types of information you need; develop search recording forms, or use existing ones such as the FAO Investment Centre online search form, available at www.fao.org/tc/tci/sectors/guidelines2.pdf (FAO Investment Centre, 1997).

(2)   *Identify and prioritize water and environment web resources* – The proliferation and variable usefulness of electronic libraries, databases, and websites requires careful selection and phasing of Web resources. The water information portals and general websites listed for Chapters 1 and 2 below can help identify water and environmental organizations, as can the more specialized organizations listed under other chapters.

(3)   *Select key search terms* – It is important to identify the search terms most relevant for your topic and the electronic sources. For topics on the relationship between water management and environmental policy, that may involve: (a) general environmental keywords; (b) specific environmental terms; (c) water sector and technology terms; and (d) geographic terms such as the names of rivers, states, or countries. Multilingual thesauruses of water and environmental terms should be used for detailed searching (FAO, 1997); and some databases include a thesaurus (e.g., Water Resources Abstracts).

(4)   *Experiment with pairs of water and environment terms* – Unless they are highly specialized (e.g., a species name), single search terms usually yield too many results to process. By contrast, using three or more search terms can omit important sources. Searching with pairs of terms has proven effective in our experience. Pairs of terms should be employed systematically across electronic sources, but different pairs will prove useful in different databases. For example, in a general database (e.g., Web of Science), broad terms such as "water" and "environment" may

yield thousands of references for a single year, while in a more specialized website (e.g., on a specific country) the same terms may yield a more manageable number.

(5) *Manage your search results* – Browsing Internet resources can quickly become a challenge like that of Theseus in the labyrinth. You can soon become lost or forget what you found in the preceding hour. It is thus helpful to record what you searched, what you found, and what you did with the search results, as you proceed. Many databases have convenient tools for downloading, emailing, or printing results. To save paper and other resources, downloading results onto computer disks and managing them electronically is recommended.

(6) *Budget time to assess and digest results* – Electronic library and Internet resources are so voluminous that it is easy to become overwhelmed by the results, or to spend all of your time searching. To avoid both pitfalls, prioritize your results as they occur, periodically stop searching to digest those results, and then resume the search. The procedures outlined here are efficient, but you need to reserve time – more time than usual given the rich resources, to use the search results effectively.

With these broad principles in mind, it is useful to consider some strategies for examining different types of Internet resources.

Strategies for systematically using Web resources

As water and environmental Web resources are identified and prioritized, the process of searching begins. All too often, the search follows a "drunkard's path," skipping from one website to another, conducting partial searches, and spending large amounts of time with unproductive search tools. Careful phasing of a search helps avoid these problems. Recognizing that different types of search have different objectives, starting points, and paths, the following general strategies seem useful:

(1) *Avoid false starts* – Do not begin with general Internet search engines. They may yield thousands of results, some of them useful; but they are just as likely to miss the most useful scientific information, yield thousands of distractions, and thus consume enormous amounts of time.

(2) *Undertake reconnaissance* – Begin with a brief visit to the major water and environmental organizations relevant to your search. Note the major types of resources their home pages contain, especially their publications, databases, and most recent newsletter.

Avoid their links pages, as that can take you off in wide-ranging directions and turn a reconnaissance into a wild goose chase.

(3) *Go to electronic libraries early and often* – Increased use of Internet websites and search engines carries the risk that electronic library catalogs will be underutilized. Electronic libraries include catalogs of research universities, research institutes, and abstracting services. Although some specialized libraries are available by subscription only, many research university catalogs have remote public access from anywhere in the world. They contain a high proportion of peer-reviewed scientific and scholarly publications. If a local library does not have a publication, it can usually order it electronically through inter-library loan. For those who have access to a major research university, the following electronic libraries constitute essential resources:

(a) Books – the OCLC and WorldCat libraries have cataloged the largest number of books in US and selected European libraries.

(b) General scientific articles – the Web of Science, Ingenta/ UnCover, and Article1st have indexed articles, in some cases with abstracts, full-text, or faxing services.

(c) Doctoral dissertations – Some of the most recent detailed research projects are searchable online (e.g., through the FirstSearch Silver service).

(d) Water resources articles – Water Resources Abstracts is the first stop for water articles.

(e) Environmental articles – Many abstracting services index ecological, toxicological, and environmental policy journals (e.g., by subscription to Dialog, FirstSearch, MEDLINE, GEOBASE, and other services).

(f) Law and policy – LexisNexis has a public service for legal and policy documents called Legal Universe and more specialized databases for lawyers by subscription.

(4) *Return to detailed searching of organization websites* – After thorough library searching, return to the most promising governmental, scientific, and non-governmental websites identified in step 2 above. These websites often have valuable "gray literature" and technical reports not available in research libraries. Many useful websites are listed below.

(5) *Check Internet search engines for unexpected treasures* – General search engines should not be used until specialized libraries and databases have been systematically consulted. However, they do often turn up unexpected gems, along with thousands of unsorted

websites. When such gems are found, the principles and strategies outlined above may be replicated. If consulted towards the
end of a literature review, they can be fruitful and efficient.

With these general principles and strategies in hand, we proceed
to a list of Internet resources that follows the organization of chapters
in this book. In a few cases websites are duplicated, appearing under
more than one chapter heading. For categories that have a large number of excellent websites, we identify up to ten good places to start
your search, listed alphabetically. These Internet resources strive for
broad international scientific coverage; a later section of the appendix
lists selected regional resources.

Chapter 1   Water and life

The Internet resources for this initial chapter are primarily "portals,"
that is, sites that provide a broad introduction, a large array of resources
and links, and tools for searching for more specific water and environmental topics and information. The gaps between water management
and environmental policy discussed in this volume have precluded the
development of a single best website. Even so, the following provide
excellent resources for gaining a broad orientation to the field and for
starting a search.

Selected major websites

Center for Earth Science Information Network – CIESIN
www.ciesin.org

H2O-Scanner
www.h2o-scanner.com

International Office for Water
www.oieau.fr/anglais

International Water Resources Association
www.iwra.siu.edu

UNESCO Portal
www.unesco.org/water

Universities Council on Water Resources
www.uwin.siu.edu

Water and Nature Initiative – IUCN
iucn.org/themes/wani

Additional websites

Earth Trends – the WRI Environmental Information Portal
earthtrends.wri.org

Environmenatal Data Interactive Exchange – EDIE
www.edie.net

Geo-Information Gateway
www.geog.le.ac.uk/cti/info.html

Global Environmental Information Center – GEIC
www.geic.or.jp

International Water Association – IWA
www.iawq.org.uk

KeyWATER
keywater.vub.ac.be

UN Environment Program – GEMS Program
www.cciw.ca/gems

UN Environment Program – Water
www.unep.org/unep/program/natres/water

Water Information Group
www.irc.nl/products/documentation/wisig/launch.html

Water Librarians Homepage
www.interleaves.org/~rteeter/waterlib.html

WaterMasters Ring
watermasters.ring.vub.ac.be

Water Web Consortium
www.waterweb.org

Wetlist – Universities Water Information Network
www.uwin.siu.edu/WaterSites/browse.html

World Water
www.worldwater.org

Chapter 2   Challenge and opportunity

In the last decade of the twentieth century, many water and environmental organizations launched global initiatives in the form of new

organizations, programs, and projects. Beginning with an International Conference on Water and Environment in Dublin in 1991 and continuing through a series of international water meetings projected through the first decade of the twenty-first century, renewed emphasis was given to global issues and institutions. Thus, the Internet resources listed for this chapter focus on programs founded in the last years of the twentieth century and first years of the twenty-first.

Global Environment Facility
www.gefweb.org

Global Water Information Network
www.globwinet.org

International Institute for Environment and Development
www.iied.org

International Rivers Network – IRN
www.irn.org

International Water Management Institute – IWMI
www.cgiar.org/iwmi

IUCN Water and Nature Initiative
iucn.org/themes/wani

Pacific Institute
www.pacinst.org

Stockholm International Water Institute
www.siwi.org/sws/sws.html

Sustainable Water Management Programme
www.undp.org/water

World Bank Water Resource Management
www.worldbank.org/water

World Conservation Monitoring Center – WCMC/UNEP
www.unep-wcmc.org

World Summit on Sustainable Development
www.johannesburgsummit.org

World Water Assessment Programme – UNESCO
www.unesco.org/water/wwap/pccp/about.shtml

World Water Council
www.worldwatercouncil.org

World Water Forum (Third Forum, Kyoto, Japan, 2003)
www.worldwaterforum.org

World Water Vision
www.worldwatercouncil.org/vision.shtml

Chapter 3   Unfolding recognition of ecosystem change

The Internet sites for this chapter concentrate on historical information, educational resources, and long-term global change websites. These help chart and advance human recognition of environmental impacts of, and on, water use. Educational resources are voluminous, ranging from pre-collegiate environmental studies programs to advanced professional training and broad public water resources education. Interestingly, Internet sites on the history and historical geography of water and environmental management are less numerous, so for those topics in particular it is essential to make full use of the electronic library resources described above.

Environment and Sustainable Development Programme of UNU: Water Crisis
www.unu.edu/env/water/water.html

Gender and Water Alliance
www.irc.nl/projects/genall

Global Change Master Directory
gcmd.gsfc.nasa.gov

Global Continental Paleohydrology Project – GLOCOPH
www.geodata.soton.ac.uk/glocoph/glocoph.html

Global International Waters Assessment – GIWA
www.giwa.net

Global Learning and Observations to Benefit the Environment – GLOBE
www.globe.gov

Global Program of Action for the Protection of the Marine Environment – GPA
www.gpa.unep.org

Global Rivers Environmental Education Network – GREEN
www.green.org

Intergovernmental Panel on Climate Change
www.ipcc.ch

International Water History Association
www.iwha.net

International Waters Learning Exchange and Resource Network – IW:LEARN
www.iwlearn.org

IUCN Wetlands and Water Resources Program
www.iucn.org/themes/wetlands

Learning to Be WaterWise
www.getwise.org

Office to Combat Desertification and Drought of UNDP – UNSO
www.undp.org/seed/unso

Project WET – Water Education for Teachers
www.projectwet.org

USGS Water Science for Schools
ga.water.usgs.gov/edu

Water Education Foundation
www.watereducation.org

World Conservation Monitoring Centre – Freshwater
www.unep-wcmc.org

World Resource Institute
www.wri.org

WWF World Water Campaign
www.panda.org/livingwaters

Chapter 4   Natural waters

A wealth of basic scientific information in the hydrologic and environmental sciences has become available. From global centers on precipitation, runoff, and water budget analysis to hydrometeorological satellite imagery, online scientific journals, and aquatic and wetland ecosystem science centers, the Internet is now unmatched as a library on "natural waters." Major international centers are listed below.

Centre For Ecology and Hydrology
www.nwl.ac.uk/ih

Global Energy and Water Cycle Experiment – GEWEX
www.gewex.org

Global Hydrological Databases Meta-Data System – IAHS
www.watsys.unh.edu/metadata

Global Hydrology and Climate Center – GHCC
www.ghcc.msfc.nasa.gov

Global Hydrology Resource Center
ghrc.msfc.nasa.gov

Hydrology and Water Resources Programme
www.wmo.ch/web/homs/hwrpframes.html

International Association for Environmental Hydrology – IAEH
www.hydroweb.com

International Association of Hydrological Sciences – IAHS
www.cig.ensmp.fr/~iahs

International Commission on Water Quality – ICWQ
www.ex.ac.uk/~BWWebb/icwq

International Hydrologic Programme
www.unesco.org/water/ihp

International Hydrology Research Group
www.watsys.unh.edu

Isotope Hydrology Section of International Atomic Energy Agency – IAEA
www.iaea.or.at/programmes/ripc/ih

*United Nations Comprehensive Assessment of Fresh Water Resources
  in the World*
www.un.org/esa/sustdev/freshwat.htm

World Hydrological Observing System – WHYCOS
www.wmo.ch/web/homs/projects/whycos.html

World Water Balance
www.ce.utexas.edu/prof/maidment/atlas/atlas.htm

Chapter 5   Plant–soil–water–ecosystem relationships

Agriculture is the largest water use sector, and has a concomitant wealth of Internet resources. Although agronomy is inherently an "environmental science," increasing emphasis is being placed on relationships between irrigation, drainage, and ecosystem management – notably in the inter-agency *Dialogue on Water, Food and Environment*, hosted by the International Water Management Institute (IWMI). Major research and information centers are listed below.

Agricultural Network Information Center
www.agnic.org

Aquaculture Network Information Center – AquaNIC
aquanic.org

Aquatic, Wetland, and Invasive Plant Database
aquat1.ifas.ufl.edu

Cemagref
www.cemagref.fr/English

Consultative Group on International Agricultural Research – CGIAR
www.cgiar.org

  CGIAR Challenge Program on Water and Food
  www.waterfood.org

  International Water Management Institute – IWMI (CGIAR Network)
  www.cgiar.org/iwmidialogue

Food and Agriculture Organization – FAO
www.fao.org

  Aquastat
  www.fao.org/waicent/faoinfo/agricult/agl/aglw/aquastat/main/
    index.stm

  Gateway to Land and Water Information
  www.fao.org/ag/agl/swlwpnr/swlwpnr.htm

  Information Systems
  www.fao.org/waicent/faoinfo/agricult/agl/lwris.htm

  International Programme for Technology and Research in Irrigation and
    Drainage – IPTRID
  www.fao.org/iptrid

  Land and Water Development Division
  www.fao.org/ag/agl

  Library Resources
  www.fao.org/library

  Participatory Training and Extension in Farmer's Water Management
  www.fao.org/ag/agl/aglw/farmerwatertraining

  Statistical Databases
  apps.fao.org

French Committee on Irrigation and Drainage
afeid.montpellier.cemagref.fr/afeideng.htm

International Commission on Irrigation and Drainage – ICID
www.icid.org

International Development Enterprises
www.ideorg.org

International Food Policy Research Institute – Water Resource Allocation
www.ifpri.org

International Irrigation Center
www.engineering.usu.edu/Departments/iic/iichome0.html

International Land Reclamation Institute – ILRI
www.ilri.nl

International Network on Participatory Irrigation Management – INPIM
www.inpim.org

Irrigation Association
www.irrigation.org

Soil and Water Management and Crop Nutrition
www.iaea.org/programmes/nafa/d1

Tropical Agriculture Association – TAA
www.taa.org.uk

Water Conservation and Use in Agriculture – WCA infoNET
www.wca-infonet.org/iptrid/infonet

WWW Virtual Library Irrigation
www.wiz.uni-kassel.de/kww/projekte/irrig/irrig_i.html

Chapter 6   Groundwater

Groundwater constitutes the largest supply of liquid freshwater on the planet, and became the largest source for domestic water use during the twentieth century. However, groundwater issues are not as well represented in libraries or on the Internet as surface water issues. The following five websites provide a good starting place, after which specific regional sites should be consulted.

Groundwater.com
groundwater.com

International Association of Hydrogeologists – IAH
www.iah.org

International Commission On Water Quality – ICWQ
www.ex.ac.uk/~BWWebb/icwq

International Groundwater Modeling Center – IGWMC
www.mines.edu/igwmc

Urban Groundwater Database – UGD
www.clw.csiro.au/UGD

Chapter 7   Lakes and wetlands

International Internet resources on lakes and wetlands range from basic
data sources on hydrology to law, policy, and environmental conservation. The International Lake and Environment Committee (ILEC) is the
first stop for information on lakes. For wetlands, the websites of IUCN,
Ramsar, and Wetlands International provide a broad perspective.

Global Lake and Catchment Conservation Database
wwwcpg.mssl.ucl.ac.uk/orgs/un/glaccd/html/more_info.html

International Association of Theoretical and Applied Limnology – SIL
www.limnology.org

International Lake Environment Committee – ILEC
www.ilec.or.jp/eg

International Society for Salt Lake Research
isslr.org

IUCN – the World Conservation Union
www.iucn.org/themes/wetlands

LakeNet
www.worldlakes.org

Living Lakes
www.livinglakes.org

Partners for Wetlands
www.partnersforwetlands.org

Ramsar Convention on Wetlands
www.ramsar.org

Society of Wetlands Scientists
www.sws.org

Wetlands International
www.wetlands.org

World Lakes Database – ILEC
www.ilec.or.jp/database/database.html

Chapter 8   River channels and floodplains

The websites listed below range from the Global Runoff Data Centre (GRDC) to international river protection organizations (e.g., International Rivers Network). While good international sites have been created on flood hazards (e.g., the Dartmouth College World Flood Database), we have not yet found a site of international scope on floodplain management.

Global Runoff Data Centre
www.bafg.de/grdc.htm

International Research and Training Center on Erosion and Sedimentation
www.irtces.com

International Rivers Network – IRN
www.irn.org

Mitigation of Climate Induced Natural Hazards – MITCH
www.mitch-ec.net

Natural Hazards Center – NHRAIC – Floods
www.colorado.edu/hazards/sites/floods.html

River Basin Analysis Centre
www.ct.tudelft.nl/rba

RiverNet
www.rivernet.org

World Flood Database
www.dartmouth.edu/~floods

Chapter 9   Impounded rivers and reservoirs

Controversies over large dams in the late twentieth century led to the development of a wealth of Internet resources, ranging from pro-dam sites (e.g., ICOLD and IHA) to anti-dam sites (e.g., IRN). However, the most important collaborative technical initiative, with associated Internet resources, was carried out by the World Commission on Dams.

Less electronic attention has been given to small dams, ranging in size from ephemeral diversions to check dams and earth or concrete dams less than 15 m high, for which the agricultural web sites listed under Chapter 5 may be helpful.

International Commission on Large Dams – ICOLD
genepi.louis-jean.com

International Energy Agency Hydropower Agreement
www.ieahydro.org

International Hydropower Association – IHA
www.hydropower.org

International Rivers Network – IRN
www.irn.org

World Commission on Dams – WCD
www.dams.org

Chapter 10   Domestic and industrial water management

International information on domestic water and sanitation was catalyzed by the Decade for Safe Drinking Water and Sanitation (1980–90). Although the Decade ended as Internet resources were becoming available, organizations created at that time, notably the International Resource Centre (IRC) and the Water Supply and Sanitation Collaborative Council (WSSCC), continued to the present and were well positioned to put their recently compiled as well as new information on the Internet (Black, 1998; IRC International Water and Sanitation Centre, 2000; WASH, 1993). The Global Environmental Sanitation Initiative advocates ecological approaches to domestic water and sanitation. Although fewer Web resources focus on industrial water management, the International Association for Water Quality (IAWQ) and electronic libraries (e.g., Water Resources Abstracts and EI Compendex) provide abstracts for a wealth of information.

Bottled Water Web
www.bottledwaterweb.com

Business Partners for Development – Water and Sanitation
www.bpd-waterandsanitation.org

Center for Ecological Pollution Prevention – CEPP
www.cepp.cc

Centers For Disease Control and Prevention – CDC
www.cdc.gov/safewater

Centre for Human Settlements – UNCHS
www.unchs.org

Desalination Directory Online
www.desline.com

Environmental Health Project
www.ehproject.org

Global Applied Research Network – GARNET
info.lut.ac.uk/departments/cv/wedc/garnet/grntback.html

International Centre for Diarrhoeal Disease Research, Bangladesh – ICDDR,B
www.icddrb.org

International Commission on Water Quality – ICWQ
www.ex.ac.uk/~BWWebb/icwq

International Desalination Association – IDA
www.idadesal.org

International Foundation for the Protection of Drinking Water
www.protectwater.org

International Network on Water, Environment and Health – UNU/INWEH
www.inweh.unu.edu/inweh

International Secretariat for Water – ISW
www.i-s-w.org

International Water Association – IWA
www.iawq.org.uk

International Water and Sanitation Center – IRC
www.irc.nl

Islamic Relief Worldwide – Water and Sanitation Program
www.islamic-relief.com

Pan American Center for Sanitary Engineering and Environmental Sciences
www.cepis.ops-oms.org/indexeng.html

Sanitation Connection
www.sanicon.net

School Sanitation and Hygiene Education – SSHE
www.irc.nl/sshe

Streams of Knowledge
www.irc.nl/stream

Urban Environmental Management – WWW Virtual Library
gdrc.org/uem

Wastewater Users Planning Group – WaPUG
www.wapug.org.uk

Water Aid
www.wateraid.org.uk

Water and Environment Health of London and Loughborough – WELL
www.lboro.ac.uk/well

Water and Sanitation – UNDP
www.wsp.org/English/regions.html

Water and Sanitation/World Health Organization – WHO
www.who.int/water_sanitation_health

WaterCan/EauVive
www.watercan.com

Water, Environment and Sanitation – WES
www.unicef.org/programme/wes

Water Environment Federation – WEF
www.wef.org

Water for People
water4people.org

Watermark
www.lboro.ac.uk/departments/cv/wedc/watermark

Water Supply and Sanitation Collaborative Council – WSSCC
www.wsscc.org

Water Technology
www.water-technology.net

World Bank Water Sanitation Program – UNDP
www.wsp.org

Chapter 11   Decision processes

Internet resources and information affect an increasing proportion of water decisions as national, state, and local governments all develop GIS, spatial databases, and decision-support systems. Collaborative networks and websites on water conflict resolution are expanding. Interactive water modeling software and sophisticated decision-support systems are also described online. Although the data resources for these decision tools are sometimes available online, the models and DSS systems themselves are often proprietary products. Moreover, the positive and negative effects of new information technologies and resources on decision processes, as well as decisions themselves, are rarely assessed.

Both ENDS
www.bothends.org

Center for Advanced Decision Support for Water and Environmental Systems –
   CADSWES
cadswes.colorado.edu

Center for International Environmental Law
www.ciel.org

Environmental Law Alliance Worldwide – ELAW
www.elaw.org

Decision Support System for Evaluation of River Basin Strategies – DESERT
www.iiasa.ac.at/Research/WAT/docs/desert.html

Dialogue on Water and the Climate
www.wac.ihe.nl

Global Water Partnership
www.gwpforum.org

Green Cross International – Water Conflict Prevention
www.gci.ch/GreenCrossPrograms/waterres/waterresource.html

Integrated Decision Support Group – CSU
www.ids.colostate.edu

International Law
www.un.org/law

International Network of Basin Organizations
www.oieau.fr

International Water Academy
www.thewateracademy.org

International Water Law Project – IWLP
internationalwaterlaw.org

International Water Law Research Institute – IWLRI
www.dundee.ac.uk/law/water

Pacific Institute
www.pacinst.org

Resolve: Center for Environmental and Public Policy Dispute Resolution
www.resolve.org

Transboundary Freshwater Dispute Database
www.transboundarywaters.orst.edu

United Nations University – UNU/INWEH
www.inweh.unu.edu/inweh

Water Conflict Chronology
www.worldwater.org/conflictIntro.htm

Chapter 12   Integrative approaches

Depending upon how it is used, the Internet may serve as a vehicle of integration or fragmentation. On the one hand, it can disseminate information far more broadly than has occurred in the past, and may facilitate compilation of diverse media, including texts, satellite images, numeric data, GIS layers, and photographs. Interactive river basin and watershed models can now be run online, with real-time data, to support decision processes. On the other hand, there is so much specialized information available on the Internet that, if not used systematically, it can lead to fragmentation and confusion. While all of the websites listed above can contribute to integration, the following deal with integrative themes explicitly.

Center for Earth Science Information Network – CIESIN
www.ciesin.org

Global International Waters Assessment Program – GIWA
www.giwa.net

Integrated Water Management Toolbox – Global Water Partnership
www.gwp.ihe.nl

International Centre for Integrated Mountain Development – Watersheds
www.icimod.org.sg/focus/watershed/wshed_toc.htm

International Development Research Center – IDRC
www.idrc.ca

International Network of Basin Organizations – INBO
www.oieau.fr/riob

International Water Assessment Center of UNECE – IWAC
www.iwac-riza.org

River Basin Initiative
genet.virtualave.net/docs/rbi-broc.pdf

Transboundary Freshwater Dispute Database
www.transboundarywaters.orst.edu

Universities Water Information Network – UWIN
www.uwin.siu.edu

Regional websites

The Internet resources listed above strive for broad international or global scientific coverage. They only occasionally include detailed country, river basin, or local information – though they often have links to those resources. Here we list some leading Internet resources for regions around the world. Although US and English-language websites are most fully covered, we strive for regional balance of different regions. To remedy the language and western library biases of this list, we recommend that researchers download the appropriate language fonts and search the national and regional libraries in any country where they are working.

United States of America

American Ground Water Trust
www.agwt.org

American Institute of Hydrology
www.aihydro.org

American Rivers
www.amrivers.org

American Water Resources Association – AWRA
www.awra.org

American Water Works Association – AWWA
www.awwa.org

Association of Groundwater Agencies
www.agwa.org

Association of State Floodplain Managers
www.floods.org

Association of State Wetlands Managers
www.aswm.org

Directory of Water Resources Expertise
www.nceas.ucsb.edu/exp

Freshwater Society
www.freshwater.org

Groundwater Foundation
www.groundwater.org

Ground-Water Remediation Technologies Analysis Center – GWRTAC
www.gwrtac.org

Hydrology and Remote Sensing Laboratory
hydrolab.arsusda.gov

National Academy of Sciences, Water Science and Technology Board
www.nationalacademies.org/wstb

National Drinking Water Clearinghouse
www.nesc.wvu.edu/ndwc

National Drought Mitigation Center
www.drought.unl.edu

National Extension Water Quality Database
hermes.ecn.purdue.edu/water

National Ground Water Association – NGWA
www.ngwa.org

National Oceanic and Atmospheric Administration
www.noaa.gov

   Current Hydrologic Information – NOAA
   www.nws.noaa.gov/oh/hic/conds.html

National Water Quality Monitoring Council
water.usgs.gov/wicp/acwi/monitoring

North American Commission for Environmental Cooperation
www.cec.org

Pesticide Action Network – PAN
www.pesticideinfo.org

Project WET – Water Education for Teachers
www.projectwet.org

River Network
www.rivernetwork.org

Sewage World
www.sewage.net

Soil and Water Conservation Society
www.swcs.org

Tennessee Valley Authority
www.tva.gov

US Army Corp of Engineers
www.usace.army.mil

   Water Resources Institute (and library)
   www.wrsc.usace.army.mil/iwr

US Bureau of Reclamation – USBR
www.usbr.gov

US Department of Agriculture
www.usda.gov

   Agricultural Research Service, Watersheds Database
   hydrolab.arsusda.gov/arswater.html

   Bibliographic Database of Water Quality
   www.nal.usda.gov/wqic/pfdr.html

   Natural Resources Conservation Service – NRCS
   www.nrcs.usda.gov

   US Salinity Laboratory – USSL
   www.ussl.ars.usda.gov

   Watershed Science Institute
   www.wcc.nrcs.usda.gov/watershed

   Watershed Technology Electronic Catalog
   www.wcc.nrcs.usda.gov/wtec

US Environmental Protection Agency – USEPA
www.epa.gov/eq

Biological Indicators of Watershed Health
www.epa.gov/bioindicators

Compliance and Enforcement
www.epa.gov/compliance

Enviromapper Watershed Information Atlas
www.epa.gov/wateratlas

Environmental Justice
www.epa.gov/compliance/environmentaljustice

Groundwater Drinking Water
www.epa.gov/ogwdw

Index of Watershed Indicators
www.epa.gov/iwi

National Drinking Water Contaminant Database
www.epa.gov/ncod

Office of Wetlands, Oceans and Watersheds
www.epa.gov/owow

Safe Drinking Water Query
www.epa.gov/enviro/html/sdwis/sdwis_query.html

Surf Your Watershed
www.epa.gov/surf

Watershed Academy
www.epa.gov/owow/watershed/wacademy

Watershed Mapper
map2.epa.gov/enviromapper

US Geological Survey, Water Resources of the US
water.usgs.gov

Advisory Committee on Water Information
water.usgs.gov/wicp

Groundwater Atlas
capp.water.usgs.gov/gwa

National Water Quality Assessment Program
water.usgs.gov.nawqa

National Wetlands Research Center – NWRC
www.nwrc.gov

NWIS-Web
water.usgs.gov/nwis

Toxic Substances Hydrology Program
toxics.usgs.gov

Water Data
water.usgs.gov/data.html

Water Education
water.usgs.gov/education.html

Water Use Data
water.usgs.gov/watuse

Water Watch
water.usgs.gov/waterwatch

US Society on Dams
www2.privatei.com/~uscold

US Water News
www.uswaternews.com

Water Education Foundation
www.watereducation.org

Wateright
www.wateright.org

Watershed Information Resource System Database
www.terrene.org

Watershed Management Council
www.watershed.org

Water Wiser – Water Conservation Clearinghouse
www.waterwiser.org

Wetlands Regulation Center
www.wetlands.com

Canada

Canadian Groundwater Association
www.cgwa.org

Canada's Water Resources Association
www.cwra.org

Environment Canada
www.ec.gc.ca/water

  Aquatic Ecosystems
  www.ec.gc.ca/water/en/nature/aqua/e_aqua.htm

  Groundwater
  www.ec.gc.ca/water/en/nature/grdwtr/e_gdwtr.htm

  Lakes
  www.ec.gc.ca/water/en/nature/lakes/e_lakes.htm

  Rivers
  www.ec.gc.ca/water/en/nature/rivers/e_rivers.htm

  Water and Climate
  www.ec.gc.ca/water/en/nature/clim/e_clim.htm

  Water Policy in Canada
  www.ec.gc.ca/water/en/policy/pol/e_wpcan.htm

  Wetlands
  www.ec.gc.ca/water/en/nature/wetlan/e_wetlan.htm

The Green Lane
www.ec.gc.ca/envhome.html

Ministry of Water, Land and Air Protection – British Columbia
www.gov.bc.ca/wlap

Pollution Probe
www.pollutionprobe.org

Water Information Network of Canada
www.riversides.org

North American transboundary water organizations

Border Environment Cooperation Commission
www.cocef.org/englishbecc.html

Great Lakes Commission (USA–Canada)
www.glc.org

Great Lakes Information Network (USA–Canada)
www.great-lakes.net

Great Lakes Water Quality Agreement (USA–Canada)
www.on.ec.gc.ca/glwqa

International Boundary and Water Commission (USA–Mexico)
www.ibwc.state.gov

International Joint Commission – Treaty Enforcement (USA–Canada)
www.ijc.org/ijcweb-e.html

North American Commission for Environmental Cooperation
www.cec.org

Central and South America

*Binational Commission for the Development of the Upper Bermejo River and
    Grande de Tarija River Basins (Transboundary: Argentina–Bolivia)*
www.cbbermejo.org.ar

*FRIEND–AMIGO – Flow Regimes from International Experimental and Network
    Data*
www.friend-amigo.org

Inter-American Water Resources Network
www.iwrn.net

Inter-Municipal Consortium of the Piracicaba and Capivari River Basins
www.agua.org.br

International Hygrological Programme for Latin America and the Caribbean
www.unesco.org.uy/phi

National Water Commission of Mexico
www.cna.gob.mx

Organization of American States – OAS
www.oas.org

Pan American Center For Sanitary Engineering and Environmental Sciences
www.cepis.ops-oms.org

Patterns and Processes of Change in the Amazon River Basin
boto.ocean.washington.edu/eos

*Water Center for the Humid Tropics of Latin America and the Caribbean –
    CATHALAC*
www.cathalac.org

Europe and Russia

Aqu@Doc Inter
www.aquadocinter.org

Blue Plan
www.planbleu.org

British Hydrological Society
www.hydrology.org.uk

Centre for Ecology and Hydrology
www.ceh.ac.uk

Chartered Institution of Water and Environmental Management – CIWEM
www.ciwem.com

Delft Hydraulics
www.wldelft.nl

Euro-Mediterranean Information System – EMWIS
www.emwis.org

European Commission – Environment
europa.eu.int/comm/environment

  Bathing Water Quality Directive
  europa.eu.int/water/water-bathing/index_en.html

  Urban Waste Water Treatment
  europa.eu.int/comm/environment/water/water-urbanwaste/
      index_en.html

  Water Framework Directive
  europa.eu.int/comm/environment/water/water-framework/
      index_en.html

European Desalination Society
www.edsoc.com

European Environment Agency – EEA
www.eea.eu.int

  EEA – Water
  themes.eea.eu.int/Specific_media/water

European Rivers Network – ERN
www.rivernet.org/ern.htm

European Water Association
www.ewpca.de

French Water Data Network
www.rnde.tm.fr

German Federal Institute of Hydrology
www.bafg.de

   Global Runoff Data Centre
   www.bafg.de/grdc.htm

German Wastewater Management
www.atv.de/english

Groundwater Forum
www.nerc-wallingford.ac.uk/gwf

HR Wallingford
www.hrwallingford.co.uk

Innovative Management of Groundwater Resources in Europe –
   IMAGE/TRAIN
www.image-train.net

Institute for Inland Water Management and Wastewater Treatment – RIZA
www.riza.nl

International Commission for the Protection of the Danube
www.icpdr.org/pls/danubis/danubis.navigator

International Institute for Applied Systems Analysis – Water
www.iiasa.ac.at/Research/WAT

   IIASA Adaptive Dynamics Network
   www.iiasa.ac.at/Research/ADN

International Institute for Infrastructural, Hydraulic and Environmental
   Engineering – IHE
www.ihe.nl

MANTRA East – Transboundary Basin Research
www.mantraeast.org

Mediterranean Action Plan of UNEP–MAP
www.unepmap.org

Mediterranean Hydrological Cycle Observing System – MED-HYCOS
medhycos.mpl.ird.fr

Natural Environment Research Council
www.nerc.ac.uk

Netherlands Water Partnership
www.nwp.nl

Peipsi Center for Trans-Boundary Cooperation
www.ctc.ee

Programme Solidarité Eau – pS-eau
www.pseau.org

Regional Cooperation of the Danube Countries
147.213.145.2/danube

State Hydrological Institute of Russia
pyramid.sr.unh.edu/~sasha/shi.com

Swedish International Development Cooperation Agency – SIDA
www.sida.se

Swedish Meteorological and Hydrological Institute – SMHI
www.smhi.se

Water in France
www.eaufrance.tm.fr

Water Research Network – WRN
water.nml.uib.no

World Wildlife Fund European Freshwater Program
www.panda.org/europe/freshwater

Asia

Aral Sea GIS
giserv.karelia.ru/aral

Asian Arsenic Network
www.asia-arsenic.*net/index-e.htm*

Asian Development Bank – Water for All
www.adb.org/Water

Asian Disaster Preparedness Centre
www.adpc.ait.ac.th

Asia-Pacific Center for Environmental Law
sunsite.nus.edu.sg/apcel

Association of Uzbekistan for Sustainable Water Resources Development –
AUSWRD
freeyellow.com/members8/abdullaev/auswrd.html

Central Asia Research and Remediation Exchange
www.geology.sdsu.edu/geology/facilities/carre

Central Water Commission for the Government of India
cwc.nic.in

Global Environmental Center in Japan
www.unep.or.jp/gec

H2O–China
www.h2o-china.com/english/index-e.asp

Hong Kong Water Supplies Department
www.info.gov.hk/wsd

India – Centre for Science and Environment (Water harvesting
*   campaign)*
www.rainwaterharvesting.org

Institute of Water Modelling – Bangladesh
www.iwmdb.org

Japan's River Bureau – Land, Infrastructure and Development
www.mlit.go.jp/river/english

Kushiro International Wetland Center
www.kiwc.net/english/main.html

Lake Biwa Research Institute in Japan
www.lbri.go.jp/default.htm

Mekong River Commission
www.mrcmekong.org

Ministry for Water Resources – India
wrmin.nic.in

Ministry of Water Resources For The People's Republic of China
www.mwr.gov.cn/english/index.htm

National Institute of Hydrology of India
www.nih.ernet.in

Nepal Water Conservation Foundation
www.panasia.org.sp/nepalnet/nwcf

Qinghai Institute of Salt Lakes in China
www.isl.ac.cn/eindex.html

Regional Humid Tropics Hydrology and Water Resources for Southeast Asia and the Pacific
htc.moa.my/htc

South Asian Consortium for Interdisciplinary Water Resources Study
www.saciwaters.org

Sustainable Development Policy Institute – Pakistan and South Asia
www.sdpi.org

UNEP Regional Resource Center for Asia and the Pacific – RRC.AP
www.rrcap.unep.org

UN ESCAP Water, Land and Mineral Resources
www.unescap.org/enrd/water_mineral/water_mineral.htm

Water and Power Development Authority – WADPA (Pakistan)
www.pakwadpa.com

Water Policy in Japan
www.idi.or.jp/river

Water Policy of the Asia Development Bank
www.adb.org/documents/policies/water

Water Resources of India – UNDP
sdnp.delhi.nic.in/resources/waterharvesting/water-frame.html

Australia, New Zealand, South Pacific

Australian Department of Environmental Protection
www.environ.wa.gov.au

Australian Water Association – AWA
www.awa.asn.au

Centre for Groundwater Studies
www.groundwater.com.au

Cooperative Research Centre for Catchment Hydrology
www.catchment.crc.org.au

CSIRO Land and Water
www.clw.csiro.au

Hydrometeorological Advisory Service
www.bom.gov.au/hydro/has

Inland Waters – Wetlands
www.ea.gov.au/water/wetlands

Land and Water Australia
www.lwrrdc.gov.au

National Centre for Groundwater Management – NCGM
groundwater.*ncgm.uts.edu.au/ncgm*

New Zealand National Institute of Water and Atmospheric Research
www.niwa.cri.nz

New Zealand Water and Waste Association
www.nzwwa.org.nz

Water and Rivers
www.wrc.wa.gov.au

Water and Rivers Commission – Western Australia
www.wrc.wa.gov.au

Water New Zealand
www.waternz.co.nz

Middle East

Arab Center for the Studies of Arid Zones and Dry Lands – ACSAD
www.acsad.org

Blue Plan
www.planbleu.org/indexa.htm

Columbia University – Middle East Studies Water Reports Online
www.columbia.edu/cu/lweb/indiv/mideast/cuvlm/water.html

*Inter-Islamic Network on Water Resources Development and Management –
INWRDAM*
www.nic.gov.jo/inwrdam

International Hydrological Programme (IHP) for Arab States
www.unesco-cairo.org/programmes/science/ihp

Mediterranean Action Plan of UNEP–MAP
www.unepmap.org

Mediterranean Water Institute
www.ime-eau.org

Middle East Desalination Research Center – MEDRC
www.medrc.org

Middle East Water Information Network – MEWIN
www.ssc.upenn.edu/~mewin

Ministry of Agriculture and Water – Saudi Arabia
www.agrwat.gov.sa

Multilateral Working Group on Water Resources
water.usgs.gov/exact

Palestinian Hydrology Group
www.phg.org

School of Oriental and African Studies, Water Issues Group
www2.soas.ac.uk/Geography/WaterIssues

South-Eastern Anatolia Project – GAP (Turkey)
www.gap.gov.tr

Water and Conflict
waternet.rug.ac.be

Water Resource Planning in Egypt – Report by Middle Eastern Environment
www.netcomuk.co.uk/~jpap/hvidt.htm

Wetlands in Africa and the Middle East
www.wetlands.agro.nl

Africa

Africa Plus – The Water Page
www.thewaterpage.com

EARS Monitoring and Early Warning
www.earlywarning.nl

Egypt's Ministry of Public Works and Water Resources
www.misrnet.idsc.gov.eg

GeoAfrica
www.geoafrica.co.za/indexalt.htm

Intergovernmental Authority on Drought and Development – IGADD
www.dfa.gov.za/for-relations/multilateral/igad.htm

*Inter-Islamic Network on Water Resources Development and Management –
  INWRDAM*
www.nic.gov.jo/inwrdam

Lake Victoria Environmental Management Project – LVEMP
www.lvemp.org

Managing Water for African Cities
www.un-urbanwater.net

Mediterranean Action Plan of UNEP–MAP
www.unepmap.org

Nile Basin Initiative
www.nilebasin.org

Nile Basin Society
nilebasin.com

Regional Association on Irrigationand Drainage in West and Central Africa –
ARID
www.hipponet.nl/arid-l

Regional Cooperation and Integration Division – Transboundary Waters
www.uneca.org/eca_programmes/regional_integration

Rennies Wetlands Project
psybergate.com/wetfix

Sahara and Sahel Observatory
www.unesco.org/oss

Sahel Weather and Crop Situation
www.fao.org/waicent/faoinfo/economic/giews/english/esahel/sahtoc.htm

Society for Urban Development in East Africa – SUDEA
user.tninet.se/~gyt516c

South African Department of Water Affairs and Forestry
www-dwaf.pwv.gov.za

South African Water Research Commission
www.wrc.org.za

Southern African Development Commission – Hydrological Cycle Observing
System (SADC–HYCOS)
www-sadchyco.pwv.gov.za

Southern Waters
www.southernwaters.co.za

Water for Children in Africa
www.waterforchildrenafrica.org

Water Institute of Southern Africa
www.wisa.co.za

World Wise Schools Water in Africa
www.peacecorps.gov/wws/water/africa

References

Abu-Zeid, M. A. and El Shibini, F. A. (1997). Egypt's High Aswan Dam. *Water Resources Development* **13**(2), 209–217.

Ackermann, W. C., White, G. F., and Worthington, E. B. (eds.) (1973). *Man-Made Lakes: Their Problems and Environmental Effects*. Geophysical Monograph 17. Washington, DC: American Geophysical Union.

Adams, R. McC. (1981). *Heartland of Cities: Surveys of Ancient Settlement and Land Use on the Central Floodplain of the Euphrates*. Chicago, IL: University of Chicago Press.

Adams, W. (1992). *Wasting the Rain: Rivers, People and Planning in Africa*. Minneapolis, MN: University of Minnesota.

Adaptive Management Practitioners' Network. (2002). http://www.iatp.org/AEAM. Last visited August 21, 2002.

Adler, R. W., Landman, J. C., and Cameron, D. M. (1993). *The Clean Water Act 20 Years Later*. Washington, DC: Island Press.

Agarwal, A. and Narain, S. (eds.) (1997). *Dying Wisdom: Rise, Fall and Potential of India's Traditional Water Harvesting Systems*. New Delhi: Centre for Science and Environment.

Agarwal, A., Narain, S., and Khurana, I. (eds.) (2001). *Making Water Everybody's Business: Practice and Policy of Water Harvesting*. New Delhi: Centre for Science and Environment.

Aladin, N. (2002). Aral Sea crisis and its rehabilitation. *ILEC Newsletter* **40**, 3.

Allan, T. (1997). "Virtual Water": A Long-term Solution for Water Short Middle Eastern Economies? Occasional Paper 3. London: School of Oriental and African Studies.

Alley K. D. (2002). *On the Banks of the Ganga: When Wastewater Meets a Sacred River*. Ann Arbor, MI: University of Michigan Press.

Alley, W. Reilly, T., and Franke, L. (1999). *Sustainability of Ground-Water Resources*. Circular 1186. Denver, CO: US Geological Survey.

Amery, H. A. and Wolf, A. T. (eds.) (2000). *Water in the Middle East: A Geography of Peace*. Austin, TX: University of Texas Press.

Anderson, J. L. (1998). Embracing uncertainty: The interface of Bayesian statistics and cognitive psychology. *Conservation Ecology* **2**(1), 1–27.

Arnold, D. (1993). *Colonizing the Body: State Medicine and Epidemic Disease in Nineteenth-Century India*. Berkeley, CA: University of California Press.

ASFPM (1999). *99 Planning Ahead: Reducing Flood Losses in the 21st Century*. Proceedings from Portland, Oregon, May 1999. Boulder: Natural Hazards Center.

(2000). *Floodplain Management 2000 and Beyond: A New Beginning in a New Millennium*. Proceedings from Austin, Texas, May 2000. Madison, WI: Association of State Floodplain Managers.

(2001). *New Trends in Floodplain Management*. Proceedings from Charlotte, North Carolina, May 2001. Madison, WI: Association of State Floodplain Managers.

(2002). *Mitigation Success Stories in the United States*, 4th edition. Madison, WI: Association of State Floodplain Managers.

Astroth, J. H. (1990). *Understanding Peasant Agriculture: An Integrated Land-Use Model for the Punjab*. Research Paper 223. Chicago, IL: University of Chicago, Department of Geography.

Bachelard, G. (1983). *Water and Dreams: An Essay on the Imagination of Matter*, trans. E. R. Farrell. Dallas, TX: Dallas Institute of Humanities and Culture.

Barlow, M. (1999). *Blue Gold: The Global Water Crisis and the Commodification of the World's Water Supply: A Special Report*. San Francisco, CA: International Forum on Globalization.

Bauer, C. J. (1998). *Against the Current: Privatization, Water Markets, and the State in Chile*. Boston, MA: Kluwer.

Baumann, D. D., Boland, J. J., and Haneman, W. M. (eds.) (1998). *Urban Water Demand Management and Planning*. New York, NY: McGraw-Hill.

Baumann, D. D. and Haimes, Y. Y. (eds.) (1988). *The Role of Social and Behavioral Sciences in Water Resources Planning and Management*. New York, NY: American Society of Civil Engineers.

Beaumont, P., Bonine, M., and McLachlan, K. (eds.) (1989). *Qanat, Kariz and Khattara: Traditional Water Systems in the Middle East and North Africa*. Cambridgeshire: MENAS Press.

Becerra, E. H. (1995). *Monitoring and Evaluation of Watershed Management Project Achievements*. FAO Conservation Guide 24. Rome: FAO.

Becker, A., Blöschl, G., and Hall, A. (eds.) (1999). Land surface heterogeneity and scaling in hydrology. Workshop proceedings (Rabat 1997). *Journal of Hydrology* **217**(3–4), 169–335.

Bedford, D. P. (1996). International water management in the Aral Sea Basin. *Water International* **21**(2), 63–69.

Bennett, J. W. (1969). *Northern Plainsmen – Adaptive Strategy and Agrarian Life*. Chicago, IL: Aldine Press.

Berkamp, G., McCartney, M., Dugan, P., McNeely, J., and Acreman, M. 2000. *Dams, Ecosystem Functions and Environmental Restoration*. Thematic Review II.1 prepared as an input to the World Commission on Dams, Cape Town. http://www.dams.org/kbase/thematic/tr21.htm. Last visited March 2, 2003.

Beverage Marketing Corporation (2000). *2000 Bottled Water in the U.S.* New York, NY: Beverage Marketing Corporation.

Biswas, A. (1970). *History of Hydrology*. Amsterdam: North-Holland.

Biswas, A. and Uitto, J. I. (eds.) (2001). *Sustainable Development of the Ganges–Brahmaputra–Meghna Basins*. Tokyo: United Nations University Press.

Black, M. (1998). *UNDP–World Bank Water and Sanitation Program. Learning What Works: 20 Years Cooperation in Water and Sanitation*. Washington, DC: World Bank.

Blaikie, P. (1985). *Political Economy of Soil Erosion in Developing Countries*. New York, NY: Wiley.

Blaikie, P. and Brookfield, H. (1987). *Land Degradation and Society*. London: Methuen.

Blake, N. (1956). *Water for Cities: A History of Urban Water Supply Problems*. Syracuse, NY: Syracuse University Press.

Bochet, J. (1986). *Management of Upland Watersheds: Participation of the Mountain Communities*. FAO Conservation Guide 8. Rome: FAO.

Boon, B. J., Davies, B. R., and Petts, G. E. (2000). *Global Perspectives on River Conservation: Science, Policy and Practice*. New York, NY: Wiley.

Boot, M. T. and Cairncross, S. (1997). Actions speak: the study of hygiene behaviour in water and sanitation projects. *Environment and Urbanization* **9**(1), 271–272.

Bosch, D. (ed.) (2002). Integrated decision making for watershed management. *Journal of the American Water Resources Association* special issues **38**(2) and **38**(4).

Boulder Area Sustainability Information Network (2003). http://bcn.boulder.co.us/basin. Last visited March 9, 2003.

Boulder Creek Watershed Initiative (2003). http://csf.colorado.edu/bcw/BCWI0.htm. Last visited March 9, 2003.

Boxer, B. (1998). China's water problems in the context of U.S.–China relations. *China Environment Series* **2**, 20–27. Washington, DC: Woodrow Wilson Center, Environmental Change and Security Project.

Boyd, C. and Slaymaker, T. (2000). Re-examining the "More people less erosion" hypothesis: special case or wider trend? *Natural Resource Perspectives* **63**. London: Overseas Development Institute.

Brady, N. C. and Weil, R. R. (1999). *The Nature and Properties of Soils*, 12th edition. Upper Saddle River, NJ: Prentice Hall.

Briscoe, J. (1997). Managing water as an economic good: rule for reformers. In: *Water: Economics, Management, and Demand*, ed. M. Kay, T. Franks, and L. Smith. London: Spon. pp. 339–361.

Brooks, D. B., Rached, E., and Saade, M. (1997). *Management of Water Demand in Africa and the Middle East: Current Practices and Future Needs*. Ottawa: International Development Research Centre.

Brooks, E. and Emel, J. (1995). The llano estacado of the American southern high plains. In: *Regions at Risk: Comparisons of Threatened Environments*, ed. J. X. Kasperson, R. E. Kasperson, and B. L. Turner II. Tokyo: United Nations University Press. pp. 255–303.

Brosius, J. P., Tsing, A. L., and Zerner, C. (1998). Representing communities: histories and politics of community-based natural resource management. *Society and Natural Resources* **11**, 157–168.

Brown, L. R., Flavin, C., Dunn, S., Mattoon, A., Sampat, P., and Starke, L. (2001). *State of the World – 2001*. New York, NY: Worldwatch Institute; London: Norton.

Brown, N. (2001). Attempts to scan old land use maps. *GEOBYTE (Royal Geographical Society with Institute of British Geographers)* **2**(8), 5.

Brunner, R. (ed.) (2002). *Finding Common Ground: Governance and Natural Resources in the American West*. New Haven, CT: Yale University Press.

Brunner, R. D. (1997). Introduction to the policy sciences. *Policy Sciences* **30**, 191–215.

Brunner, U. (2000). The ancient Marib Dam in Yemen – an example of irrigation techniques adapted to the local environmental conditions. In: *Water and History*, ed. H. Fahlbusch. Second World Water Forum. The Hague: International Commission on Irrigation and Drainage. pp. 70–80.

Brunner, U. and Haefner, H. (1986). The successful floodwater farming system of the Sabeans, Yemen Arab Republic. *Applied Geography* **6**, 77–86.

Brush, L. M., Wolman, M. G., and Huang, B. W. (1987). *Taming the Yellow River: Silt and Floods*. Dordrecht: Kluwer.

Bruun, C. (1991). *The Water Supply of Ancient Rome: A Study of Roman Imperial Administration*. Helsinki: Societas Scientiarum Fennica.

Burchi, S. (1994). *Preparing National Regulations for Water Resources Management: Principles and Practice.* FAO Legislative Study 52. Rome: FAO.

Butzer, K. W. (1976). *Early Hydraulic Civilization in Egypt: A Study in Cultural Ecology.* Chicago, IL: University of Chicago Press.

   (1990). The realm of cultural-human ecology: adaptation and change in historical perspective. In: *The Earth as Transformed by Human Action,* ed. B. L. Turner II *et al.* Cambridge: Cambridge University Press. pp. 685–701.

Cairncross, S. and Feachem, R. (1993). *Environmental Health Engineering in the Tropics,* 2nd edition. Chichester: Wiley.

Cameron, T. (1999). Economic literature relevant to Grand Canyon management. In: *Downstream: Adaptive Management of Glen Canyon Dam and the Colorado River Ecosystem* (National Research Council). Washington, DC: National Academy Press. pp. 201–220.

Campbell, C. S. and Ogden, M. H. (1999). *Constructed Wetlands in the Sustainable Landscape.* New York, NY: Wiley.

Cantor, L. M. (1970). *A World Geography of Irrigation.* New York, NY: Praeger.

Caponera, D. A. (1973). *Water Laws in Moslem Countries.* Irrigation and Drainage Paper 20. Rome: FAO.

Carney, J. (1998). The role of African rice and slaves in the history of rice cultivation in the Americas. *Human Ecology* 24(4), 525.

Carson, R. (1962). *Silent Spring.* Boston, MA: Houghton Mifflin.

CEQ (1981). *Environmental Trends.* Washington, DC: Council on Environmental Quality.

Chapman, G. P. and Thompson, M. (eds.) (1995). *Water and the Quest for Sustainable Development in the Ganges Valley.* London: Mansell.

Chappell, W. R., Abernathy, C. O., and Calderon R. (eds.) (2001). *Arsenic Exposure and Health Effects.* Proceedings of the Fourth International Conference on Arsenic Exposure and Health Effects, July 18–22, 2000. San Diego, California. New York, NY: Elsevier.

Chave, P. (2001). *The EU Water Framework Directive: An Introduction.* London: International Water Association.

Chow, V. T. (ed.) (1964). *Handbook of Applied Hydrology.* New York, NY: McGraw-Hill.

Clark, W. C. and Dickson, N. M. (2001). Civic science: America's encounter with global environmental risks. In: *Learning to Manage Global Environmental Risks,* ed. the Social Learning Group. Cambridge, MA: MIT Press. pp. 259–264.

Clean Water Action (2000). Unified federal policy for a watershed approach to federal land and resource management. *Federal Register* 65(202), 62566–62572.

Cohon, J. (1978). *Multiobjective Programming and Planning.* New York, NY: Academic Press.

Cooke, G. D., Welch, E. B., Peterson, S. A., and Newroth, P. R. (1993). *Restoration and Management of Lakes and Reservoirs,* 2nd edition. Ann Arbor, MI: Lewis.

Coomaraswamy, A. K. (1993). *Yakshas: Essays in the Water Cosmology.* Delhi: Oxford University Press.

Cosgrove, D. and Petts, G. (eds.) (1990). *Water, Engineering and Landscape.* London: Belhaven Press.

Cosgrove, W. J. and Rijsberman, F. R. (2000). *World Water Vision: Making Water Everybody's Business.* For the World Water Council, Conseil Mondial de l'Eau. London: Earthscan.

Costanza, R., Norton, B. G., and Haskell, B. D. (1992). *Ecosystem Health: New Goals for Environmental Management.* Washington, DC: Island Press.

Cotruvo, J. A. and Vogt, C. D. (1990). Rationale for water quality standards and goals. In: *Water Quality and Treatment: A Handbook of Community Water Supplies,* 4th edition. New York, NY: McGraw-Hill.

Cowling, E. (1982). Acid precipitation in historical perspective. *Environmental Science and Technology*, February, 110A–123A.

Cowling, E. and Nilsson, J. (1995). Acidification research: lessons from history and visions of environmental futures. *Water, Air and Soil Pollution* **85**, 279–292.

Creese, W. L. (1990). *TVA's Public Planning: The Vision, the Reality*. Knoxville, TN: University of Tennessee Press.

Crouch, D. P. (1993). *Water Management in Ancient Greek Cities*. Oxford: Oxford University Press.

Crow, B., Lindquist, A., and Wilson, D. (1995). *Sharing the Ganges: The Politics and Technology of River Development*. New Delhi: Sage.

Curtis, A. and DeLacy, T. (1996). Landcare in Australia: does it make a difference? *Journal of Environmental Management* **46**(2), 119–137.

Curtis, J. and Profeta, T. (1993). *After Silent Spring: The Unsolved Problems of Pesticide Use in the United States*. Washington, DC: Natural Resources Defense Council.

Darby, H. C. (1956). *The Draining of the Fens*, 2nd edition. Cambridge: Cambridge University Press.

Dartmouth Flood Observatory (2003). *Dartmouth Flood Observatory*. http://www.dartmouth.edu/artsci/geog/floods. Last visited March 29, 2003.

De Bernardi, R. and Giussani, G. (1995). *Guidelines of Lake Management. Vol. 7. Biomanipulation in Lakes and Reservoirs Management*. Shiga: ILEC Foundation and UN Environment Programme.

Deakin, A. (1893). *Irrigated India, an Australian View of India and Ceylon: Their Irrigation and Agriculture*. London: W. Thacker & Co.

Delli Priscoli, J. (2000). Water and civilization: using history to reframe water policy debates and to build a new ecological realism. *Water Policy* **1**(6), 623–636.

Denevan, W. M. (2001). *Cultivated Landscapes of Native Amazonia and the Andes*. Oxford: Oxford University Press.

Dikshit, D. D. (1986). *Agriculture, Irrigation and Horticulture in Ancient Sri Lanka*. Delhi: Bharatiya Vidya Prakashan.

Dinar, A. and Subramaniam, A. (1997). *Water Pricing Experiences: An International Perspective*. World Bank Technical Paper 386. Washington, DC: World Bank.

Dinar, A., Seidl, P., Olem, H., Jorden, V., Duda, A., and Johnson, R. (1995). *Restoring and Protecting the World's Lakes and Reservoirs*. World Bank Technical Paper 289. Washington, DC: World Bank.

Dixit, A. (ed.) (1994). *Himalaya Ganga: Contending with Complexity. Water Nepal* **4**, 1–328.

Doolette, J. B. and Magrath, W. B. (eds.) (1990). *Watershed Development in Asia: Strategies and Technologies*. World Bank Technical Paper 127. Washington, DC: World Bank.

Doolittle, W. E. (2000). *Cultivated Landscapes of Native North America*. Oxford: Oxford University Press.

Dougherty, T. C. and Hall, A. W. (1995). *Environmental Impact Assessment of Irrigation and Drainage Projects*. FAO Irrigation and Drainage Paper 53. Rome: FAO.

Dreiseitl, H., Grau, D., and Ludwig, K. (2001). *Waterscapes: Planning, Building and Designing with Water*. Basel: Birkhauser.

Dreze, J., Samson, M., and Singh, S. (eds.) (1997). *The Dam and the Nation: Displacement and Resettlement in the Narmada Valley*. Delhi: Oxford University Press.

Dubash, N. K., Dupar, M., Kothari, S., and Lissu, T. (2001). *A Watershed in Global Governance? An Independent Assessment of the World Commission on Dams*. Washington, DC: World Resources Institute.

Dubois, R. (1990). *Soil Erosion in a Coastal River Basin: A Case Study from the Philippines*. Geography Research Paper 232. Chicago, IL: Department of Geography, University of Chicago.

Duffy, J. (1990). *The Sanitarians: A History of American Public Health*. Urbana, IL: University of Illinois Press.

Dundes, A. (1988). *The Flood Myth*. Berkeley, CA: University of California Press.

Dunne, T. and Leopold, L. B. (1978). *Water in Environmental Planning*. San Francisco, CA: Freeman.

Duram, L. A. (1999). Factors in organic farmers' decisionmaking: Diversity, challenge, and obstacles. *American Journal of Alternative Agriculture* **14**, 2–11.

Dussart, B.H., White, G.F., Szesztay, K.S., Larkin, P.T., and Lagler, K. (1972). *Man-Made Lakes as Modified Ecosystems*. SCOPE Report 2. Paris: ICSU.

Easter, K. W., Dixon, J. A., and Hufschmidt, M. M. (eds.) (1986). *Watershed Resources Management: An Integrated Framework with Studies from Asia and the Pacific*. Boulder, CO and London: Westview Press.

Eccles, D. H. (1974). An outline of the physical limnology of Lake Malawi (Lake Nyasa). *Limnology and Oceanography* **19**, 730–743.

Edmonds, R. (1992). The Sanxia (Three Gorges) Project: the environmental arguments surrounding China's super dam. *Global Ecology and Biogeography Letters* **2**(4), 105–125.

Eliade, M. (1963). The waters and water symbolism. In: *Patterns in Comparative Religion*. New York, NY: Meridian. pp. 60–73.

El-Katsha, S. and White, A. U. (1989). Women, water and sanitation: Household behavioral patterns in two Egyptian villages. *Water International* **14**, 103–111.

Elliot, R. (1997). *Faking Nature: The Ethics of Environmental Restoration*. Special issue of *Ecological Restoration*. London: Routledge.

Encyclopedia Britannica (1974a). Groundwater. *Macropedia* **8**, 438. Chicago, IL: Encyclopedia Britannica.

  (1974b). Springs and wells. *Macropedia* **17**, 517–518. Chicago, IL: Encyclopedia Britannica.

Environmental Planning Collaborative (1998). *Sabarmati Riverfront Development*. Ahmedabad: VIKAS Centre for Development.

Esrey, S., Gough, J., Rapaport, D., *et al*. (eds.) (1998). *Ecological Sanitation*. Stockholm: SIDA.

European Environment Agency (2001). *Sustainable Water Use in Europe*. Luxembourg: Office for Official Publications of the European Communities.

European Parliament (2000). Directive of the European Parliament and of the Council: establishing a framework for Community action in the field of water policy. 2000/60/EC (23 October 2000) L 327/1. *Official Journal of the European Communities*. 22.12.2000.

Evans, H. B. (1994). *Water Distribution in Ancient Rome: The Evidence of Frontinus*. Ann Arbor, MI: University of Michigan Press.

Evenari, M., Shanan, L., and Tadmor, N. (1971). *The Negev, the Challenge of a Desert*. Cambridge, MA: Harvard University Press.

Falkenmark, M., Andersson, L., Catsenson, R., and Sunblad, K. (1999). *Water: A Reflection of Land Use*. Stockholm: Swedish Natural Science Research Council.

FAO (1993). *Watershed Management Training in Asia and the Pacific Region. Afghanistan, Bangladesh, Bhutan, The People's Republic of China, India, Myanmar, Nepal, Pakistan, Sri Lanka, and Thailand. Project Findings and Recommendations*. Rome: FAO.

  (1995a). *Reforming Water Resources Policy*. FAO Irrigation and Drainage Paper 52. Rome: FAO.

  (1995b). *Land and Water Integration and River Basin Management*. FAO Land and Water Bulletin 1. Rome: FAO.

(1996a). Computer-assisted watershed planning and management: technologies for national planning. *FAO Conservation Guide* **28**(1).

(1996b). *Support to Watershed Management in Asia. Regional Asia. Project Findings and Recommendations.* FO: DP/RAS/86/107. Rome: FAO.

(1997). *AGROVOC: Multilingual Agricultural Thesaurus*, 3rd edition. Rome: FAO.

FAO Investment Centre (1997). *Obtaining Environmental Information On-line.* Environmental Impact Guidelines 2. Rome: FAO. http://www.fao.org/tc/tci/sectors/ guidelines2.pdf. Last visited March 2, 2003.

Farrington, J., Turton, C., and James, A. J. (eds.) (1999). *Participatory Watershed Development: Challenges for the Twenty-First Century.* Delhi: Oxford University Press.

Faruqui, N. I., Biswas, A. K., and Bino, M. J. (eds.) (2001). *Water Management in Islam.* Tokyo: United Nations University Press.

Farvar, M. T. and Milton, J. P. (eds.) (1972). *The Careless Technology: Ecology and International Development.* Garden City, NY: Natural History Press.

Fauveau, V. (ed.) (1994). *MATLAB: Women, Children and Health.* Dhaka: International Centre for Diarrhoeal Disease Research.

Federal Interagency Stream Restoration Working Group (2001). *Stream Corridor Restoration: Principles, Processes, Practices*, revised edition. Washington, DC: Government Printing Office.

Fekete, B. M., Vorosmarty, C. J., and Grabs, W. (2002). High resolution fields of global runoff combining observed river discharge and simulated water balance. *Global Biogeochemical Cycles* **16**(3), 1–6.

Feldhaus, A. (1995). *Water and Womanhood: Religious Meanings of Rivers in Maharashtra.* Delhi: Oxford University Press.

Feldman, D. L. (1991). *Water Resources Management: In Search of an Environmental Ethic.* Baltimore, MD: Johns Hopkins University Press.

Fergusson, B. (1994). *Stormwater Infiltration.* Chelsea, MI: Lewis.

Fisher, W. F. (ed.) (1995). *Toward Sustainable Development? Struggling over India's Narmada River.* Armonk, NY: Sharpe.

Fisk, D. W. (ed.) (1989). *Proceedings Wetlands: Concerns and Successes.* Meeting of the American Water Resources Association, Tampa, FL, 17–22 September. Bethesda, MD: American Water Resources Association.

Fiske, G. and Yoffe, S. (2002). Use of GIS for analysis of indicators of conflict and cooperation over international freshwater resources. Unpublished paper in review. http://www.transboundarywaters.orst.edu/projects/bar/BAR_chapter3.htm. Last visited March 21, 2003.

Forman, R. T. T. (1995). *Land Mosaics: The Ecology of Landscapes and Regions.* Cambridge: Cambridge University Press.

France, R. (ed.) (2002). *Handbook of Water Sensitive Planning and Design.* Boca Raton, FL: CRC Press.

Galat, D. L., Lider, E. L., Vigg, S., and Robertson, S. R. (1981). Limnology of a large, deep, North American terminal lake, Pyramid Lake, Nevada, U.S.A. *Hydrobiologia* **82**, 281–317.

Galbraith, H., Strzepek, K., and Yates, D. (2001). *Moving Beyond the Vision: The Importance of Case Studies in Reconciling Water for Nature and Agriculture.* Dialogue Working Paper 2. Colombo: Dialogue Secretariat.

Galloway, G. (1980). *Ex Post Evaluation of Regional Water Resources Development: The Case of the Yazoo-Mississippi Delta.* Fort Belvoir, VA: US Army Corps of Engineers, Institute for Water Resources.

Gandhi, M. K. (1957). *Gandhi, An Autobiography: The Story of My Experiments with Truth.* Boston: Beacon Press.

Garbrecht, G. (1996). Historical water storage for irrigation in the Fayum Depression (Egypt). *Irrigation and Drainage Systems* **10**(1), 47–76.

Geddes, P. (1949). Valley section. In: *Cities in Evolution*. London: Williams and Norgate. First published 1911.

Germany. Federal Ministry for the Environment (2001). *Water – A Key to Sustainable Development*. Bonn International Conference on Freshwater. Bonn: Courir-Druck.

Getches, D. (1996). *Water Law in a Nutshell*, 3rd edition. St. Paul, MN: West Group.

Ghassemi, F., Jakeman, A. J., and Nix, H. A. (1995). *Salinisation of Land and Water Resources: Human Causes, Extent, Management and Case Studies*. Sydney: University of New South Wales Press.

Gilmour, A., Walderden, G., and Scandol, J. (1999). Adaptive management of the water cycle on the urban fringe: three Australian case studies. *Conservation Ecology [online]* **3**(1). http://www.consecol.org/vol3/iss1/art11. Last visited March 2, 2003.

Glacken, C. (1968). *Traces on the Rhodian Shore: Nature and Culture in Western Thought from Ancient Times to the end of the Eighteenth Century*. Berkeley, CA: University of California Press.

Gleick, P. H. (ed.) (1993). *Water in Crisis: a Guide to the World's Fresh Water Resources*. Oxford: Oxford University Press.

(1996). Basic water requirements for human activities: meeting basic needs. *Water International* **21**, 83–92.

(1998a). The human right to water. *Water Policy* **1**, 487–503.

(1998b). *The World's Water: The Biennial Report on Freshwater Resources*. Washington, DC: Island Press.

(1998c). The status of large dams, the end of an era? In: *The World's Water*, ed. P. H. Gleick. Washington, DC: Island Press. pp. 75–104.

(2000a). *The World's Water, 2000–2001: The Biennial Report on Freshwater Resources*. Washington, DC: Island Press.

(ed.) (2000b). *Water: The Potential Consequences of Climate Variability and Change*. A Report of the National Water Assessment Group for the US Global Change Research Program. Oakland, CA: Pacific Institute.

(2002). *The World's Water, 2002–2003: The Biennial Report on Freshwater Resources*, Washington, DC: Island Press.

Goldsmith, E. and Hildyard, N. (eds.) (1984). *The Social and Environmental Effects of Large Dams*, vol. 1. Camelford: Wadebridge Ecological Centre.

(eds.) (1986a). *The Social and Environmental Effects of Large Dams*, vol. 2. Camelford: Wadebridge Ecological Centre.

(eds.) (1986b). *The Social and Environmental Effects of Large Dams: A Review of the Literature*, vol. 3. Camelford: Wadebridge Ecological Centre.

Gosnell, H. (2001). Section 7 of the Endangered Species Act and the art of compromise: the evolution of a reasonable and prudent alternative for the Animas-La Plata project. *Natural Resources Journal* **41**(3), 561–626.

Goubert, J. P. (1986). *The Conquest of Water: The Advent of Health in the Industrial Age*, trans. A. Wilson. Princeton, NJ: Princeton University Press.

Grigg, N. (1988). *Infrastructure Engineering and Management*. New York, NY: Wiley.

(1996). *Water Resources Management: Principles, Regulations, and Cases*. New York, NY: McGraw-Hill.

Gruntfest, E. (1997). *Twenty Years Later: What We Have Learned Since the Big Thompson Flood*. Special Publication 33. Boulder, CO: Natural Hazards Research and Applications Information Center.

Gruntfest, E. and Montz, B. (1986). Changes in American urban floodplain occupancy since 1958: the experience of nine cities. *Applied Geography* **15**, 325–338.

Guillerme, A. (1983). *The Age of Water: The Urban Environment in the North of France, A.D.300–1800.* College Station, TX: Texas A&M University Press.

Gumprecht, B. (1999). *The Los Angeles River: Its Life, Death and Possible Rebirth.* Baltimore, MD: Johns Hopkins University Press.

Gunderson, L. (1999). Resilience, flexibility, and adaptive management – antidotes for spurious certitude? *Conservation Ecology [online]* 3(1). http://www.consecol.org/vol3/iss1/art7. Last visited March 2, 2003.

Gunderson, L. and Holling, C. S. (2001). *Panarchy: Understanding Transformations in Human and Natural Systems.* Washington, DC: Island Press.

Gunderson, L., Holling, C. S., and Light, S. S. (eds.) (1995). *Barriers and Bridges to the Renewal of Ecosystems and Institutions.* New York, NY: Columbia University Press.

Gyawali, D. (2001). *Water in Nepal.* Kathmandu: Himal Books.

H. John Heinz III Center for Science, Economics and Environment (2002). *Dam Removal: Science and Decision-Making.* Washington, DC: H. John Heinz III Center.

Haan, C. T., Johnson, H. P., and Brakensiek, D. L. (eds.) (1982). *Hydrologic Modelling of Small Watersheds.* St. Joseph, MI: American Society of Agricultural Engineers.

Haberman, D. (2000). River of love in an age of pollution. In: *Hinduism and Ecology*, ed. C. K. Chapple and M. E. Tucker. Cambridge, MA: Harvard University Press. pp. 339–354.

Haestad Methods (2002). *Water Security.* http://www.watersecurity.org. Last visited 21 August 2002.

Haggart, K., Huq, S., Rahman, A. A., Haq, E., Majumder, M. K., and Miranda, C. (1994). *Rivers of Life: Bangladeshi Journalists Take a Critical Look at the Flood Action Plan.* London: PANOS.

Haimes, Y., Moser, D., and Stakhiv, E. (1994). *Risk-Based Decision Making in Water Resources VI.* New York, NY: American Society of Civil Engineers.

Halvorson, S. (2000). *The Geography of Children's Vulnerability: Households and Water-Related Disease Hazard in a Mountain Community in Northern Pakistan.* Doctoral dissertation. Boulder, CO: University of Colorado.

Haney, A. and Power, R. (1996). Adaptive management for sound ecosystem management. *Environmental Management* **20**, 879–886.

Harlin, J. M. and. Lanfear, K. J. (eds.) (1993). *Proceedings of the Symposium on Geographic Information Systems and Water Resources.* Bethesda, MD: American Water Resources Association.

Harrison, R. W. (1961). *Alluvial Empire: A Study of State and Local Efforts Toward Land Development in the Alluvial Valley of the Lower Mississippi River.* Little Rock, AR: Pioneer Press.

Hasan, A. (1993). *Scaling Up of the OPP's Low-cost Sanitation Programme.* Karachi: Orangi Pilot Project.

(1997). *Working with Government.* Karachi: City Press.

Haury, E. (1976). *The Hohokam: Desert Farmers & Craftsmen.* Tucson, AZ: University of Arizona Press.

Heaney, J. (2002). *Environmental Center of the Rockies Demonstration Project, Technical Details.* http://bcn.boulder.co.us/basin/local/envirocenter.html. Last visited March 2, 2003.

Helms, D. (1992). *History of Soil and Water Conservation Services.* Washington, DC: Soil Conservation Service.

Herring, J. ed. (2003). Changes in Water Management: Lessons Learned. *Water Resources IMPACT* **5**(1), 3–27.

Hewitt, K. (1982) Natural dams and outburst floods of the Karakoram Himalaya. In: *Hydrological Aspects of Alpine and High-Mountain Areas*, ed. J. W. Glen. International Commission on Snow and Ice (ICSI) Symposium, Exeter, UK, 19–30

July 1982. International Association of Hydrological Sciences Publication 138. Wallingford: IAHS. pp. 259–269.

Hilgard, E. W. (1900). *Nature, Value and Utilization of Alkali Lands*. Sacramento, CA: California State Printing Office.

Hillel, D. (1992). *Out of the Earth: Civilization and the Life of the Soil*. Berkeley, CA: University of California Press.

Hippocrates (1978). Airs, waters, places. In: *Hippocratic Writings*, trans. J. Chadwick and W. Mann. Harmondsworth: Penguin. pp. 148–169.

Holling, C. S. (ed.) (1978). *Adaptive Environmental Assessment and Management*. New York, NY: Wiley.

Hoque, B. A., Hoque, M. M., Ali, N., and Coghlan, S. E. (1994). Sanitation in a poor settlement in Bangladesh – a challenge for the 1990s. *Environment and Urbanization* 6(2), 79–86.

Hori, H. (2000). *Mekong: Environment and Development*. Tokyo: United Nations University Press.

Howe, C. W. (1997). Dimensions of sustainability: geographical, temporal, institutional and psychological. *Land Economics* 73(4), 597–607.

Hughes, D. (1994). *Pan's Travail: Environmental Problems of the Ancient Greeks and Romans*. Baltimore, MD: Johns Hopkins University Press.

Hutchinson, G. E. (1975). *A Treatise on Limnology. Vol. 1. Part 1, Geography and Physics of Lakes*. New York, NY: Wiley.

ICID (1957). *Can Man Develop a Permanent Irrigation Agriculture?* Proceedings. New Delhi: International Commission on Irrigation and Drainage.

ICOLD (1998). *World Register of Dams*. Paris: International Commission on Large Dams.

ICOLD, IHA, and ICID (2001). Open letter from ICOLD, IHA and ICID on the Final Report of the World Commission on Dams. http://www.dams.org/report/reaction/reaction_icold_et_al.htm. Last visited March 1, 2003.

ICWE (1992). *The Dublin Statement on Water and Sustainable Development*. Dublin: International Conference on Water and the Environment.

IDNDR–UNESCAP (1999). *Water Hazards, Resources and Management for Disaster Prevention: A Review of the Asian Conditions, IDNDR 1991–1999*. Bangkok: UN Economic and Social Commission for Asia and the Pacific.

ILEC (1994–96). *Data Book of World Lake Environments*. Kusatsu: International Lake Environment Committee.

  (1995). *Data Book of World Lake Environments, Asia and Oceania*. Kusatsu: International Lake Environment Committee.

  (1996). *Conservation and Management of Lakes/Reservoirs in India*. Kusatsu: International Lake Environment Committee.

  (2002). *World Lakes Database*. http://www.ilec.or.jp/database/database.html. Last visited March 27, 2003.

ILEC and UNEP (1995). *Biomanipulation in Lakes and Reservoirs Management*. Kusatsu: ILEC.

Iles, A. (1996). Adaptive management: Making environmental law and policy more dynamic, experimentalist and learning. *Environmental and Planning Law Journal* 13, 288–308.

ILRI (2002). *International Land Reclamation Institute*. http://www.ilri.nl. Last visited March 2, 2003.

International Federation for Information and Documentation (FID) (2000). *Key Issues in Water Information*. Delft: IRC International Water and Sanitation Centre.

IPCC (1995). *Second Assessment Report: Climate Change*. Cambridge: Cambridge University Press.

(2001a). *The Regional Impacts of Climate Change: An Assessment of Vulnerability.* Cambridge: Cambridge University Press.

(2001b). *Climate Change 2001: Impacts, Adaptation and Vulnerability.* Working Group II. Cambridge: Cambridge University Press.

(2001c). *Working Group II: Impacts, Adaptation, and Vulnerability.* Technical Summary. Intergovernmental Panel on Climate Change. Cambridge: Cambridge University Press.

IRC International Water and Sanitation Centre (2000). World Water Forum (5): priority for sanitation? *Source Weekly [online]* **12–14.** http://www.irc.nl/source/weekly/00124.html#sanitation. Last visited March 2, 2003.

Islam, M. A. (1995). *Environment, Land Use, and Natural Hazards in Bangladesh.* Dhaka: Dhaka University.

IUCN (2000). *Red List Categories.* Version 3.1. Gland, Switzerland: International Union for Conservation of Nature and Natural Resources.

(2002). *Wetlands and Water Resources Programme.* http://www.iucn.org/themes/wetlands/wetlands.html. Last visited March 2, 2003.

IUCN and World Bank (1996). *Large Dams: Learning from the Past, Looking at the Future.* Proceedings from a conference on 11–12 April 1996 in Gland, Switzerland. Gland: IUCN; Washington, DC: World Bank.

Ives, J. D. (1986). *Glacial Lake Outburst Floods and Risk Engineering in the Himalaya.* Occasional Paper 5. Kathmandu: International Centre for Integrated Mountain Development.

IWA (2001). *Efficient Water Management: Making It Happen.* Berlin: World Water Congress.

IWMI (2001). *Dialogue on Water, Food and Environment. Proposed Final Version.* Colombo: International Water Management Institute. http://www.iwmi.cgiar.org/dialogue. Last visited March 31, 2003.

Jacobs, J. W. (1995). Mekong Committee history and lessons for river basin development. *Geographical Journal* **161**(2), 135–148.

Jacobs, J. W. and Wescoat, J. L., Jr. (2002). Managing river resources: lessons from Glen Canyon Dam. *Environment* March 2002, 8–19.

Jansen, M., Mulloy, M., and Urban, G. (eds.) (1991). *Forgotten Cities on the Indus.* Mainz: Philipp von Zabern.

Japan Map Centre (ed.) (1982). *Maps of Japanese Lakes.* Technical Data D1-No. 221. Tsukuba: National Geographical Institute.

Joardar, S. D. (1998). Carrying capacities and standards as bases towards urban infrastructure planning in India: a case of urban water supply and sanitation. *Habitat International* **22**(3), 327–337.

Johnson, B. (1999). Introduction to the special feature: adaptive management – scientifically sound, socially challenged? *Conservation Ecology [online]* 3(1), 1–6. http://www.consecol.org. Last visited March 2, 2003.

Johnston, D. M. (2003). The digital river basin: interactive real-time visualization of landscape processes. Proceedings of international symposium on Landscape Modeling. Anhalt University, Germany.

Jonsson, A. and Satterthwaite, D. (2000). Overstating the provision of safe water and sanitation to urban populations: a critical review of the quality and reliability of official statistics and of the criteria used in defining what is "adequate" and "safe". Background paper prepared for the National Academy of Science's Panel on Urban Population Dynamics. London: International Institute for Environment and Development.

Kates, R. W. and Burton, I. (eds.) (1986). *Geography, Resources and Environment,* vol. 1: Selected writings of G. F. White; vol. 2: Themes from the work of G. F. White. Chicago, IL: University of Chicago Press.

Kates, R. W., Clark, W. C., Correll, R. *et al.* (2001). Sustainability science. *Science* **292**, 641–642.

Kemmer, F. N. (1998). *The NALCO Water Handbook.* New York, NY: McGraw-Hill.

Kenney, D. (1997). *Resource Management at the Watershed Level: An Assessment of the Changing Federal Role in the Emerging Era of Community-Based Watershed Management.* Boulder, CO: Natural Resources Law Center.

Khan, A. H. (1994). *Orangi Pilot Project Programs,* 3rd edition. Karachi: Orangi Pilot Project.

   (1996). *The Orangi Pilot Project: Reflections and Reminiscences.* Karachi: Oxford University Press.

Kirkby, M. J. (1978). *Hillslope Hydrology.* New York, NY: Wiley.

Kluger, J. R. (1992). *Turning on Water with a Shovel: The Career of Elwood Mead.* Albuquerque, NM: University of New Mexico Press.

Knapp, G. (1991). *Andean Ecology: Adaptive Dynamics in Ecuador.* Boulder, CO: Westview Press.

Knopf, J. (1991). *The Xeriscape Flower Gardener.* Boulder, CO: Johnson Books.

Kobori, I. and Glantz, M. H. (eds.) (1998). *Central Eurasian Water Crisis: Caspian, Aral and Dead Seas.* Tokyo: United Nations University Press.

Kondolf, G. M. (1995). Five elements for effective evaluation of stream restoration. *Restoration Ecology* **3**, 133–136.

   (1997). Hungry water: Effects of dams and gravel mining on river channels. *Environmental Management* **21**, 533–551.

Kotwicki, V. (1986). *Floods of Lake Eyre.* Adelaide: Engineering and Water Supply Department.

Kreutzmann, H. (ed.) (2000). *Sharing Water: Irrigation and Water Management in the Hindukush, Karakorum, Himalaya.* Delhi: Oxford University Press.

Kromm, D. E. and White, S. (eds.) (1992). *Groundwater Exploitation in the High Plains.* Lawrence, KS: University of Kansas Press.

Kumar, S. V. (1983). *The Pauranic Lore of Holy Water-Places.* New Delhi: Munshiram Manoharlal.

Kusler, J. and Kentula, M. (eds.) (1990). *Wetland Creation and Restoration: The State of the Science.* Washington, DC: Island Press.

L. R. Johnston Associates (1992). *FloodplainManagement in the United States: an Assessment Report.* Report FIA-18. Washington, DC: Federal Interagency Floodplain Management Task Force.

Lagler, K. F. (ed.) (1969). *Man-Made Lakes: Planning and Development.* Rome: FAO.

Lal, P., Lim-Applegate, H., and Scoccimarro, M. (2001). The adaptive decision-making process as a tool for integrated natural resource management: focus, attitudes, and approach. *Conservation Ecology [online]* **5**(2), 11. http://www.consecol.org/vol5/iss2/art11. Last visited April 7, 2003.

Lansing, J. S. (1991). *Priests and Programmers: Technologies of Power in the Engineered Landscape of Bali.* Princeton, NJ: Princeton University Press.

Lachavanne, J.-B. (1980). Les manifestations de l'eutrophisation des eaux dans un grand lac profond, le Léman (Suisse). *Schweizerische Zeitschrift fur Hydrologie* **42**(2), 127–154.

Leatherman, S. P. (2002). *Get Ready 2002: Hurricane Preparedness Guide. What to do Before, During and After a Hurricane.* Miami, FL: International Hurricane Center, Florida International University.

Lee, K. N. (1993). *Compass and Gyroscope: Integrating Science and Politics for the Environment.* Washington, DC: Island Press.

   (1999). Appraising adaptive management. *Conservation Ecology [online]* **3**(2), 3. http://www.consecol.org/vol3/iss2/art3. Last visited March 2, 2003.

Leopold, A. (1991). *A Sand County Almanac*. New York, NY: Ballantine Books. First published 1949.

Leopold, L. and Maddock, T. (1954). *The Flood Control Controversy: Big Dams, Little Dams, and Land Management*. New York, NY: Ronald Press.

Lightfoot, D. (1997). The nature, history, and distribution of Lithic mulch agriculture: an ancient technique of dryland agriculture. *Agricultural History Review* **44**(2), 206–222.

Lightfoot, D. R. and Eddy, F. W. (1995). The construction and configuration of Anasazi pebble–mulch gardens in the Northern Rio Grande. *American Antiquity* **60**(3), 459–470.

Litton, R. B., Tetlow, R. B., Sorenson, J., and Beatty, R.A. (1974). *Water and Landscape: An Aesthetic Overview of the Role of Water in the Landscape*. Port Washington, NY: Water Information Center.

Liverman, D. M. (1999). Adaptation to drought in Mexico. In: *Drought*, ed. D. Wilhite. New York, NY: Routledge. vol. 2, pp. 35–45.

Liverman, D. M., Yarnal, B., and Turner, B.L. II. (in press). Human dimensions of global change. In: *Geography in America at the Dawn of the 21st Century*, ed. G. Gaile and C. Wilmott. Oxford: Oxford University Press.

Livy (1960). *The Early History of Rome*, trans. A. de Selincourt. Harmondsworth: Penguin.

Lohmann, U. (2002). Interactions between anthropogenic aerosols and the hydrological cycle. *International Geosphere Biosphere Programme: Global Change Newsletter* **49**, 14–19.

Lowdermilk, W. C. (1944). *Palestine: Land of Promise*. New York, NY: Harper and Brothers.

(1953). *Conquest of the Land Through 7,000 Years*. Agriculture Information Bulletin 99. Washington, DC: Government Printing Office.

Lowe-McConnell, R. H. (ed.) (1966). *Man-Made Lakes, Proceedings*. London: Published for the Institute of Biology; New York, NY: Academic Press.

Lowrance, R., Dabney, S., and Schultz, R. (2002). Improving water and soil quality with conservation buffers. *Journal of Soil and Water Conservation* **57**(2), special issue.

L'vovich, M. and White, G. F. (1990). Use and transformation of terrestrial water systems. In: *The Earth as Transformed by Human Action*, ed. B. L. Turner II *et al.* Cambridge: Cambridge University Press. pp. 236–237.

Maass, A. (1962). *Design of Water Resource Systems*. Cambridge, MA: Harvard University Press.

MacDonnell, L. J. (1999). *From Reclamation to Sustainability: Water, Agriculture and the Environment in the American West*. Niwot, CO: University Press of Colorado.

Macinko, G. (1963). The Columbia Basin Project: expectations, realizations, implications. *Geographical Review* **53**(2), 185–199.

(1975). *The Columbia Basin Project Re-Appraised*. Working paper 24, UNDP/UN Interregional Seminar on River Basin and Interbasin Development. Proceedings of a conference in Budapest, Hungary, September 1975. New York, NY: United Nations Department of Economic and Social Affairs.

Malanson, G. (1993). *Riparian Landscapes*. Cambridge: Cambridge University Press.

Margat, J. (1996). Groundwater component. *Comprehensive Global Freshwater Assessment*. New York, NY: United Nations.

Marsh, G. P. (1864). *Man and Nature: Or, Physical Geography as Modified by Human Action*. Cambridge, MA: Belknap Press (1965 reprint).

Mathur, A. and da Cunha, D. (2001). *Mississippi Floods: Designing a Shifting Landscape*. New Haven, CT: Yale University Press.

Maxey, G. B. (1964). Hydrogeology. In: *Handbook of Applied Hydrology*, ed. V. T. Chow. New York, NY: McGraw-Hill. pp. 4–35.

McCuen, R. A. (1989). *Hydrologic Analysis and Design*. Englewood Cliffs, NJ: Prentice-Hall.

McCully, P. (1996). *Silenced Rivers: The Ecology and Politics of Large Dams*. London: Zed Books.

McDonough, W. and Braungart, M. (2002). *Cradle to Cradle:Remaking the Way We Make Things*. New York, NY: North Point Press.

McGranahan, G. and Kjellen, M. (1997). *Urban Water: Towards Health and Sustainability*. Stockholm: Stockholm Environment Institute.

Meade, R. H. (ed.) (1995). *Contaminants in the Mississippi River, 1987–92*. Circular 1133. Washington, DC: US Geological Survey.

Melosi, M. V. (1999). *The Sanitary City: Technical Choices, Urban Growth, and Environmental Services from Colonial Times to the Present*. Baltimore, MD: Johns Hopkins University Press.

Merritt, R. H. (1984). *The Corps, the Environment, and the Upper Mississippi River Basin*. EP 870-1-19. Ft. Belvoir, VA: US Army Corps of Engineers.

Michel, S. (2000). *Place, Power, and Water Pollution in the Californias: A Geographical Analysis of Water Quality Politics in the Tijuana-San Diego Metropolitan Region*. Doctoral dissertation. Boulder, CO: Department of Geography, University of Colorado.

Micklin, P. P. (1992). The Aral crisis: introduction to the special issue. *Post-Soviet Geography* **33**(5), 269–283.

Micklin, P. P. and Williams, W. D. (eds.) (1996). *The Aral Sea Basin*. NATO Workshop, 1994, Tashkent. New York, NY: Springer.

Mileti, D. S. (1999). *Disasters by Design*. Washington, DC: Joseph Henry Press.

Mitchell, B. (ed.) (1990). *Integrated Water Management*. New York, NY: Belhaven Press.

Mitchell, W. P. and Guillet, D. (eds.) (1994). *Irrigation at High Altitudes: The Social Organization of Water Control Systems in the Andes*. Society for Latin American Anthropology Monograph 12. Society for Latin American Anthropologists.

Mitsch, W. and Gosselink, J. (2000). *Wetlands*, 3rd edition. New York, NY: Wiley.

Moench, M., Caspari, E., and Dixit, A. (eds.) (1999). *Rethinking the Mosaic: Investigations into Local Water Management*. Kathmandu: Nepal Water Conservation Foundation; Boulder, CO: Institute for Social and Environmental Transition.

Mommsen, T. and Krueger, P. (1985). *The Digest of Justinian*. 4 vols, ed. A. Watson. Philadelphia, PA: University of Pennsylvania Press.

Montz, B. and Gruntfest, E. (1986). Changes in American floodplain occupancy since 1958: the experiences of nine cities. *Applied Geography* **6**, 325–338.

Morse Commission (1992). *Sardar Sarovar: The Report of the Independent Review*. Ottawa: Resources for the Future International.

Muir, J. (1910). The Hetch-Hetchy Valley: a national question. *Sierra Club Bulletin* **16**(5), 263–269.

Munn, M. D. and Gilliom, R. J. (2001). *Pesticide Toxicity Index for Freshwater Aquatic Organisms*. Denver, CO: US Geological Survey.

Natural Resources Law Center (2000). *The New Watershed Source Book: A Directory and Review of Watershed Initiatives in the Western United States*. Boulder, CO: University of Colorado, Natural Resources Law Center.

Nordstrom, D. K. (2002). Worldwide occurrences of arsenic in groundwater. *Science* **296**, 2144–2145.

NRC (1989a). *Alternative Agriculture*. Washington, DC: National Academy Press.
    (1989b). *Irrigation-Induced Water Quality Problems*. Washington, DC: National Academy Press.

(1990). *Alternative Agriculture.* Washington, DC: National Academy Press.

(1992). *Restoration of Aquatic Ecosystems.* Washington, DC: National Academy Press.

(1993a). *Ground Water Vulnerability Assessment: Contamination Potential Under Conditions of Uncertainty.* Washington, DC: National Academy Press.

(1995). *Wetlands: Characteristics and Boundaries.* Washington, DC: National Academy Press.

(1996a). *A New Era for Irrigation.* Washington, DC: National Academy Press.

(1999a). *Groundwater and Soil Cleanup: Improving Management of Persistent Contaminants.* Washington, DC: National Academy Press.

(1999b). *Downstream: Adaptive Management of Glen Canyon Dam and the Colorado River Ecosystem.* Washington, DC: National Academy Press.

(1999c). *New Strategies for America's Watersheds.* Washington, DC: National Academy Press.

(1999d). *Our Common Journey. A Transition Toward Sustainability.* Washington, DC: National Academy Press.

(2000a). *Risk Analysis and Uncertainty in Flood Damage Reduction Studies.* Washington, DC: National Research Council.

(2000b). *Water for the Middle East.* Washington, DC: National Academy Press.

(2000c). *Watershed Management for Potable Water Supply.* Washington, DC: National Academy Press.

(2000d). *Watershed Management for Potable Water Supply: Assessing the New York City Strategy.* Washington, DC: National Academy Press.

(2001). *Growing Population, Changing Landscapes: Studies from India, China and the United States.* Washington, DC: National Academy Press.

(2002). *Privatization of Water Services in the United States: an Assessment of Issues and Experience.* Washington, DC: National Academy Press.

NRCS (1998). *National Watershed Manual.* Washington, DC: US Government Printing Office.

(2000). *A Report to Congress on Aging Watershed Infrastructure: an Analysis and Strategy for Addressing the Nation's Aging Flood Control Dams.* Washington, DC: US Department of Agriculture.

Olami, Y. and Peleg, Y. (1977). The water supply system of Caesarea Maritima. *Israeli Exploration Journal* **27**(2–3), 127–137.

O'Reilly, W. (1999). *Sustainable Landscape Design in Arid Climates.* Geneva: The Aga Khan Trust for Culture; Washington, DC: Dumbarton Oaks.

Ortolano, L., Kao Cushing, K., and contributing authors (2000). *Grand Coulee Dam and the Columbia Basin Project, USA.* Cape Town: World Commission on Dams.

Ostiani, L. F. and Patrizio, W. (eds.) (1996). *Steps Towards a Participatory and Integrated Approach to Watershed Management. Bolivia, Burundi, Nepal, Pakistan, and Tunisia.* GCP/INT/5422/ITA. Rome: FAO.

Oswald, W. J. (1995). Ponds in the 21st century. *Water Science and Technology* **31**(2), 1–8.

Parson, E. A. and Clark, W. C. (1995). Sustainable development as social learning: theoretical perspectives and practical challenges for the design of a research program. In: L. Gunderson *et al.*, 1995. pp. 428–460.

Penning-Rowsell, E. (1996). *Improving Flood Hazard Management Across Europe. Euroflood.* Middlesex: Flood Hazards Centre.

Pereira, H. C. (1989). *Policy and Practice in the Management of Tropical Watersheds.* Boulder, CO: Westview Press.

Person, H. (1936). *Little Waters: A Study of Headwater Streams and other Little Waters, Their Use and Relations to the Land.* Washington, DC: Government Printing Office.

Pielke, R. A., and Bravo de Guenni, L. (eds.) (in press). How to evaluate the vulnerability in changing environmental conditions. In: *Vegetation, Water, Humans and the Climate. A Synthesis of the ICBP Core Project, Biospheric Aspects of the Hydrologic Cycle*, ed. P. Kabat *et al.* Heidelberg: Springer.

Pitlick, J. and Van Steeter, M. (1998). Geomorphology and endangered fish habitats of the Upper Colorado River. 2. Linking sediment transport to habitat maintenance. *Water Resources Research* **34**(2), 303–316.

Plato (1965). *Critias*, trans. D. Lee. Harmondsworth: Penguin.

Platt, R. H., Rowntree, R. A., and Muick, P. C. (eds.) (1994). *The Ecological City: Preserving and Restoring Urban Biodiversity.* Amherst, MA: University of Massachusetts Press.

Poland, J. F., (1981). Subsidence in United States due to ground-water withdrawal. *American Society of Civil Engineers, Journal of the Irrigation and Drainage Division* **107**(IR2), 115–135.

Postel, S. (1999). *Pillar of Sand: Can the Irrigation Miracle Last?* New York: Norton.

Powell, J. W. (1879). *Report on the Lands of the Arid Region.* Washington, DC: Government Printing Office.

Prince, H. (1997). *Wetlands of the American Midwest: A historical geography of Changing Attitudes.* Chicago, IL: University of Chicago Press.

Prince of Orange (2002). *No Water, No Future. A Water Focus for Johannesburg.* http://www.nowaternofuture.org. Last visited August 31, 2002.

Pulwarty, R. S. and Redmond, K. T. (1997). Climate and salmon restoration in the Columbia River Basin: the role and usability of seasonal forecasts. *Bulletin of the American Meteorological Society* **78**, 381–397.

PWRPC (1950). *The Report.* 3 vols. Washington, DC: Government Printing Office.

Rached, E., Rathgeber, E., and Brooks, D. (1996). *Water Management in Africa and the Middle East: Challenges and Opportunities.* Ottawa: International Development Research Centre.

Ramsar Convention on Wetlands (1999). *The Ramsar Convention Definition of "Wetland" and Classification System for Wetland Type.* http://www.ramsar.org/key_ris_types.htm. Last visited March 9, 2003.

   (2000). *The Annotated Ramsar List. The List of Wetlands of International Importance.* Gland: The Bureau of the Convention on Wetlands.

   (2001). *What are wetlands?* Ramsar Information Paper 1. http://www.ramsar.org/about_infopack_1e.htm. Last visited March 27, 2003.

Reid, G. K. (1961). *Ecology of Inland Waters and Estuaries.* New York, NY: Reinhold.

Reuss, M. (1998). *Designing the Bayous: The Control of Water in the Atchafalaya Basin, 1800–1995.* Alexandria, VA: US Army Corps of Engineers, Office of History.

Revenga, C., Murray, S., Abramovitz, J., and Hammond, A. (1998). *Watersheds of the World: Ecological Value and Vulnerability.* Washington, DC: World Water Resources Institute.

Richards, J. and Flint, E. (1994). *Historic Land Use and Carbon Estimates for South and Southeast Asia 1880–1980.* ORNL/CDIAC-61 NDP-046. Knoxville, TN: Oak Ridge National Laboratory.

Riebsame, W. E., Strzepek, K. M., Wescoat, J. L. Jr., *et al.* (1995). Complex river basins. In: *As Climate Changes: International Impacts and Implications*, ed. K. M. Strzepek and J. B. Smith. Cambridge: Cambridge University Press. pp. 57–91.

Riley, A. L. (1998). *Restoring Streams in Cities: A Guide for Planners, Policymakers, and Citizens.* Washington, DC: Island Press.

Rogers, P. and Lydon, P (eds.) (1997). *Water in the Arab World: Perspectives and Prognosis.* Cambridge, MA: Harvard University Press.

Rogers, P., Lydon, P., and Seckler, D. (1989). *Eastern Waters Study: Strategies to Manage Flood and Drought in the Ganges–Brahmaputra Basin.* Alexandria, VA: US Agency for International Development.

Rogers, P., Lydon, P., Seckler, D., and Pitman, K. (1994). *Water and Development in Bangladesh: A Retrospective on the Flood Action Plan.* Alexandria, VA: US Agency for International Development.

Rosegrant, M. W., Cai, X., and Cline, S. A. (2002). *World Water and Food to 2025.* Washington, DC: International Food Policy Research Institute.

Rosen, H. and Keating, A. (1991). *Water and the City: The Next Century.* Chicago, IL: Public Works Historical Society.

Ruxin, J. N. (1994). Magic bullet: the history of oral rehydration therapy. *Medical History* **38**, 363–397.

Saleth, R. M. (1996). *Water Institutions in India: Economics, Law, and Policy.* New Delhi: Commonwealth Publishers.

Schlesinger, W. H. (1991). *Biogeochemistry – An Analysis of Global Change.* San Diego, CA: Academic Press.

Scobie, A. (1986). Slums, sanitation, and mortality in the Roman world. *Klio* **68**, 399–433.

SCOPE (1999). *Emerging Environmental Issues for the 21st Century: A Study for GEO-2000.* Paris: Scientific Committee on Problems of the Environment.

Seckler, D., Amarasinghe, U., Molden, D, de Silva, R., and Barker, R. (1998). *World Water Demand and Supply, 1990–2025: Scenarios and Issues.* Research report 19. Colombo: International Water Management Institute.

Semple, E. C. (1911). *Influences of Geographical Environment.* New York, NY: Henry Holt.

Shah, T. (1993). *Groundwater Markets and Irrigation Development: Political Economy and Practical Policy.* New York, NY: Oxford University Press.

   (2000). *Pedal Pump and the Poor: Social Impact of a Manual Irrigation Technology in South Asia.* Colombo: International Water Management Institute.

Shallat, T. (1994). *Structures in the Stream: Water, Science and the Rise of the U. S. Army Corps of Engineers.* Austin, TX: University of Texas Press.

Sharma, P. (ed.) (1995). *Asian Watmanet.* Newsletter. Kathmandu: International Centre for Integrated Mountain Development.

Sharma, P. N. (ed.) (1996). *Recent Developments, Status, and Gaps in Participatory Watershed Management Education and Training in Asia.* PWMTA–FARM Field Document 6. RAS/93/0622. Kathmandu: International Centre for Integrated Mountain Development.

   (1997). *Recent Development, Status and Gaps in Participatory Watershed Management Education and Training in Asia.* PWMTA/FARM/UNDP/FAO Report 78. Kathmandu: International Centre for Integrated Mountain Development.

Sharma, P. N. and Wagley, M. P. (eds.) (1996a). *The Status of Watershed Management in Asia.* RAS/93/0622. Kathmandu: International Centre for Integrated Mountain Development.

   (eds.) (1996b). Case studies of people's participation in watershed management in Asia. Part I: Nepal, China, India. PWMTA-FARM Field Document 4. RAS/93/0622. Kathmandu: International Centre for Integrated Mountain Development.

Sheaffer, J. R. (2000). *Water Reuse.* Abstracts. Illinois State Water Survey Conference. July 18–20, 2000. Chicago, IL: Illinois State Water Survey. http://www.sws.uiuc.edu/hilites/watercon/abstracts.htm. Last visited March 2, 2003.

Sheaffer, J. R. and Stevens, L. A. (1983). *Future Water: An Exciting Solution to America's Most Serious Resource Crisis.* New York, NY: William Morrow.

Sherwood, C. B., Bruington, A. E., Drescher, W. J. (1969). Saltwater intrusion in the United States. *American Society of Civil Engineers, Journal of the Hydraulics Division* **95**(5), 1651–1669.

Shiklomanov, I. A. (1993). World fresh water resources. In: *Water in Crisis: A Guide to the World's Fresh Water Resources*, ed. P. H. Gleick. New York, NY: Oxford University Press. pp. 13–24.

(1999). *World water resources and their use: A joint SHI/UNESCO product.* http://webworld.unesco.org/water/ihp/db/shiklomanov. Last visited March 20, 2003.

(2000). Appraisal and assessment of world water resources. *Water International* **25**, 11–32.

Sit, V. and Taylor, B. (eds.) (1998). *Statistical Methods for Adaptive Management Studies.* Land Management Handbook 42. Victoria, BC: British Columbia Ministry of Forests.

SIWI (2000). *Water Security for Multinational Water Systems: Opportunity for Development.* 2000 Seminar. Stockholm: Stockholm International Water Institute.

Smit, J. and Nasr, J. (1992). Urban agriculture for sustainable cities: using wastes and idle land and water bodies as resources. *Environment and Urbanization* **4**(2), 141–152.

Smith, D. (1994). Change and variability in climate and ecosystem decline in Aral Sea Basin deltas. *Post-Soviet Geography* **35**, 142–165.

(1995). Environmental security and shared water resources in post-Soviet Central Asia. *Post-Soviet Geography* **36**, 351–370.

Smith, J. R. (1922). *Springs and Wells in Greek and Roman Literature, Their Legends and Locations.* New York, NY: G. P. Putnam's Sons.

Snow, J. (1855). *On the Mode of Communication of Cholera.* London: John Churchill.

Solley, W. B., Pierce, R. R., and Perlman, H. A. (1998). *Estimated Use of Water in the U. S. in 1995.* US Geological Survey Circular 1200. Washington, DC: US Geological Survey.

Spirn, A. W. (1984). *The Granite Garden: Urban Nature and Human Design.* New York, NY: Basic Books.

(1998). *The Language of Landscape.* New Haven, CT: Yale University Press.

(2000). Ian McHarg, landscape architecture and environmentalism: Ideas and methods in context. In: *Environmentalism in Landscape Architecture*, ed. M. Conan. Washington, DC: Dumbarton Oaks. pp. 97–114.

Stakhiv, E. Z. (2002). Improving environmental benefits analysis. In: *Balancing Economy and Environment.* US Army Corps Of Engineers Economic And Environmental Analysis Conference, New Orleans, July 16–18, 2002. http://www.usace.army.mil/inet/functions/cw/cecwp/eande2002/TrackB1_stakhiv_abs.doc. Last visited March 2, 2003.

Stanley, E.H., Luebke, M. A., Doyle, M. W., and Marshall, D. W. (2002). Short-term changes in channel form and macroinvertebrate communities following low-head dam removal. *Journal of the North American Benthological Society* **21**, 172–187.

Stanley, N. F. and Alpers, M. P. (1975). *Man-Made Lakes and Human Health.* London: Academic Press.

Steinberg, T. (1991). *Nature Incorporated: Industrialization and the Waters of New England.* Studies in Environment and History. Cambridge: Cambridge University Press.

Strabo (1917–32). *The Geography of Strabo*, with English translation by H. L. Jones. Cambridge, MA: Harvard University Press.

Swyngedouw, E. A. (1995). The contradictions of urban water provision – a study of Guayaquil, Ecuador. *Third World Planning Review* **17**(4), 387–405.

Tarr, J. (2000). *The Search for the Ultimate Sink: Urban Pollution in Historical Perspective.* Akron, OH: University of Akron Press.

Teclaff, L. (1996). Evolution of the river basin concept in national and international law. *Natural Resources Journal* **36**, 359–391.

Terrene Institute (1995). *Water: Taking a New Tack on Nonpoint Source Pollution.* Alexandria, VA: Terrene Institute.

Third World Water Forum (2003). *World Water Actions.* Kyoto: World Water Forum.

Thomas, W. L., Jr. (ed.) (1959). *Man's Role in Changing the Face of the Earth.* Chicago, IL: University of Chicago Press.

Thompson, J., Porras, I., Katui-Katua, M., *et al.*, (2001). *Drawers of Water II.* London: International Institute for Environment and Development.

Thompson, J. O. and Cairncross, S. (2002). Drawers of water: assessing domestic water use in Africa. *Bulletin of the World Health Organization* **80**, 1–2.

Thorne, C. R., Hey, M., and Newson, M. (eds.) (1997). *Applied Fluvial Geomorphology for River Engineering and Management.* Chichester: Wiley.

Tiffen, M., Mortimore, M., and Gichuki, F. (1994). *More People Less Erosion: Environmental Recovery in Kenya.* London: Wiley.

Tiner, R. W. (1989). An update of Federal wetland delineation techniques. In: *Wetlands: Concerns and Successes*, ed. D. Fisk. Bethesda, MD: American Water Recourses Association. pp. 13–23.

Toepfer, K. (2002). Moving forward together. *Confluence. Newsletter of the Dams and Development Project* **1**. Cape Town: UN Environment Programme. http://www.unep-dams.org. Last visited March 5, 2003.

Trimble, S. W. (1997). Streambank fish-shelter structures help stabilize tributary streams in Wisconsin. *Environmental Geology* **32**(3), 230–234.

Tuan, Y.-F. (1968a). *The Hydrologic Cycle and the Wisdom of God.* Toronto: University of Toronto, Department of Geography.

(1968b). Discrepancies between environmental attitudes and behaviour: examples from Europe and China. *The Canadian Geographer* **12**, 176–191.

Turner, B. L. II, Clark, W. C., Kates, R. A., Richards, J. F., Mathews, J. T., and Meyer, W. B. (eds.) (1990). *The Earth as Transformed by Human Action. Global and Regional Changes in the Biosphere over the Past 300 Years.* Cambridge: Cambridge University Press.

Turner, B. L. II, Skole, D., Sanderson, S., Fischer, G., Fresco, L., and Leemans, R. (1995). *Land-Use and Land-Cover Change Science/Research Plan.* IGBP Report 35; HDP Report 7. Geneva: International Social Science Council.

UN Commission on Sustainable Development (1997). *Comprehensive Assessment of the Freshwater Resources of the World. Report of the Secretary-General.* Report E/CN.17/1997/9. New York, NY: United Nations.

UN Economic and Social Council (2002). *The Right to Water.* Articles 11 and 12 of the International Covenant on Economic, Social and Cultural Rights. UN Doc. E/C.12/2002/11. New York, NY: United Nations.

UN Statistics Division (2003). *International Standard Industrial Classification.* Revision 3.1. http://unstats.un.org/unsd/cr/registry/regcst.asp?Cl=17. Last visited April 4, 2003.

UNCED (1992). Protection of the quality and supply of freshwater resources: application of integrated approaches to the development, management and use of water resources. *Agenda 21*, chapter 18. New York, NY: United Nations.

UNCHS (1996a). *Managing Water Resources for Large Cities and Towns.* Report of the Beijing Water conference. Nairobi: United Nations Centre for Human Settlements.

(1996b). *An Urbanizing World: Global Report on Human Settlements (1996).* New York, NY: Oxford University Press.

(1998). *Best Practices Database.* http://www.bestpractices.org. Last visited March 2, 2003.

(2001). *Cities in a Globalizing World.* London: Earthscan.

(2003). *Urban Indicators Toolkit.* http://www.unhabitat.org/programmes/guo/guo_guide.asp. Last visited April 4, 2003.

UNEP (1998). *Sourcebook of Alternative Technologies for Freshwater Augmentation in Some Countries in Asia.* Technical Publication Series. Tokyo: United Nations Environment Programme.

(1999). *Global Environmental Outlook 2000.* London: Earthscan.

UNEP/IETC (1999). *Planning and Management of Lakes and Reservoirs: An Integrated Approach to Eutrophication.* Nairobi: United Nations Environment Programme.

UNESCO (2003). *Water for People – Water for Life. The United Nations World Water Development Report.* Executive summary pre-release. http://unesdoc.unesco.org/images/0012/001295/129556e.pdf. Last visited March 21, 2003.

UNFCCC (1997). *Kyoto Protocol.* http://unfccc.int/resource/convkp.html. Last visited March 5, 2003.

United Nations (1949). *Scientific Conference on the Conservation and Utilization of Resources.* New York, NY: United Nations.

(1957). *Integrated River Development.* New York, NY: United Nations.

(1997). *Convention on the Law of the Non-Navigational Uses of International Watercourses.* UN Doc. A/51/869. New York, NY: United Nations.

Uphoff, N. (1992). *Learning from Gal Oya: Possibilities for Participatory Development and Post-Newtonian Social Science.* Ithaca, NY: Cornell University Press.

US 1990 Decennial Census (1995). *Housing of American Indians on Reservations – Plumbing.* Statistical Brief SB/95–9. Washington, DC: US Department of Commerce.

US Commission on Organization of the Executive Branch of the Government (1955). *Water Resources and Power: A Report to the Congress.* Washington, DC: US Government Printing Office.

US Congress (1911). *Weeks Act.* 61st Cong. 3d sess., ch. 186, 1911, pp. 961–963.

(1969). *National Environmental Policy Act of 1969.* Public Law 91–190, 42 US Code 4321–4347, as amended.

US Department of the Interior (1987). *Design of Small Dams.* Washington, DC: US Government Printing Office.

US Natural Resources Conservation Service 1998. *National Watershed Manual.* Washington, DC: Department of Agriculture.

USBR (1941–47). *Columbia Basin: Joint Investigations. 26 problems.* Washington, DC: US Government Printing Office.

(1946). *The Colorado River: A Natural Menace Becomes a National Resource.* Washington, DC: US Government Printing Office.

(1995). *Removal of Elwha and Glines Canyon Dams.* Elwha Technical Series PN-95-7. Elwha River Ecosystem and Fisheries Restoration Project, United States. Boise, ID: Bureau of Reclamation.

(2001). *Quality of Water – Colorado River Basin Progress Report. 20th Biennial report.* Denver, CO: US Bureau of Reclamation.

USEPA (1994). *Water Quality Standards Handbook,* 2nd edition. EPA-823-B-94-005. Washington, DC: Environmental Protection Agency.

(1997). *Technical Guidance Manual for Developing Total Maximum Daily Loads. Book 2. Rivers and Streams; Part 1, Biochemical Oxygen Demand/Dissolved Oxygen & Nutrient Eutrophication* (PDF, 88M) EPA-823-B-97-002. Washington, DC: Environmental Protection Agency.

(2002a). *Protecting Drinking Water through Underground Injection Control.* EPA-816-K-02-001. Washington: Environmental Protection Agency.

(2002b). *Training Materials on Source Water Protection Best Management Practices.* http://www.epa.gov/safewater/protect/swpbmp.html. Last visited March 2, 2003.

(2003). *List of Drinking Water Contaminants & MCLs.* http://www.epa.gov/safewater/mcl.html. Last visited March 9, 2003.

USGS (1984) *National Water Summary, 1983.* Water Supply Paper 2250. Washington, DC: Government Printing Office.

(1988). *Basic Ground-Water Hydrology.* Water Supply Paper 2220. Washington, DC: Government Printing Office.

(1989). *National and Regional Trends in Water-Well Drilling in the Untied States, 1964–84.* Open File Report. Reston, VA: US Geological Survey.

(2003). *Ground-Water Data for the Nation.* http://waterdata.usgs.gov/nwis/gw Last visited March 26, 2003.

USHUD (1999). *American Housing Survey for the United States 1997.* Current Housing Reports H150/97. Washington, DC: Department of Commerce.

(2000). *American Housing Survey for the United States.* H150/99. Washington, DC: Department of Commerce.

USSL (2002). *United States Salinity Laboratory.* http://www.ussl.ars.usda.gov. Last visited August 31, 2002.

Van der Hoek, W., Sakthivadivel, R., Renshaw, M., Silver, J. B., Birley, M. H., and Konradsen, F. (2001). *Alternate Wet / Dry Irrigation in Rice Cultivation: A Practical Way to Save Water and Control Malaria and Japanese Encephalitis?* IWMI Research Report 47. Colombo: International Water Management Institute.

Van der Leeden, F., Troise, F. L., and Todd, D. K. (1990). *The Water Encyclopedia*, 2nd edition. Chelsea, MI: Lewis.

Verghese, G. B. and Iyer, R. R. (eds.) (1993). *Harnessing the Eastern Himalayan Rivers: Regional Cooperation in South Asia.* New Delhi: Centre for Policy Research.

Wallach, B. (1996). *Losing Asia: Modernization and the Culture of Development.* Baltimore, MD: Johns Hopkins University Press.

Walters, C. J. (1986). *Adaptive Management of Natural Resources.* New York, NY: McGraw-Hill.

(1997). Challenges in adaptive management of riparian and coastal ecosystems. *Conservation Ecology [online]* **1**(3). http://www.consecol.org/vol1/iss2/art1. Last visited March 2, 2003.

Walters, C. J. and Holling, C. S. (1990). Large-scale management experiments and learning by doing. *Ecology* **71**, 2060–2068.

Ward, J. V. and Stanford, J. A. (1995). The serial discontinuity concept: extending the model to floodplain rivers. *Regulated Rivers: Research and Management* **10**, 159–168.

Ward, R. (1978). *Floods.* London: Methuen.

Ware, E. F. (1905). *Roman Water Law.* St. Paul, MN: West Publishing Co.

Waring, G. A. (1965). *Thermal Springs of the United States and Other Countries of the World.* US Geological Survey Professional Paper 492. Washington, DC: US Government Printing Office.

WASH (1993). *Lessons Learned in Water, Sanitation, and Health: Thirteen Years of Experience in Developing Countries.* Alexandria, VA: Water and Sanitation for Health Project.

Water Supply and Sanitation Collaborative Council (1999). *Water for People: a Shared Vision for Hygiene, Sanitation, and Water Supply; and a Framework for Mobilisation of Action.* http://www.worldwatercouncil.org/Vision/Documents/VISION21FinalDraft.PDF. Last visited April 5, 2003.

WCD (2000). *Dams and Development: a New Framework for Decision-Making.* London: Earthscan.

(2002). *Reactions to the Final Report.* http://www.dams.org/report/reaction. Last visited August 31, 2002.

WCED (1987). *Our Common Future* [the Brundtland Report]. Oxford: Oxford University Press.

Weatherford, G. (2000). *From Basin to "Hydrocommons": Integrated Water Management Without Regional Governance*. DP05. Boulder, CO: Natural Resources Law Center.

Webb, R. H., Schmidt, J. C., Marzolf, G. R., and Valdez, R. A. (eds.) (1999). *The Controlled Flood in Grand Canyon*. Washington, DC: American Geophysical Union.

Wescoat, J. L., Jr. (1995a). Main currents in multilateral water agreements: a historical–geographic perspective, 1648–1948. *Colorado Journal of International Environmental Law and Policy* **7**, 39–74.

(1995b). The right of thirst for animals in Islamic water law: a comparative perspective. *Environment and Planning D: Society and Space* **3**, 637–654.

(1995c). Waterworks and culture in metropolitan Lahore. *Asian Art and Culture* SpringSummer 1995, 21–36.

(2000). "Watersheds" in regional planning. In: *The American Planning Tradition: Culture and Policy*, ed. R. Fishman. Washington, DC: Wilson Center, Smithsonian Institution. pp. 147–172.

(2002). Beneath which rivers flow: water, geographic imagination and sustainable landscape design. In: *Landscapes of Water: History, Innovation and Sustainable Design*, ed. U. Fratino, A. Petrillo, A. Petruccioli, and M. Stella. Bari: Unigrafica Corcelli Editrice. vol. 1, pp. 13–34.

Wescoat, J. L., Jr. and Halvorson, S. J. (2000). *Ex-Post Evaluation of Dams and Related Water Systems*. Report to the World Commission on Dams. Capetown: WCD.

Western Governors' Association (1997). *Watershed Partnerships: A Strategic Guide for Local Conservation Efforts in the West*. Denver, CO: Western Governors' Association. http://westgov.org/wga/publicat/wsweb.htm. Last visited March 2, 2003.

Western Water Policy Review Advisory Commission (1998). *Water in the West*. Denver, CO: Western Water Policy Review Advisory Commission.

Whitcombe, E. (1994). The environmental costs of irrigation in British India: waterlogging, salinity, and malaria. In: *Nature, Culture, Imperialism: Essays on the Environmental History of South Asia*, ed. D. Arnold and R. Guha. Delhi: Oxford University Press. pp. 237–259.

White, G. F. (1945). *Human Adjustment to Floods*. Research Paper 29. Chicago, IL: University of Chicago, Department of Geography.

(1957). A perspective of river basin development. *Law and Contemporary Problems* **22**(2), 157–187.

(1964). *Choice of Adjustment to Floods*. Research Paper 93. Chicago, IL: University of Chicago, Department of Geography.

(1974). Domestic water supply: right or good? *Human Rights and Health (Ciba Foundation)* **23**, 41–59.

(1976). Formation and role of public attitudes. In: *Environmental Quality in a Growing Economy: Essays from the Sixth RFF Forum*, ed. H. Jarret. Baltimore, MD: Johns Hopkins University Press. pp. 105–127.

(ed.) (1977). *The Environmental Effects of Complex River Development*. Boulder, CO: Westview Press.

(1988a). When may a post-audit teach lessons? In: *The Flood Control Challenge: Past, Present, and Future*, ed. M. Reuss. Washington, DC: Public Works Historical Society. pp. 53–65.

(1988b). The environmental effects of the High Aswan dam. *Environment* **30**(7), 4ff.

(1997). Watersheds and streams of thought. In: *Reviews in Ecology: Desert Conservation and Development*, ed. H. Barakat and A. Hegazy. Cairo: Metropole. pp. 89–97.

(1998). Reflections on the 50-year international search for integrated water management. *Water Policy* **1**, 21–27.

White, G. F., Bradley, D., and White, A. U. (1972). *Drawers of Water*. Chicago, IL: University of Chicago Press.

White, G. F., Calef, W. C., Hudson, J. W., Mayer, H. M., Sheaffer, J. R., and Volk, D. J. (1958). *Changes in Urban Occupance of Flood Plains in the United States*. Geography Research Papers 57. Chicago, IL: University of Chicago.

White, G. F. with the Committee (1971). *Integrated River Basin Development*. New York, NY: UN Department of Economic and Social Affairs.

White, G. F. with the Task Force (1966). *A Unified National Program for Managing Flood Losses*. House Document 465. Washington, DC: US Congress.

White, G. F. and White, A. U. (1986). Potable water for all: the Egyptian experience with rural water supply. *Water International* **11**, 54–63.

WHO (1989). *Guidelines for the Safe Use of Wastewater and Excreta in Agriculture and Aquaculture*. Geneva: WHO.

Wigington, P. J., Jr. (2001–02). Riparian ecology and management in multi-land use watersheds. *Journal of the American Water Resources Association* special issues **37**(6) and **38**(3).

Wilkinson, C. F. (2000). *Messages from Frank's Landing: A Story of Salmon, Treaties, and the Indian Way*. Seattle, WA: University of Washington Press.

Williams, M. (1991). *Wetlands: A Threatened Landscape*. Oxford: Blackwell.

Wittfogel, K. A. (1981). *Oriental Despotism: A Comparative Study of Total Power*. New York, NY: Vintage. First published 1957.

WMO (1997). *A Comprehensive Assessment of the Freshwater Resources of the World*. Geneva: World Meteorological Organization.

Wolf, A. T. (1995). *Hydropolitics along the Jordan River: The Impact of Scarce Water Resources on the Arab–Israeli Conflict*. Tokyo: United Nations University Press.

(1999a). Criteria for equitable allocations: the heart of international water conflict. *Natural Resources Forum* **23**(1), 3–30.

(1999b). The transboundary freshwater dispute database project. *Water International* **24**(2), 160–163.

(ed.) (2002). *Atlas of International Freshwater Agreements*. Nairobi: United Nations Environment Programme.

Wolf, A. T., Natharius, J. A., Danielson, J. J., Ward, B. S., and Pender, J. (1999). International river basins of the world. *International Journal of Water Resources Development* **15**(4), 387–427.

World Bank (2001). *Agenda for Water Sector Strategy for North China*. Report 22040-CHA. Washington, DC: World Bank.

WRC (1973). Principles and standards for planning water and related land resources. *Federal Register* **38**(174), Part III (September 10, 1973), 24, 777–724, 869.

(1978). *Second National Water Assessment: The Nation's Water Resources 1975–2000*. Washington, DC: US Water Resources Council.

WWC (2000). *World Water Vision. Commission Report. A Water Secure World. Vision for Water, Life and the Environment*. Marseille: World Water Council.

WWW Virtual Library Irrigation (2003). University of Kassel. http://www.wiz.uni-kassel.de/kww/projekte/irrig/irrig_i.html. Last visited March 1, 2003.

Zagona, E., Fulp, T., Shane, R., Magee, T., and Goranflo, H. (2001). Riverware: a generalized model for complex reservoir system modeling. *Journal of the American Water Resources Association* **37**(4), 913–929.

Index